Child Protection

Risk and the Moral Order

Child Protection

Risk and the Moral Order

Nigel Parton,
David Thorpe
and
Corinne Wattam

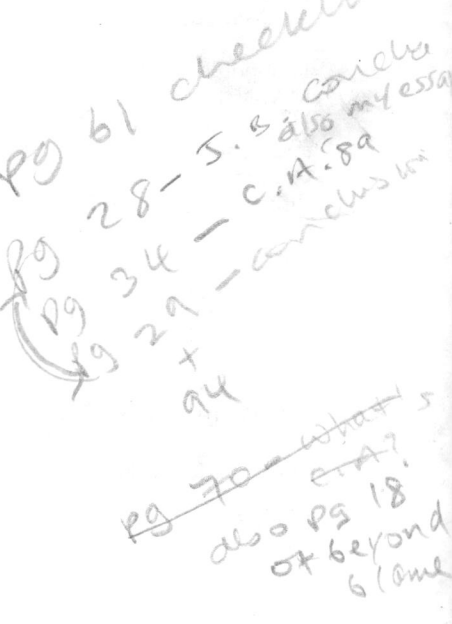

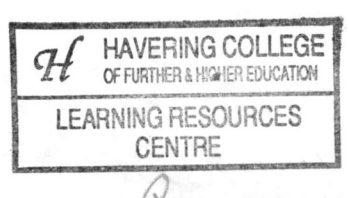

First published 1997 by
MACMILLAN PRESS LTD
Houndmills, Basingstoke, Hampshire RG21 2XS
and London
Companies and representatives
throughout the world

ISBN 0–333 62947–7

A catalogue record for this book is available from the British Library.

10   9   8   7   6   5   4   3   2   1
06 05 04 03 02 01 00 99 98 97

Typset by EXPO Holdings, Malaysia

Printed in Hong Kong

For Chris, Kusminder and Suzanne

Contents

List of Figures and Tables

Figures

Tables

Preface

Since the early 1980s all three of us have been working, researching and writing in the area of child protection (Parton, 1985, 1991; Thorpe, 1994; Wattam, 1992). In the early 1990s, however, via a chance meeting and subsequent series of phone calls, we came to realise that our different but complementary areas of interest and expertise provided a stimulating and productive arena for developing our analyses and ideas both separately and together. We were also conscious of a considerable amount of research being carried out in Britain, much of it funded by the Department of Health, which was likely to have a major impact on the way we thought about and developed child protection policy and practice. While sympathetic and supportive of much of this research, we were also uncomfortable with how it might be interpreted and understood. In particular, we were concerned that it may not address and analyse the nature of child protection work and how this is experienced and carried out by practitioners. It is now clear that the publication of the research has opened up a major debate on the future direction of policy and practice in this highly sensitive area (Dartington Social Research Unit, 1995). It is also clear that the current debates are not confined to Britain. Very similar discussions are taking place elsewhere, particularly North America and Australia, about future priorities and directions.

This book brings together our current thinking and analyses and draws on our own empirical research. In the process it develops a series of arguments and raises a number of questions which are central to contemporary child protection policy and practice. The book thus makes an explicit contribution to these current debates. At various stages over recent years we have shared our ideas with numerous practitioners, managers, policy-makers and researchers who have provided new insights and critical perspectives. Much of this has taken place at various conferences where we have been invited to speak. These have proved invaluable.

We would, however, like to thank Barbara Hearn, Philip Noyes, Des Semple and Sue Wise, all of whom have actively participated in our journey at various times, and Sue Hanson who helped bring it all together at the end. It is important to stress, however, that we are completely responsible for what follows.

NIGEL PARTON
DAVID THORPE
CORINNE WATTAM

1
Current Issues in Child Protection and Child Abuse: Some Common International Themes

Child protection systems and practices are currently being subjected to a fundamental interrogation and re-appraisal. It is perhaps not an exaggeration to suggest that child welfare practitioners and managers are feeling embattled and even under seige in a context of growing referrals and increasingly severe caseloads but where there are insufficient resources to do the job expected of them. Increasingly major questions are being posed about the efficacy, impact and outcomes for children, parents and professionals of a system which has been developed and refined since the early 1970s.

This is an important period of debate about the future direction of policy and practice in child protection, and this book aims to make an explicit contribution to these debates. While the focus for our analysis and discussions is primarily the UK we will also demonstrate and argue that the issues are not exclusive to the UK alone. Parallel trends, developments and debates are taking place across the English-speaking Western world. As we will illustrate, this is most clearly the case in the USA, Canada and Australia. Not only can we learn from these wider global experiences, but it is also intended that our analyses and arguments will have relevance and significance to a much wider world than just the UK.

Trends in Child Abuse and Neglect Reports

There can be little doubt that child welfare agencies have been virtually overwhelmed in recent years by an explosion of child abuse and neglect reports and referrals (Lindsey, 1994).

1

In the USA the number of official reports of child abuse to child protection agencies has increased inexorably since the late 1960s from 9,563 in 1967 to 669,000 in 1976 to over 2 million in 1987. By 1992 the figure was over 2.9 million (see Figure 1.1). What is also apparent, however, is that

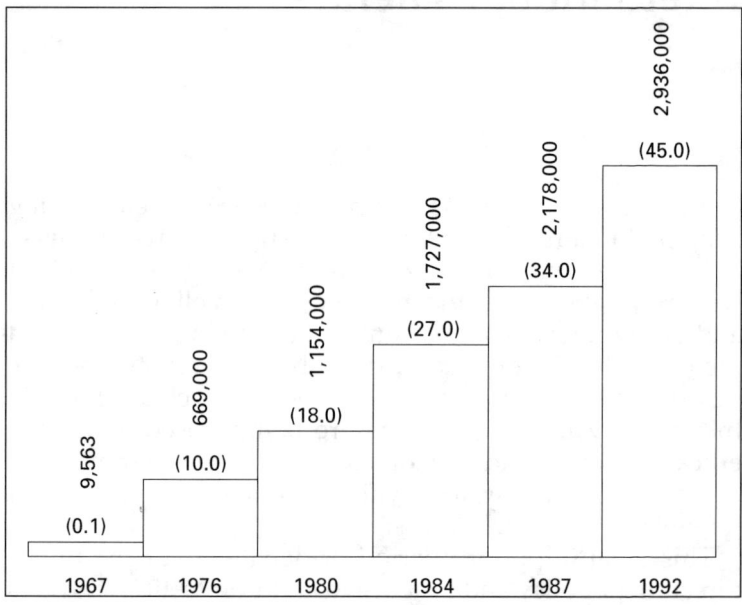

Figure 1.1   Child abuse and neglect reports in the United States, 1967–92 (rate per 1,000 in brackets)
Source: McCurdy and Daro (1993)

well over 50 per cent of reported cases are now either determined as being unfounded or not substantiated. While in 1976 60 per cent were classed as substantiated, by 1987 this figure had dropped to 40 per cent. A very similar pattern of trends has been identified in Canada (Johnson and Chisholm, 1989).

The trends are perhaps even more dramatic in Australia. In the State of Victoria notifications of child abuse/neglect went up more than 5,000 per cent between 1977/8 and 1993/4 (see Figure 1.2). These increases in Victoria were also matched by a tremendous growth in the budget for child protection (see Figure 1.3).

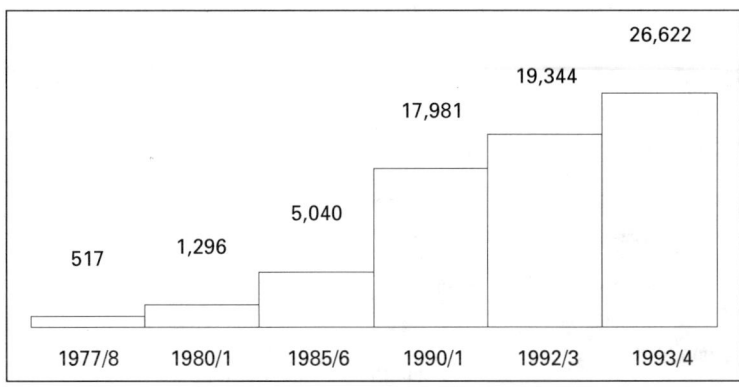

Figure 1.2   Notifications of child abuse and neglect, Department of Health and Community Services, Victoria, Australia, 1977/8–1993/4

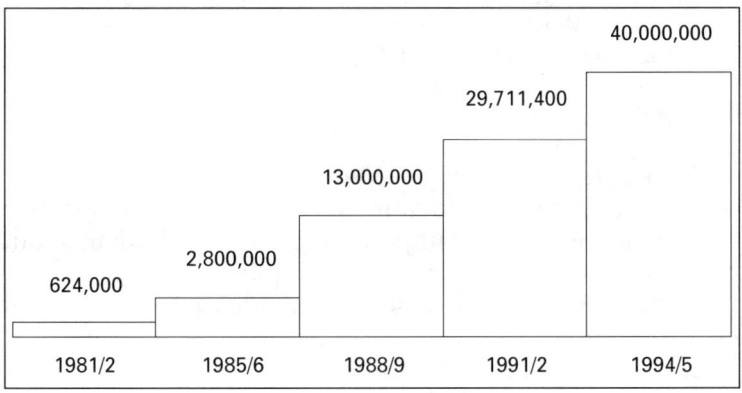

Figure 1.3   Protective service budget, Department of Health and Community Services, Victoria, Australia, 1981/2–1993/4

A review of child protection data in Western Australia (Cant and Downie, 1994) demonstrated that allegations had increased from less than 3,000 in 1989/90 to nearly 8,000 in 1993/4. However the number of substantiated allegations had remained fairly constant in line with population growth (see Figure 1.4).

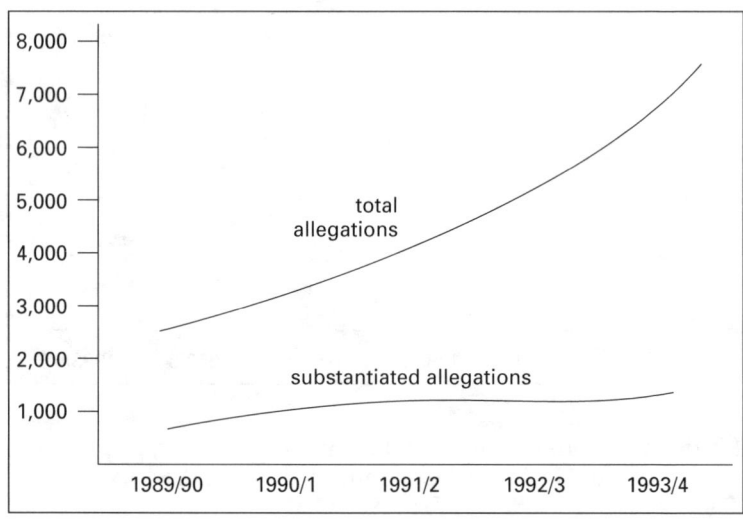

Figure 1.4   Child maltreatment allegations, 1989/90–1993/4,
               Western Australia
Source: Cant and Downie (1994)

The Western Australian review also argued that many of the reports of child maltreatment could more appropriately be seen as concerns about parenting style rather than about harm to children. They were about parents not providing what the community considered an adequate standard of care.

In the UK there are no comparable statistics. While it has recently been estimated that there are currently 160,000 child protection referrals per year (Dartington Social Research Unit, 1995), there has been no systematic attempt to collect and collate statistics on child protection referrals. The nearest equivalent statistics relate to the numbers on child protection registers and it is only since 1988 that these statistics have been collected nationally. Prior to that we were dependent on figures extrapolated by the National Society for the Prevention of Cruelty to Children (NSPCC) from the registers it administered covering 9 per cent of the child population of England. The statistics prior to 1988 in Table 1.1 thus relate to extrapolations from

Table 1.1 Numbers of children on child protection registers in England by category for selected years 1978–94

Category of abuse	1978	1984	1986	1988	1989	1990	1991	1992	1993	1994
Physical abuse	7,944	7,856	10,422	11,100	10,000	10,200	10,600 (23%)	10,700 (28%)	11,900 (37%)	13,000 (37%)
Physical neglect	289	933	1,888	4,900	5,300	5,600	6,800 (15%)	7,700 (20%)	8,500 (26%)	10,300 (30%)
Sexual abuse	89	1,088	5,922	5,800	5,800	5,900	6,000 (13%)	6,600 (17%)	8,300 (26%)	9,600 (28%)
Emotional abuse	0	200	455	1,700	2,000	2,200	2,600 (6%)	2,800 (7%)	3,500 (11%)	4,400 (13%)
Grave concern	3,533	2,312	5,133	14,400	16,300	17,900	21,100 (47%)	12,900 (34%)	2,700 (8%)	500 (2%)
Total	11,844	12,389	23,820	39,200	41,200	43,600	45,300 (100%)	38,600 (100%)	32,500 (100%)	34,900 (100%)

Source: NSPCC (1978–86); DoH (1988–94)

NSPCC registers and since 1988 to those from the Department of Health. It should also be noted that after 1991 the Department of Health recommended that the 'grave concern' category be dropped from local registers. By 1994 it was describing this category as 'not recommended'. There has, however, been a marked decline in the number of cases categorised under 'grave concern', indicating that most areas are now following Department of Health guidance.

The numbers of children on registers can be seen to have quadrupled between 1978 and 1991 but, following the most recent Department of Health guidance, they declined by a quarter by 1993 to increase somewhat in 1994. However, this does not give an adequate representation of the changing size and nature of the overall workload. In many respects it is the number of reports or allegations which is key and it is clear the workload has increased dramatically since the early 1970s.

Increasingly, however, it is being suggested that the fact that less than 50 per cent of reports/referrals are substantiated poses a major question about the utility and efficacy of current systems and practices. Besharov has estimated the number of unfounded or unsubstantiated reports in the USA as running between 55 and 65 per cent of total reports (Besharov, 1990, p. 10).

Funnels and Filters: Professional Response to Child Abuse Reports

The 1990s have witnessed the completion of a number of research studies which have provided major insights into the operation, decision-making and outcomes of child protection systems and processes, and in many ways it is these which have posed the major questions for policy-makers and practitioners and opened up debates about the future direction(s) for child protection.

During the design phase of a child protection information system, Thorpe (1994) collected data on a 100 per cent sample of reports of abused and neglected children in Western Australia in 1987. Figure 1.5 shows the decisions made by social workers on these 655 reports. These decisions are represented as a funnel.

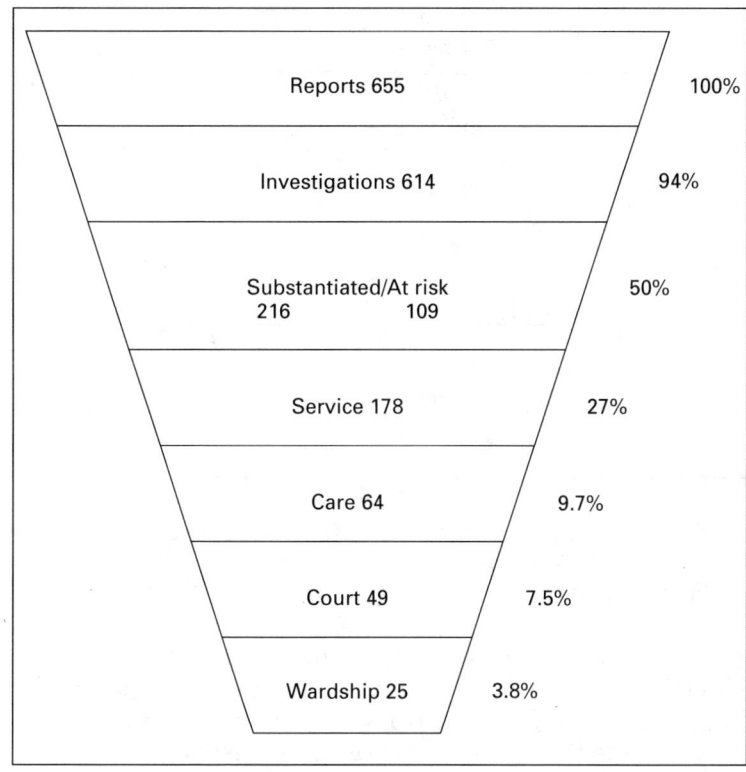

Figure 1.5   Funnelling and filtering child abuse reports in
Western Australia, 1987

Figure 1.5 shows that, after investigation, only 33 per cent
(216) of the reports were considered to concern abused children, while a further 16.6 per cent (109) cases were judged to
be 'at risk' of abuse or neglect. Despite these assessments,
just 27 per cent (178) cases received a service, of which 64
(9.7 per cent of the original 655 reports) were taken into care.
The proportion of the original 655 reports taken to the
Children's Court on 'care and protection' grounds was less
then 10 per cent, while only 25 children (3.8 per cent) were
made state wards. This pattern of filtering in Western
Australia was again evident when the results of allegations
for 1994/5 were also analysed (see Figure 1.6).

A similar study (Thorpe, 1994) was carried out in 1991 in
a local authority social services department in South Wales
in the UK, when a 100 per cent sample of child abuse

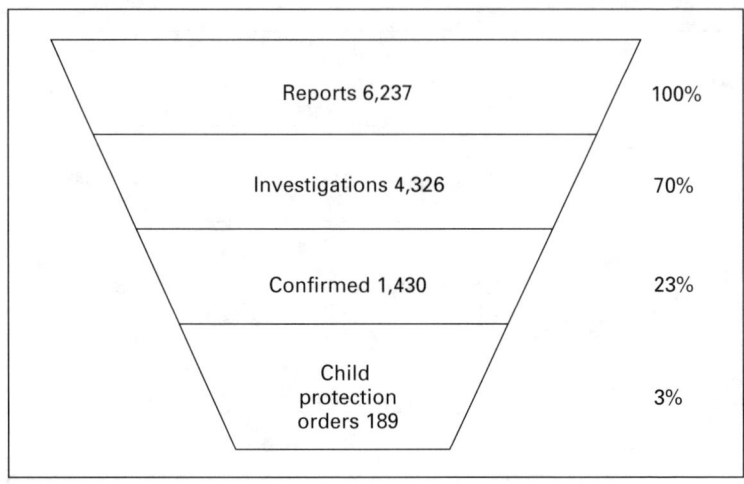

Figure 1.6   Funnelling and filtering child abuse reports in
              Western Australia, 1994/5
Source: Department of Family and Children's Services (1995)

reports were followed up for nine months after referral. Child protection laws and procedures in England and Wales are quite different from those in Western Australia: they include the case conference mechanism and a registration procedure where it is considered appropriate. However, as Figure 1.7 demonstrates, the process of filtering was very similar to that applied in Western Australia.

The issue of the significance of filters in child protection systems and decision-making has been a major contributor to the current re-think and re-evaluation of child protection policy and practice in the UK. Two studies in particular have been important in this respect. Giller, Gormley and Williams (1992) looked at four Area Child Protection Committee (ACPC) areas and found that over 75 per cent of cases 'dropped out' of the child protection system between the time of becoming a referral and the conclusion of a case conference with a view to registration. They noted that this represented a considerable volume of child protection work, even though registration was not the end result.

However, the key research which has exercised the minds and sensibilities of researchers, civil servants and ministers in the UK was that carried out by Gibbons, Conroy and Bell (1995). A central objective of the research

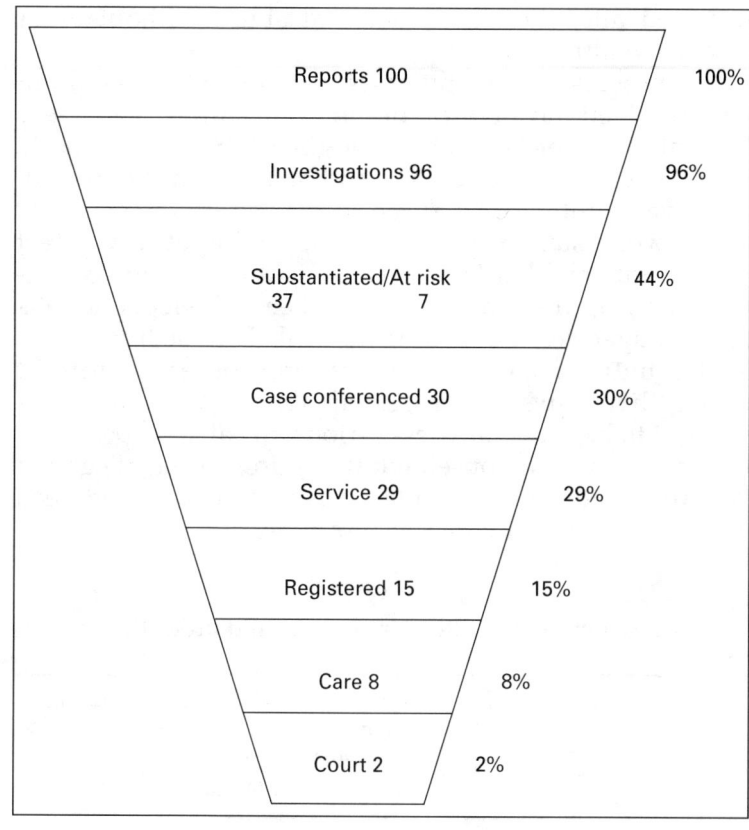

Figure 1.7   Funnelling and filtering child abuse reports in
              South Wales, UK

was to describe the processes that led to a child's name
being placed on a child protection register. Detailed study
took place in eight different English authorities (two outer
London boroughs, four inner London boroughs and two
counties). Over a 16-week period in 1992 children referred
for investigations were identified and their progress
through the child protection system was tracked for up to
26 weeks through social work records and minutes of conferences. Most of the 1,888 referrals (44 per cent) were for
suspected physical abuse, followed by suspected sexual
abuse (28 per cent), and neglect (21 per cent) or fears for
the child's safety (4 per cent). Only 3 per cent of referrals

involved allegations of emotional abuse without other forms of maltreatment.

The processes whereby cases were quickly filtered out and received no service or no 'protection' were very evident (see Table 1.2). Of the original 1,888 allegations 42 were lost from the outset and could not be traced. However, another 478 (26 per cent) were filtered out by social work staff at the duty stage without any direct contact with child or family. This might have involved discussions with the senior social worker and telephone calls to other agencies. Cases were more likely to be filtered out at this initial stage if the allegations concerned neglect rather than physical or sexual abuse, the abuse was thought to be physically less serious, the alleged perpetrator was not in the household, the source of the allegation was anonymous or from a lay person and there had been no previous contact with social services.

Table 1.2   Operation of filters in English child protection system

	No. of cases at each stage (percentage of original total given in brackets)	No. filtered out at each stage
ENTRY POINT New incident	1,888	42 'lost' cases
FIRST FILTER Checks	1,846 (100%)	478 (26%)
SECOND FILTER Investigation	1,368 (74%)	925 (50%)
THIRD FILTER Child protection conference	443 (24%)	128 (7%)
RETAINED IN SYSTEM AFTER CONFERENCE	315 (17%)	
ON REGISTER	272 (15%)	

Source: adapted from Gibbons, Conroy and Bell (1995)

The second filter was the investigation itself, where the senior social worker or manager was seen as the crucial decision-maker. About two thirds of the cases actually investigated (925 of the 1,368 investigated) were filtered out and never reached an initial child protection conference. The nature of the abuse and the source of the referral were again influential, as were any previous history of suspected maltreatment and any recorded parental problems such as criminality or substance abuse.

The third filter was operated by the initial child protection conference. In 51 per cent of the conferenced cases the child was registered, 10 per cent were already on the register, 10 per cent were deferred and 29 per cent were not registered. Compared with those not registered, cases placed on the register had more previous investigations for abuse, and had more indicators of poverty, parental deviance and domestic violence.

Gibbons, Conroy and Bell concluded that about six of every seven children who entered the child protection system at referral were filtered out without needing to be placed on a child protection register. Just 15 per cent of original referrals ever found their way onto a child protection register. Crucially, in a high proportion (44 per cent of those actually investigated) the investigation led to no actions at all. There was no intervention to protect the child, nor were any other family support services provided. In only 4 per cent of all the cases referred were children removed from home under a legal order during investigation. The researchers also estimated that the proportion of unsubstantiated allegations (those which were assessed as untrue or having alternative explanations or insufficient evidence) was 49 per cent of the total.

Despite the differences in legislation and procedures, the patterns of filtering and decision-making in the USA, Canada, Western Australia and the UK are remarkably similar. Thus while there is an elaborate procedural overlay in the English and Welsh child protection system compared with Western Australia, and the USA has a mandatory reporting system, this does not seem to have a significant impact on the way the system operates nor on outcome. There are clear patterns to child protection intervention which are reflected in all four countries. These patterns also reveal that the majority of reports or referrals for child abuse (however much they escalate) receive few services. The system, in effect, operates as a process of 'diagnostic deflation'.

Child Protection: the Current Issues

It is perhaps not surprising that a number of commentators are now suggesting that child protection policy and practice needs to be re-thought. In the UK this has taken place primarily in the context of the publication of a number of major research studies funded by the Department of Health, to which the study by Gibbons, Conroy and Bell (1995) was a major contributor. In many respects the studies, together, can be seen as the most significant coordinated research programme into child protection that has ever taken place. Not only have they helped set the terms of the debate that is taking place in the UK, but they have provided the most detailed and comprehensive insights into child protection processes and systems and their outcomes anywhere in the world. Their findings and recommendations for change are thus of considerable importance.

In June 1995 the Department of Health launched its overview report (Dartington Social Research Unit, 1995) which summarised the main messages of the 20 research projects. Eight of the studies were also published (Birchall and Hallett, 1995; Cleaver and Freeman, 1995; Farmer and Owen, 1995; Ghate and Spencer, 1995; Gibbons, Conroy and Bell, 1995; Gibbons, Gallagher, Bell and Gordon, 1995; Hallett, 1995; Thoburn, Lewis and Shemmings, 1995).

The political nature of the launch was explicit in that the Minister at the Department of Health, John Bowis, launched the document at a major press conference which received considerable coverage in all sections of the media. In his Foreword to the document, John Bowis stated that it provided 'a significant contribution to thinking and practice in child protection' and he urged managers and trainers to 'assist front-line practitioners to use the research base to inform and improve their day-to-day practice'.

The decision to fund the research in the late 1980s was a direct consequence of the fall-out from the Cleveland inquiry (Secretary of State, 1988; and see Chapter 2 of this book), the recognised paucity of knowledge in the area of child abuse and the manifest confusions in the reactions of the investigative agencies. The programme of research aimed to explore different aspects of child abuse which would, in combination, help to provide a more comprehensive assessment of current practices. Rather than being primarily concerned with researching the nature and form of child abuse itself, particularly via clinical studies as previously, the primary focus was the processes and outcomes of child protection interventions. The initiative was different from most previous child abuse research in that its focus was not to be restricted to the deviant behaviour of children and parents. It included studies of the behaviour of normal families, agency processes and decision-making. In most of the studies there was a particular concern with both short- and longer-term outcomes.

The overview document paid particular attention to questions of *definition*, particularly the questions – what is child abuse and what is meant by child protection? It is argued that any '*incident* has to be seen in *context* before the extent of its harm can be assessed and appropriate interventions agreed' (Dartington Social Research Unit, 1995, p. 53, original emphasis). Many of the studies demonstrated that 'with the exception of a few severe assaults and some sexual maltreatment' (p. 53), long-term difficulties for children seldom follow from a single abusive event or incident – rather they are more likely to be a consequence of living in an unfavourable environment, particularly one which is *low in warmth and high in criticism*. Only in a small proportion of the cases studied was the abuse seen as extreme, warranting more immediate and formal child protection interventions. It is suggested that if we put 'to one side the severe cases' (p. 19) the most deleterious situations in terms of longer-term outcomes for children are those of *emotional neglect* (p. 20), where the primary concern is the *parenting style* which fails to compensate for the inevitable deficiencies that become manifest in the course of the 20 years or so it takes to bring up a child. Unfortunately the studies suggested that these were just the situations where the child protection system seemed to be least successful. What the research seemed to demonstrate was that, while there was little evidence that children were being missed and suffering harm unnecessarily at the hands of their parents (as implied by most child abuse inquiries – see Chapter 2 of this book) and was thus 'successful' according to a narrow definition of child protection, this was at a cost. Many children and parents felt alienated and angry and there was an over-emphasis on forensic concerns with far too much time spent on investigations and a failure to develop longer-term coordinated treatment, counselling and preventative strategies.

It was concluded that many investigations were undertaken, many families were visited and case conferences called, but that, in the end, little support was offered to the family. Not only did the parents become alienated, angry and bewildered, but the children were not helped. Perhaps most crucially, valuable time and resources were wasted, particularly on investigations, with little apparent benefit. This conclusion had been rehearsed 12 months previously in an Audit Commission Report (1994). In both reports, the key research informing this was the study carried out by Gibbons, Conroy and Bell (1995) on the operation of the child protection system based on data from eight local authorities.

In the light of the research programme it is being argued that there needs to be a *rebalancing* of child protection work so that there is a greater concentration on *children in need* and, by implication, 'parenting style', that investigations should be reframed as 'inquiries' and carried out 'with a lighter touch', and that as a consequence fewer children and families should be dragged into the child protection *net*. Gibbons, Conroy and Bell's analogy between a fishing net and the child protection system provided a powerful way of representing the current situation and was one of the few direct quotes from the studies included in the overview document (Dartington Social Research Unit, 1995, p. 32). They argued that

> the child protection system might be considered as a small-meshed net, in which are caught a large number of minnows as well as a smaller number of marketable fish. The minnows have to be discarded but no rules exist about the correct size of

the mesh. Each fishing fleet may therefore set its own. The 'meshes' are the organisational filters operated by local child protection systems. A child who enters the system must pass through a number of organisational 'filters' before his or her name is placed on a child protection register. (Gibbons, Conroy and Bell, 1995, p. 51)

The implication is that not only are far too many resources concerned with trying to operate the nets, but far too many children and families are caught up who should never be there. Not only are they hurt and confused as a result, but their needs, in most cases, are not being met and they are offered few services and little help.

In this context the research overview made a number of suggestions as to how 'children's safety' could be improved. It emphasised the following: the importance of sensitive and informed professional/client relationships where honesty and reliability are valued; an appropriate balance of power between participants where serious attempts are made at partnership; a wide perspective on child protection which is not simply concerned with investigating forensic evidence but also with notions of welfare, prevention and treatment; that priority should be afforded to effective supervision and the training of social workers; and that the most effective protection from abuse is brought about by generally enhancing children's quality of life. More specifically in terms of current policy in England and Wales, it calls for a rebalancing of child protection work which prioritises Section 17 and Part 3 of the Children Act 1989 in terms of helping and supporting families with 'children in need' and thereby keeping notions of policing, surveillance and coercive interventions to a minimum. It similarly suggests that Section 47 should be read essentially as the power to *inquire* in the first instance rather than simply as the forensically determined investigation.

Conclusion

In many respects the research provides a real opportunity and it has certainly made a major contribution to and helped open up the debates that are now taking place about the future direction(s) for child protection. If it means that in future policy and practice will be informed by detailed empirical research which looks at a full range of cases which are typical of day-to-day practice, rather than simply by the dramatic case which has gone wrong and been subject to public inquiry and media opprobrium, this must be a positive development. In the process it will provide an opportunity to re-think and take stock of a number of assumptions and priorities which have never before been seriously addressed.

However, as one of us has argued previously (Parton, 1996b), none of the research, including the overview document, seriously addresses *why* child welfare services have been reconstructed as child protection, why the work takes the form that it does and *how* practitioners resolve the wider social and organisational responsibilities and tensions placed upon them. This is the central focus of this book. Our primary concern is to make a contribution to understanding the contemporary nature of child protection work, why and how it takes the form that it does, and thereby make an explicit contribution to the current debates about the future direction of policy and practice.

What we argue is that it is the notion of *risk* which, for all practical purposes, has become the key signifier for child abuse, both in policy developments and for practical decision-making. Debates about risk must thus lie at the heart of attempts to reframe and redirect future policy. Drawing on a detailed analysis of developments in the UK, Chapter 2 sets out the social and political context(s) whereby this has come about and how policy guidance and legislation has been reframed. However, the way risk has been analysed and understood in research does not resolve the problems for policy-makers and practitioners. In many ways such research has become a major part of the problem and contributed to it. This is the focus of Chapter 3. Chapter 4 sets out the central conceptual and methodological approaches which inform our approach. It starts from the premise that it is crucial to understand the nature of child protection *work* and how this is carried out and operationalised by practitioners. Our approach is then developed and applied in a variety of situations which we identify as central for understanding the nature of contemporary child protection. We analyse the way children are constructed in child protection records in Chapter 5; the way social workers identify risk assessment criteria at the point of referral in their practice in Chapter 6; the nature and form of advice and guidance offered to children and families under the auspices of child protection and how this is received in Chapter 7; and the outcomes in cases of alleged sexual abuse in Chapter 8. Finally, in Chapter 9 we bring together our argument(s), which have developed from our analysis of our empirical work, and consider the implications for current debates concerning the future(s) for child protection policy and practice.

2
The Contemporary Discourse of Child Protection

For much of the time since the early 1970s child abuse has been seen as a significant and growing social problem and has been subject to considerable media, public and political interest and debate (Aldridge, 1994; Franklin and Parton, 1991). In the UK a whole range of detailed policies and procedures have been developed and new legislation introduced. When we survey the changes between the early 1970s and mid 1990s, at one level it seems that we have seen little more than the general growth and refinement of procedures which in themselves have reflected wider developments and changes in thinking and understanding. While procedures have grown and the general priority and significance given to this area of work has increased, the changes, superficially, seem incremental. Effectively the system of child abuse management established in the early to mid 1970s seems to be still with us even though the labels and language may have changed.

At another level, however, there have been some dramatic changes which go much deeper than simply the introduction of a new language. While in the 1970s and the early 1980s the focus was the development of policies and procedures to identify and respond to the problems of the battered baby, non-accidental injury and subsequently child abuse, since 1987, in the UK, the focus has been somewhat different. The Cleveland affair and debates and developments since have helped shift the emphasis. Increasingly our energies have been focused on refining and modifying the systems and procedures themselves. We have been concerned not so much with trying to do something about *child abuse* but *doing something about child protection*.

As we will argue, this is not to say that the notion of child abuse is not embedded in day-to-day practice, as well as being a key term used by practitioners to make sense of decisions and often referred to in local policies and procedures. However, central government guidance has been reframed in quite fundamental ways to the point where the term 'child abuse' has been virtually dropped from official discourse. As we will argue, the shift to framing policies and procedures in terms of child protection in part reflects an important, though subtle, development in conceptions of what the term 'child abuse' is signifying. However, child protection is concerned with much more complex issues related to the nature and balance of *relationships* between and *responsibilities* of various state agents and private households, primarily parents and carers in the rearing of children. It is in this context that contemporary debates about child protection take on their particular significance.

The central argument of this chapter and a central theme throughout the book is that there has been an important shift in the relationships and hierarchies of authority between different agencies and professionals in key areas of decision-making. While at the moment of its modern (re)-emergence in the 1960s child abuse was constituted as essentially a medico-social reality, where the expertise of doctors was seen as central, increasingly it has been constituted as a socio-legal problem, where legal expertise takes pre-eminence. Whereas previously the concern was with diagnosing, curing and preventing the 'disease' or syndrome, increasingly the emphasis has become investigating, assessing and weighing 'forensic evidence'.

The focus of this chapter is thus to outline and analyse the factors that have influenced and circumscribed the policies and practices we now call *child protection* and how these differ from what went before. What are the essential elements of the discourse of child protection and how have these come about? How is the discourse of child protection related to wider changes in the relationship between state and family? And crucially, how do these reflect and feed into changing notions of the authority and legitimacy of the different health and welfare experts? While the analysis draws on developments and changes in England and Wales and while we recognise that there are important differences in law and policy in other countries, we argue that the issues and themes have a much wider significance.

The Children Act 1989 and the Criminal Justice Act 1991, together with the guidance of *Working Together Under the Children Act 1989* (Home Office et al., 1991) and the *Memorandum of Good Practice on Video Recorded Interviews with Child Witnesses for Criminal Proceedings* (Home Office, 1992), can be seen as the fruition of a series of heated and sometimes contradictory arguments in England and Wales from the mid 1970s onwards. What they address at their heart is a problem which has been a major, though sometimes submerged, tension for the liberal state since the mid 19th century: namely, how can we devise a *legal* basis for the power to intervene into the family to protect children which does not convert *all* families into clients of the state? Such a problem is posed by the contradictory demands of, on the one hand, ensuring that the family is experienced by its members as autonomous and the primary sphere for rearing children, while on the other recognising that there is a need for intervention in some families where they are seen as failing in this primary task and in a context where such laws are supposed to act as the general norms applicable to all (Parton, 1991).

The Emergence of Child Abuse as a Medico-Social Problem in the Context of Welfarism

The establishment of the child-care service in England and Wales in the post-war period can be seen as a particular instance of the growth and rationalisation of social interventions associated with the establishment of welfarism (Rose and Miller, 1992). The key innovations of welfarism lay in the attempts to link the fiscal, calculative and bureaucratic capacities of the state in order to encourage national growth and well-being via the promotion of *social responsibility* and the mutuality of *social risk* and was premised on notions of *social solidarity* (Donzelot, 1988). Welfarism rested on the twin pillars of Keynesianism and Beveridgianism.

A number of assumptions characterised welfarism: the institutional framework of universal social services were seen as the best way of maximising welfare in modern society, and the nation state worked for the whole society and was the best way of progressing this. The social services were instituted for benevolent purposes, meeting social needs, compensating socially-caused 'diswelfares' and promoting social justice. Their underlying functions were ameliorative, integrative and redistributive. *Social progress* would continue to be achieved through the agency of the state and professional intervention so that increased public expenditure, the cumulative extension of statutory welfare provision and the proliferation of government regulations backed by expert administration represented the main guarantee of equity, fairness and efficiency. *Scientific knowledge* was given a pre-eminence in ordering the rationality of the emerging professions who were seen as having a major contribution to developing individual and social welfare and thereby operationalising increasingly sophisticated mechanisms of social regulation.

The emergence of social work with children and families, originally under the auspices of local authority children's departments, in the context of welfarism, was itself imbued with a considerable optimism, for it was believed that measured and significant improvements could be made in the lives of individuals and families via judicious professional interventions. Social work operated quietly and confidently and in a relatively uncontested way which reflected a supportive social mandate. It harmonised with a central plank of the post-war reconstruction which believed that a positive and supportive approach to the family was required, so that the state and the family should work in partnership to ensure that children were provided with the appropriate conditions in which to develop.

The high point of this optimistic growth and institutionalisation of social work in the context of welfarism came with the establishment of social services departments in 1971. They reflected the belief of the Seebohm Report (1968) that social problems could be overcome via state intervention by professional social workers with social scientific knowledge and skills in the use of relationships, and envisaged a progressive, universal service available to all and with wide community support.

The consensus which underpinned the development of social work with children and families during this period had a number of dimensions. It was assumed that the interests of the social workers and hence the state were similar to, if not the same as, the people they were trying to *help*. It was essentially a benign, but maternalistic relationship. Interventions in the family were not conceived as a potential source of antagonism between social workers and individual family members – whether parent(s) or child(ren) – who were not seen as having interests or rights distinct from the unitary family itself. When a family required modification this would be via casework, help and advice, and if an individual did come into state care this was assumed to be in their interests. Interventions which had therapeutic intentions necessarily had beneficial outcomes so that social work required and was allowed a large degree of independence and discretion to carry out its work.

The growth of social work and its claims to expertise during the 20th century were characterised by its increasing allegiance to social casework. Not only did casework provide a systematic approach to practice, but it provided an internally coherent knowledge base derived from psychodynamic theory and ego-psychology (Payne, 1992; Pearson, Treseder and Yelloly, 1988). It provided a focus for its professionalisation which aspired to medicine and psychiatry and which thereby framed the focus of its work and the way it was carried out. Therapy and counselling provided the core of professional practice, while the law simply provided the context for the work. The law was not conceptualised as in any significant way constituting the nature of social work or informing the skills required of social workers and the types of relationships deemed appropriate for work with clients. When more coercive aspects were drawn upon, these were primarily seen as a tool for fulfilling these more significant therapeutic goals.

Such an approach is well illustrated in the early work of the NSPCC Battered Child Research Unit in London, where the crucial factor for the social worker was not to establish whether the law had been broken and whether the parents were guilty or innocent. The main objective was to form a 'consistent, trusting, professional relationship' (Okell and Butcher, 1969, p. 9). Intervention was to be based on a careful psycho-social diagnosis and should provide a 'transfusion of mothering ... in the hope they will identify with us and eventually interject a less punitive self-image' (Court, 1969, p. 15). The main feature of such a 'nurturing model' was an emphasis on intrapsychic and social factors, particularly emotional and social deprivations, as determining family relationships. History was seen to dominate, therapy was restitutive and parental maturation, or rather maternal maturation, was the goal. The social workers assumed that the parents were not responsible for the situation and in effect were powerless to do anything about it. As a result the social workers accepted considerable responsibility on the parents' behalf for trying to bring about improvements.

Not only were the courts and the legal system seen as secondary and as simply providing the mandate for such therapeutic interventions, but the police were seen as marginal and a potential source of difficulty. 'Since our main emphasis was to be on treatment and rehabilitation, we felt we would prefer that they [the police] were not involved in our families, as we did not believe they had a therapeutic role to play in battered baby cases' (Baher et al., 1976, p. 106).

The way child abuse was conceptualised and explained from the early years of its modern (re)discovery was dominated by the 'disease' or public health model (Parton, 1985, chapter 6). As the Beckford Report commented, quoting the work of Henry Kempe, 'child abuse is a disease whose carrier is the parent and whose victim is the child' (London Borough of Brent, 1985, p. 88). With such a model it was assumed that child abuse was an illness and that clinical medico-scientific procedures were the best way of explaining, identifying and responding to it.

Such an approach was crucial in influencing the way central government guidance developed during the 1970s and into the mid 1980s. It was assumed that child abuse, or the battered baby, constituted a medical reality which had previously been denied and which professionals had failed to identify and respond to. The primary purpose of official government guidance was to encourage the *discovery* of such cases via diagnosis, treatment and prevention.

In 1970 the Chief Medical Officer and the Chief Inspector of the Children's Department jointly circulated a memorandum entitled *The Battered Baby* (DHSS, 1970). It was described as a clinical condition and the memorandum outlined its incidence, aetiology, clinical picture and management. Both the nature of the condition and the recommended responses very much followed those previously suggested by the British Paediatric Association (1966) and a report from the NSPCC (Skinner and Castle, 1969). The problem was seen as a clinical entity akin to a syndrome and where medical officers of health, paediatricians and children's officers (social workers) were keys to recognising the symptomatology and the identifying factors. Even though the way the problem was officially defined broadened during the 1970s from 'the battered baby' to 'non-accidental injury' (DHSS, 1974) to 'child abuse' (DHSS, 1980), the notion of the battered baby continued to be the root metaphor.

The 1974 memorandum explicitly named physical signs on the child's body and in the home as means for identifying non-accidental injury to children:

> It is vital that all concerned with infants and young children should be alert for the *first signs* of non-accidental injury. Older children are not immune. The *first signs* may be very slight – for example:
>
> (a) minor injuries such as facial bruises, damage in the mouth or small burns;
> (b) bruising which could indicate that the child had been gripped tightly and possibly shaken; or
> (c) an unexplained failure to thrive.
>
> *Other signs* may be given by the behaviour of parents including delays in seeking advice, a plausible explanation of an injury which does not quite fit the case, very severe distress or over frequent attendances at clinics or surgeries without convincing reasons. Once suspicion is aroused the behaviour of the parents is always a factor to consider and where possible attention should be paid to the condition of any other children and to the general situation in the home. Older children and relatives sometimes support dubious statements made by

parents or guardians or may themselves invent false explanations. (DHSS, 1974, para 2, our emphasis)

The system of child abuse management was effectively
inaugurated with the issue of this DHSS memorandum in
April 1974 in the wake of the Maria Colwell inquiry
(Secretary of State, 1974), and underlined the need for
teamwork and 'strongly recommended' the establishment
of case conferences, area review committees and registers,
all of which quickly followed. The problem was defined as
essentially of a health and welfare nature. The roles of paediatricians, GPs, health visitors and social workers were
seen as vital and the social services department, as the
statutory child-care agency, central. The police, at this stage,
were not seen as crucial and it was a further circular in 1976
(DHSS, 1976) which recommended that a senior police
officer should be included on all area review committees
and case conferences. While there is evidence of a tension
between the health and welfare and the law and order
agencies, the medico-scientific model remained dominant.

Again the emphasis in the 1974 circular was to
'strengthen measures to prevent, diagnose and manage
cases' and it outlined the 'first signs' of non-accidental
injury (NAI). When suspected the 'first action' should be to
admit the child to hospital 'at once. ... Anything less
would expose him [sic] to unacceptable risk'. While this is
the first time that 'risk' enters the official discourse, the
essential assumption is that NAI exists as a reality and has
certain physical bodily signs which professionals, social
workers and doctors, can diagnose and identify. Where
'professional judgment' felt that the risk at home was
unacceptable, a court order should be applied for. In effect
the doctor and the hospital, together with the social
worker and the welfare office, were seen as the crucial
locus of power and conduits of decision-making. The court
and the agencies of law were secondary and subservient to
tackling the hidden medico-social reality.

The 1980 circular (DHSS, 1980) was primarily concerned
with broadening and refining the register system. For
the first time the problem was officially defined as *child
abuse*. Further, however, the medico-social reality and the

tance of the medical examination and the social assessment were underlined, for the 'diagnosis of child abuse will normally require both medical examination of the child and social assessment of the family background' (DHSS, 1980, para 2.2(a)). The discussion of the criteria for registration, while less categorical, clearly indicates that it is assumed there are medical and physical signs that indicate child abuse.

The Seeds of Discontent

However, the optimism and confidence evident in social work and the welfarist child-care system more generally was increasingly subject to a number of critiques from the mid 1970s onwards and these increased further during the 1980s. Some of the anxieties emanated from within social work itself and concerned the apparent poor and even deteriorating quality of child-care practice in the newly created social service departments. The poor quality of skills and the failure to capitalise on the emphasis on prevention in the 1960s were the central concerns of the National Children's Bureau Working Party (Parker, 1980), and were similarly to prove central to the various Department of Health and Social Security (DHSS, 1985b) and Economic and Social Research Council (ESRC) studies and the work of the Parliamentary Select Committee (Social Services Committee, 1984).

More widely, however, a whole variety of different concerns were developing which became increasingly important in influencing the parameters of the debate as it developed in the 1980s. While the criticisms represented somewhat different, though overlapping, constituencies, their net effect was to undermine the optimistic welfare consensus in child care.

First, from the 1960s onwards, with the growth of the women's movement and the recognition of violence in the family, it was argued that not only may the family not be the haven it was assumed to be, but that its more powerless members, women and children, were suffering a range of abuses at the hands of men. Much of the early critical analysis and action was directed to improving the position of women, and it was only in the late 1970s with the growing concerns about sexual abuse that much of the energy was directed to the position of children (C. Parton, 1990; N. Parton, 1990). Such critiques helped to effect a fundamental questioning of the family 'blood-tie', to disaggregate the interests of individual family members and to support the sometimes contradictory growth of the Children's Rights Movement (Freeman, 1983; Franklin, 1986; Freeman, 1987/8; Franklin, 1995). During the 1980s this was to find something of a common ground with the more traditional child rescue sentiments which received their most explicit expression with the establishment of ChildLine in late 1986, the first national telephone helpline for children and young people.

Second was the growth from the late 1960s of a more obviously 'civil liberties' critique which concentrated upon the apparent extent and nature of intervention in people's lives that was allowed, unchallenged, in the name of welfare: initially, this was directed at the issues of mental illness and delinquency (see Taylor et al., 1980; Unsworth, 1987). In the child-care field, such arguments were associated with critiques specifically related to Parental Rights Resolutions[1] and the reform of juvenile courts, but were increasingly focused upon criticisms of the Place of Safety Order.[2] More generally, they were concerned with protecting the inherent rights of 'parents' over the 'natural' sphere of the private family from state interference (Morris et al., 1980; Geach and Szwed, 1983). Very much related to these developments we have articulated the critiques of liberal, due-process lawyers, who drew attention to the way the administration of justice was unfairly and often unjustly applied in various areas of child care. It was argued that the priorities of practitioners, together with the processes of decision-making, failed to give due weight and consideration to the different and perhaps competing interests of family members as opposed to the concerns of the professionals themselves and their agencies, which may be overly influenced by protecting themselves from outside criticism.

These elements made their most explicit appearance with the establishment of a number of pressure groups, which put particular emphasis on the need to protect and enhance individual clients' rights. The National Association for One Parent Families, Justice for Children, the Children's Legal Centre and the Family Rights Group were perhaps the best known. They helped to construct a new set of priorities and debates around child care rarely articulated in the post-war period.

While quite different in terms of their social location and their focus of concern, we can see a growing number of constituencies in the polity developing from the late 1970s which were critical of the post-war welfarist consensus in child care and the medico-social professional dominance and constitution of child abuse in particular. This was to prove of importance from the mid 1980s onwards, particularly when the parents' lobby gained its most articulate voice with the establishment of Parents Against INjustice (PAIN) in 1985. Although a small group with few resources, its appearance proved to be significant in helping to frame the issues surrounding the Cleveland inquiry which were to be subsequently replayed in Rochdale, Orkney and elsewhere – particularly in the way they were portrayed in the media. As a consequence, the rights of parents and the rights of children to be left at home, free of state intervention and removal, were placed on political and professional agendas. The medico-social definition and approach to child abuse and the practices of health and welfare professionals themselves, as well as parental violence, were identified as being actually and potentially abusive. No longer could it be assumed that child abuse was a hidden reality which could be discovered and unearthed in an uncontested way by professional and scientific interventions and practices.

The Cleveland affair and subsequent inquiry did not simply undermine the legitimacy of the medico-social approach to child abuse, but it punctured any cosy, paternalist or maternalist assumptions about what constituted child abuse itself. The Cleveland inquiry provided the crucial watershed in this respect. For while up until this point the priority in policy and procedures had been to improve and refine our systems for *identifying child abuse*, subsequently the focus was to refine and improve the *systems of child protection* themselves.

Child Abuse Inquiries

Throughout it was child abuse inquiries which were the catalyst for bringing about change in policy, practice and procedure. While earlier inquiries had been primarily concerned with improving the identification of non-accidental injury and subsequently child abuse, the Cleveland inquiry was concerned with both protecting children *and* protecting the privacy of the family and the rights and responsibilities of parents. This fundamental shift in emphasis was articulated in central government guidance which followed and embodied the way the roles and responsibilities of social workers were to be reconstituted. For it is *through* debates about the nature and efficacy of social work that these issues about the role of the state and the relationship between the public and the private have been fought out and reframed. It is important to recognise that child abuse inquiries have not primarily been about child abuse *per se* but about the focus, priorities and competences of social workers and, to a lesser extent, other health and welfare professionals. Not only did they provide detailed accounts of what had gone wrong in the particular cases, but they critically commented on the current state of policy and practice more generally and made recommendations as to what should be done (DHSS, 1982; DoH, 1991).

Up until the mid 1980s the 30 plus inquiries had all been concerned with the deaths of children at the hands of their parents or caretakers. Many of the children had been under the legal supervision of social workers. All had died as a result of physical abuse and neglect and often suffered emotional neglect and failure to thrive. The child-care professionals, particularly social workers, were seen to have failed to protect the children with horrendous consequences.

Rather than simply seeing the deaths as resulting from individual incompetencies on behalf of the professionals involved, though these were often central, the incompetencies were usually seen as particular instances of the current state of policy, practice, knowledge and skills and the way particular professionals and occupations approached their tasks and understood their own and others' roles and responsibilities. There was a particular emphasis on the need to reformulate the *management* of the problem at the inter-agency, agency and individual case level.

Initially, social work was subject to two sets of checks and balances. The first was located in the developing inter-professional child abuse management systems associated with Area Review Committees, case conferences and registers. The other was to underline the importance of medical expertise in the identification of child abuse. Medical knowledge and medical technologies were seen as much more trustworthy, reliable and scientific than those of social workers acting alone.

The need to improve and rationalise inter-professional and inter-agency cooperation and coordination was a continual theme and priority throughout (Hallett and Birchall, 1992). Increasingly, however, the emphasis was placed on the need to recognise the importance of statutory powers and the law more generally in framing this area of work, rather than medicine. Social workers were seen as too naive and sentimental with parents and as failing to concentrate on the interests of children and to use the statutory authority vested in them. The picture presented was one of social workers going about their work but crucially unaware of their statutory mandate.

This argument was most forcefully and coherently articulated in 1985 with the publication of the inquiry into the death of Jasmine Beckford.[3] The inquiry argued that Jasmine 'became the victim of persistent disfunctioning social work while the law demanded, above all, her protection' (London Borough of Brent, 1985, p. 127). The report recommended that the local authority legal department, the police and the crown prosecuting service be included in the decision-making, so that important decisions, particularly when returning a child home, should only be made after full legal consultation in the multi-disciplinary case conference. Not only were lawyers seen as crucial to decision-making, but social work practice was perceived and evaluated via the legal gaze. This emerging emphasis on the law was not simply concerned with social workers' and others' technical knowledge of the statutes, but aimed to change attitudes and the direction of practice in order to protect children. Attempts to rationalise and improve the multi-disciplinary frameworks and to improve practitioners knowledge of the signs and symptoms indicative of child abuse were insufficient on their own. There was also a need for social workers to use the authority vested in them by statute to intervene in families and protect children from abuse and neglect.

The Cleveland affair and the subsequent inquiry report (Secretary of State, 1988), however, was concerned with a quite different set of issues and circumstances and *seemed* to provide a quite different set of interpretations of what was wrong and how we should respond (see Parton, 1991, chapter 4, for a more extensive analysis of the Cleveland inquiry). This time paediatricians as well as social workers had failed to recognise the rights of parents and had intervened too prematurely and in a too heavy-handed way into the private family. Over a hundred children were removed on Place of Safety Orders on the basis of questionable medical diagnoses of sexual abuse. A number of new techniques for diagnosing and identifying sexual abuse developed by medical experts (particularly paediatricians and child psychiatrists) and social work professionals were subjected to close critical scrutiny – particularly the anal dilation test, the use of anatomically correct dolls and 'disclosure' work. Cleveland was to prove a key moment in the recent history of child protection policy and practice. Not only was it the first inquiry concerned with *sexual abuse*, but *medical science* was found terribly wanting under the legal scrutiny of the inquiry.

The reasons for the crisis were seen as again residing primarily in inter-agency and inter-professional misunderstandings and poor cooperation. However, because the area of sexual abuse and how it could be identified was so contested in Cleveland, and the medical and social work techniques and methods came under such disrepute with such dire consequences for the parents and children involved, the law was seen as central to re-thinking how we should respond. Not only did the law itself need to be changed, but there was the need to recognise that professionals should be much more careful and accountable in identifying the 'evidence', forensically framed, for what constituted sexual abuse and child abuse more generally. All needed to recognise, professionals and family members alike, that the auspices, and hence ultimate accountability for social and medical practices and interventions, lay with the law and its representatives, particularly the police, lawyers, the crown prosecution service and, ultimately, the courts. It was not simply a question of getting the right balance between family autonomy and state intervention, but also getting the right balance between the power, discretion and responsibilities of the various juridical, social and medical experts and agencies. In this respect the juridical was prioritised and the central focus was to be investigation, identification and ultimately the weighing of forensic evidence.

1987 was to prove a watershed in shifting the focus of official concerns from child abuse to child protection. This is most explicit in a comparison of the draft guidance produced in 1986 (DHSS, 1986) primarily in response to the Beckford inquiry and the final guidance produced in 1988 (DHSS, 1988) in the aftermath of Cleveland. While apparently very similar, the differences were such as to fundamentally alter the focus of the documents and the issues they were attempting to address. While the 1986 draft guidance was concerned with doing something about *child abuse*, the 1988 guidance was concerned with *child protection*. The draft was entitled *Child Abuse – Working Together: A Draft Guide to Arrangements for Inter-Agency Cooperation for the Protection of Children*, but the final version was called *Working Together: A Guide to Inter-Agency Cooperation for the Protection of Children from Abuse*. While the aim of the former was 'to provide a guide to all the agencies concerned in working together to *prevent child abuse*' (our emphasis), the aim of the latter was to 'provide a guide to all agencies involved in working together to protect children from abuse'. Again, while the draft had moved a long way from conceptualising child abuse as a clinical entity, it did assume there is something called child abuse without attempting to define it. Its first substantive section was entitled 'What is child abuse?' and it offered a definition as: 'parents or carers can harm children either by direct acts, or by failure to provide proper care, or both' and included physical injury, neglect, emotional ill-treatment, sexual abuse, and potential abuse. In contrast, the term 'child abuse' hardly figures in the 1988 guidance where the focus has moved to 'the protection of children from abuse' or more commonly 'the protection of children'. Any suggestion that child abuse can be identified by physical signs on the child's body has been dropped.

The term 'child abuse' appears in just two places in the 1988 guidance. At the beginning, in paragraph 1.1, we are informed that 'child abuse which requires local authority intervention falls within the provisions of section 1(2)(a) and (c) of the Children and Young Persons' Act 1969'. At the outset therefore child abuse is located *within* a legal discourse. The only other reference is in paragraph 5.31 where the different categories for registration purposes are outlined. We are told that 'the term "child abuse" in this guide is intended to cover all these categories'. It is not by chance that 'child abuse' is put in inverted commas, thus questioning the validity of the term. There are other important differences between the two documents which one of us has discussed elsewhere (see Parton, 1991, chapter 5).

In other respects, however, the 1986 draft guide had already recommended that the system in terms of case conferences, registers and area review committees should become re-named as child protection. The 1988 guide reinforced this. However, the key development, apart from virtually expunging the term 'child abuse' from the official vocabulary, was the heightened explicit location of this area of work in its legal context. Whereas in the Beckford Report and the 1986 draft guide the law was crucial to protect children, in the Cleveland Report and the 1988 guide the law is important to protect *both* the children *and* the rights and interests of parents and hence the privacy and sanctity of the family. The significance and social functions of the law take on an added importance in periods of considerable uncertainty where there are particular problems concerned with managing disappointed expectations and conflict. In situations where conflict is heightened and where social cohesion and individual rights are experienced as being under threat, social responses often take on a legalistic form (King and Piper, 1995; King and Trowell, 1992).

Within an emphasis on legalism, the rule of law as ultimately judged by the court takes priority at the expense of other considerations, including those which may be deemed by the professional 'experts' as optimally therapeutic or 'in the best interests of the child'. It involves the superimposition of legal duties and rights upon the therapeutic and preventative responsibilities, essentially for the protection of both children and parents.

Recent Legislative Changes and Practice Guidance

The Children Act 1989 was described by the Lord Chancellor as 'the most comprehensive and far reaching reform of child care law which has come before Parliament in living memory' (Hansard, House of Lords, 6 December 1988, 2nd reading, col. 488).

In many respects the Act took much of its inspiration from the Short Report (Social Services Committee, 1984), the Review of Child Care Law (DHSS, 1985a) and the various ESRC and DHSS research projects (DHSS, 1985b) which informed them. As a consequence, the central principles of the Act encouraged an approach to child care based on *negotiation* with families and *involving* parents and children in *agreed* plans. The guidance and regulations accompanying the Act encouraged professionals to work in *partnership* with parents and young people and to consult them throughout. Similarly the Act strongly encouraged the importance of *supporting* families with children in need[4] in preventative work and thus keeping the use of care proceedings and emergency interventions to a minimum. Throughout it is clear that social workers and others need to be honest and open with clients and that working agreements in order to make their respective roles and responsibilities clear were central. However, the primary political momentum for the Act was concerns about child protection.

More particularly, the Act was concerned with trying to construct a new consensus. This was clearly spelt out by David Mellor when introducing the Bill to the Commons at a second reading when he said:

> As I hope I made clear, we have high ambitions for this Bill. We hope and believe that it will bring order, integration, relevance and a better *balance* to the law – a better *balance* not just between the rights and responsibilities of individuals and agencies, but most vitally, between the need to protect children and the need to enable parents to challenge intervention in the upbringing of their children. Recent well-publicised cases, including the tragic case of Kimberley Carlile, Doreen Mason and the events in Cleveland in 1987, has graphically shown the consequences of getting that *balance* wrong. Of course, of itself, legislation cannot stop such tragedies, but we

hope *a clear legal* framework will help to make more likely clear-eyed judgments by key people involved in child welfare, whether they are in social services departments, health authorities, the police, education or the courts. (Hansard, HOC, 27 April 1989, 2nd reading, col. 1107–1108, our emphasis)

While it was 'the welfare of the child' which was the Act's overriding principle, this was constituted via attempts to clarify individual rights and an emphasis on legalism. The other crucial element to emerge was in terms of the *criteria* to be used for making decisions – the threshold for state intervention. The assessment of 'high risk' had become central (Parton and Parton, 1989a; 1989b; Parton, 1991, chapters 3 and 5). In theory, the identification of the actually or potentially 'high risk' individual or family provides the mechanism for ensuring that children are protected while avoiding unwarrantable interventions. It provides the social and professional rationale for satisfying the demands of both the child rescue lobby and the parental rights lobby. In the Children Act the criteria for state intervention for care proceedings, supervision orders and emergency protection orders is 'that the child concerned is suffering, or is likely to suffer significant harm' (31(2)(a)). For the first time the criteria for state intervention includes a prediction of what may or is likely to occur in the future. The necessity to identify 'high risk' is thus embedded at the core of the legislation.

The same conditions of possibility which emphasised the need for greater legalism also underlined the need to identify 'high risk'. More generally it had become a major topic in discussions for reforming systems of state regulation in the penal and mental health fields (Bottoms, 1977). The increased official interest in the idea of identifying the 'high risk' had coincided with the growing tendencies to advocate or impose more severe interventions for those regarded as 'really serious', while advocating a reduced intervention for the 'low risk'. For such a *bifurcation* to take place one has to believe in the possibility of separating the dangerous or 'high risk' from the rest and have the expertise to carry that through. Assessments of actual or potential 'high risk' thus become *the* focal concern and activity.

In the context of child protection work, where the consequences for getting decisions wrong are so considerable, it is perhaps not surprising if those decisions are not left with the health and welfare experts alone. The decisions and the accountability for them are ultimately lodged with the court in the new legal framework based on what constitutes actual or likely significant harm in particular cases. It is thus the legal gaze and the weighing of forensic evidence which has become primary, but subjected to a variety of checks and balances set in place via the need to work in 'partnership' with children and families and 'working together' with a range of agencies and professionals.

In the process, representatives of the law and order agencies have moved centre stage in a way that was not evident previously. This is well illustrated in relation to the role now played by the police and the legal profession as outlined in the rewritten guidance *Working Together Under the Children Act 1989* (Home Office et al., 1991).

The latest version of *Working Together* was produced and published by the Home Office, the Department of Health, the Department of Education and Science and the Welsh Office, rather than by the Department of Health and Social Security as previously. The central elements which frame the guidance are spelt out in the introduction when we are reminded of the 'need to work in partnership with families', that it is the 'legal framework' which is crucial, and that the focus of working together in child protection is the child 'at risk'. For 'it is essential that ACPC procedures provide a mechanism whereby, wherever one agency becomes concerned that a child may be at *risk*, it shares its information with other agencies' (para. 1.11, our emphasis).

However, it is in the Preface that we are given the clearest rationale both for the guidance and for how practitioners should understand their work:

> It is well established that good child protection work requires good inter-agency cooperation. It is important for all professionals to combine an open minded attitude to alleged concerns about a child with decisive action when this is clearly indicated. ... Public confidence in the child protection system can only be maintained if a proper balance is struck avoiding

unnecessary intrusion in families while protecting children at risk of significant harm. (p. iii)

The guide's focus is to reconstruct the balance between the protection of children and the protection of the privacy of the family in order to maintain public confidence. Any reference to child abuse is virtually expunged, for the focus has become 'protecting children at risk of significant harm'. The term 'risk' takes on a strategic and central significance. For example, the decision to de-register a case 'must be based on a careful and thorough analysis of current risk' (para. 6.44).

The key investigating agencies are now explicitly recognised as the police and social services and it is seen as essential that there is an early 'strategy discussion to plan the investigation, the role of each agency and the extent of joint investigation' (para 28). It is explicitly stated that such cases 'involve both child care and law enforcement issues' (para 5.14.4).

Central to the process is making a social assessment drawing on the Department of Health publication *Protecting Children: A Guide for Social Workers Undertaking a Comprehensive Assessment* (DoH, 1988). This document has played an important role in framing practice at the individual case level. For it was apparent during the 1980s that it was not sufficient to rationalise and formalise the mechanisms for inter-agency working and the framework of the law alone. If 'risk' was going to be weighed and identified it was crucial to improve and clarify the role of the social assessment – for which social workers were crucially responsible. As David Pithers has highlighted, 'the guide addresses the key issue of whether a family is considered safe for a child, or whether it can be made safe, or whether it is so potentially dangerous that alternatives have to be found' (Pithers, 1989, p. 18).

The guide was an attempt to ensure that the rationalisation of inter-agency procedures was matched by attempts to develop practice skills in the assessment of individual cases. However, it accepted that child protection could never be straightforward and that there were no easy formulas for success in terms of outcome. What it did was outline the *processes* that should be followed and the questions that should be asked in constructing an assessment which should be systematic and thereby provide a better basis for decision-making. It would also 'provide opportunities for more effective supervision and management of the social work task' (p. 3).

In effect, the guide formalised the process of assessing 'high risk' which has become central to child protection work. Not only did it provide a framework for trying to objectify the subjective realities of children and other family members, but it also provided a further mechanism for opening up to scrutiny the activities of social workers and the basis on which they make decisions and thereby make them further accountable. The guide and the 167 questions and sub-questions itemised in it do not provide a formula for identifying high-risk *per se*, but rather provide a basis for making *professional judgements* about viability in the context of what is known, the potential for change and the resources available to bring about such changes. The social worker is asked to make recommendations on the basis of 'the *professional judgements* about the relative weightings of the various considerations of factors' (p. 69, our emphasis). Ultimately, however, the mandate and legitimacy for such work, and hence the ultimate accountability, is provided by the law and the court – something which social workers should be conscious of and explicit about with family members, for in some cases 'in the final analysis, the matter will be decided by the courts and parents and children must be made fully aware of their legal rights' (p. 70).

What the various guidances attempt to do is develop and formalise the contemporary nature of child protection work. The multi-agency inter-professional elements are crucial not only in piecing together information, but also in providing a set of checks and balances where the police and social services are now constituted as the key agencies, particularly in terms of investigation. Social workers are central in acting not as counsellors or therapists but as case managers – coordinating and taking the central responsibility for assessing 'risk' and monitoring and evaluating progress and thereby managing 'risk' in the future. This takes place in a context where procedures formalise the *process* for carrying out the work and, potentially, making

policy and practice more explicit and accountable, where
this accountability is essentially to the parents and, to a
lesser extent, the children on the one hand and to the court
on the other. This is not to say that all cases go to court, far
from it, but that the court and the legal gaze frames and
ultimately constitutes child protection work.

Such developments have been further reinforced following the practices and procedures set in place following the
Criminal Justice Act 1991 and the *Memorandum of Good
Practice* (Home Office, 1992) concerning the prosecution of
offenders and the video evidence of children. More than
ever the mechanisms for gathering evidence in relation to
both the processes of prosecution of offenders and the protection of the child have been combined. While prompted
by concerns about child sexual abuse cases, the wide range
of offences pertaining to the admissibility of pre-recorded
video evidence, under the Criminal Justice Act 1991,
means that increasingly this process is being used for most
types of harm, injury and alleged abuse. While it has been
concerns about how to respond to alleged cases of sexual
abuse, following Cleveland, which have been at the centre
of the reform of child protection policy and practice, they
have implications well beyond this original focus for
concern.

The *Memorandum of Good Practice* attempted to
harmonise 'the interests of justice and the interest of the
child' (Foreword). It had long been recognised that the
workings of criminal courts were not able to provide an
appropriate vehicle for receiving the evidence of children
who were usually the key witnesses in sex abuse prosecution cases. Not only were children not believed, but they
often withdrew their statements, and the processes of
giving evidence, examination and cross-examination could
themselves be seen as abusive to children. In 1988 the government decided to allow child witnesses to give evidence
from outside the courtroom via a special television link
and to ease the rules about child witnesses. This was
extended in the Criminal Justice Act 1991. For the first time
video-recordings of earlier interviews with police and
social workers could be played to the court as part of the
trial. The *Memorandum of Good Practice* produced guidance
about how this could be done which, while sensitive to the

child, tried to ensure that the evidence could stand up in a criminal court.

While the nature of evidence and hence the standard of proof under civil proceedings as constituted by the Children Act 1989 is different from and less than that in criminal proceedings under the Criminal Justice Act 1991, it seems that the two are becoming confused and that it is the latter which is pre-eminent and frames the former (Wattam, 1992). The shift towards combining the role of the police and social workers in carrying out investigations and hence combining the gathering of evidence for the purposes of the Criminal Justice Act 1991 and the Children Act 1989, particularly under the auspices of the *Memorandum of Good Practice*, has had the effect of raising the threshold for identifying what constitutes significant harm. In many respects the ratchet of legalism already set in place by the Children Act 1989 is tightened further. This has implications not only for which cases are proceeded against in a formal legal sense, but also for the way resources and expertise are allocated and priorities set. The investigation thus dominates all areas of the work.

Conclusions: the Nature of Contemporary Child Protection

The emphasis on the need to investigate 'high risk', in a context where notions of working together are set out in increasingly complex yet specific procedural guidelines and where the work is framed by a narrow emphasis on legalism and the need for forensic evidence, helps us to understand the key elements of the contemporary nature and import of child protection as articulated in recent legislation and official guidance. Work in this area from the mid 1980s onwards has increasingly been reframed and constituted in terms of the language of child protection. We now have child protection strategy meetings, child protection case conferences, Area Child Protection Committees and child protection registers. Similarly most social services departments have child protection officers and teams, as does the NSPCC, while many health authorities, health trusts and police forces have staff specifically designated as specialising in child protection. There has also been a growth in various aspects of child protection training.

We can note a number of important contextual factors which have fed into this. First, the nature of the problem of child abuse has been officially broadened to include neglect, physical abuse, sexual abuse, emotional abuse and, most recently, organised abuse (DoH, 1991). As Robert Dingwall (1989, p. 28) has noted, over the past 30 years the problem of child abuse has undergone consider-able 'diagnostic inflation'. The label of 'child abuse' now covers a wide variety of symptoms, behaviours and con-texts which is very different to the original 'battered baby syndrome'. In the process, however, the term itself has fallen into some dispute and, as we have seen, has been virtually dropped from official language.

Second, and running in parallel with this, public, profes-sional and political awareness has grown considerably. The net result, as we saw in Chapter 1, is that the number of reports coming to official notice has escalated tremendously.

Third, this broadening definition and the growth in awareness has taken place in a context where social workers and others now have to take responsibility not only for ensuring that children do not suffer in the family, but also that parental responsibilities and family autonomy are not undermined. Child protection involves a fine balance. As we have demonstrated, the notion of protec-tion subsumes within it not only the protection of the child but also the protection of parents and family privacy from unwarrantable state interventions.

Fourth, however, these developments have taken place in a changing economic and social environment which has had a direct impact on social services departments and social work practice with children and families. The amount of need and potential clients has grown as increas-ing sections of the population have become marginal-ised from the mainstream of the economy. The most recent official figures (*Households Below Average Income 1979–1990/91*, 1993) demonstrate that a total of 13.5 million people (24 per cent of the population), including 3.9 million children (31 per cent of all under-16s), were living on less than half the average income in 1990/91. In 1979 the equivalent figures were 5 million people and 1.4 million children, indicating a virtual threefold increase during the 1980s. To make the situation worse the poorest families suffered a cut of 14 per cent in their real income between 1979 and 1990/91, while the average household had an increase of 36 per cent. For the bottom group it is as if the £100 they had in 1979 was worth £86 by 1990/91, while for the mean it was worth £136. However, the changes in social security since the early 1980s have left claimant families with greater financial responsibility and reduced access to additional financial support from the state (Graham, 1994).

Similarly numerous reports and surveys have been published demonstrating increased social isolation and insecurity, growing inequalities in income and wealth, poor housing and homelessness and the impact of unemployment on children and families (Barclay, 1995; Hills, 1995; Utting, 1995). All this when local government, the voluntary sector and other areas of health and welfare services are subject to reduced resources and almost perpetual reorganisation.

While the Children Act 1989 put considerable extra responsibilities and demands upon social services departments following its introduction in October 1991 for family support for children in need, it is clear that resources required are not available (Health Committee Second Report, 1991). A national survey carried out by the Association of Directors of Social Services in 1991 found that, of 83 authorities who responded to the survey, over half anticipated either a reduced or standstill budget in 1991–2; 28 of them anticipated reductions. In London budgets were reported to have been reduced in nine of the 17 boroughs who responded to the survey, three anticipated a standstill and five were providing for growth in 1991–2 (quoted in Health Committee Second Report, 1991, p. xvi). In effect, resources were grossly inadequate at a time when local authorities, and other agencies, faced new responsibilities (Schorr, 1992).

This increased actual and potential demand in the context of reduced or, at best, maintained resources means that social workers and social services departments are finding it almost impossible to develop the more wideranging preventative family support strategies included in the Children Act 1989 (DoH, 1993; 1994). Priorities and choices have to be made, but not just between family support for children in need and responding to child abuse, but also choices and priorities in relation to child abuse itself. It is in this respect that the assessment of 'high risk' takes on its particular purchase and gets to the heart of what it means to do child protection work. The focus becomes differentiating the 'high risk' from the rest, so that children can be protected, parental rights and responsibilities can be respected and scarce resources directed to where they will, in theory, be most effective.

The comments of the Beckford Report encapsulate the situation and why it is seen to be of such significance:

> Society should sanction, in 'high risk' cases, the removal of such children from an appropriate time. Such a policy, we calculate, might save many of the lives of the 40 to 50 children who die at the hands of their parents every year, and at the same time would concentrate scarce and costly resources of Social Services Departments to the 'grey areas' of cases where something more than supervision and something less than long-term removal is indicated. (London Borough of Brent, 1985, p. 289)

It is in these 'grey areas' that the recently constituted systems, policies and practices of child protection operate. Resources and skills are focused on assessing and sifting out 'high risk', particularly when 'high risk' cannot be clearly demarcated. Where there is insufficient knowledge to demonstrate that the family or situation is safe, systems of monitoring, observation and surveillance take on a major significance. While strictly operating outside the courtroom and the formal legal mechanisms, the legal gaze has become pervasive. Increasingly the focus is concerned with weighing and assessing forensic evidence so that policy and practice, crucially dependent upon professional judgement is framed in terms of legalism and procedures. The more voluntary, indirect and universal child-care services have been remodelled because of concerns about child protection. While originally conceived in socio-medical terms, increasingly child protection has been conceptualised and operationalised in a socio-legal framework where the assessment of 'high risk' becomes central.

While *Working Together under the Children Act 1989* (Home Office et al., 1991) recommended that the more generalised category of 'grave concern' (previously 'high risk') be removed as a category for the purposes of registering cases on child protection registers and most ACPCs have done so, what we are suggesting is that the notion of 'high risk' is now embedded in and in effect is *the* key signifier of child abuse and thereby lies at the heart of child protection work.

As we demonstrated in Chapter 1, child protection policy and practice is now seen to be exemplified by systems overload. Numerous commentators are now arguing that too many cases are unnecessarily being dragged into the child protection net and that far too much time and resource is being used up in investigating child protection referrals. What is of considerable interest is that a recent well publicised and authoritative analysis (Audit Commission, 1994) has argued that this could be controlled and better managed by the use of tighter criteria for pursuing an investigation and having clearer and more precise risk indicators. It is to the issue of risk factors and indicators in child abuse that we turn in the next chapter.

3
Orthodox Approaches to Child Abuse Risk: A Critical Appraisal

Central to current thinking and embedded in policy guidance is the assumption that child protection work is fundamentally concerned with the identification of 'high risk'. As we argued in Chapter 2, the primary focus of research and the development of policy and practice since the early 1970s has been increasingly concerned with the development and refinement of policies, practices and technologies concerned with identifying 'high risk' and thereby differentiating and categorising cases. For, in theory, the identification of the actually or potentially 'high risk' individual or family provides the mechanism for ensuring that children are protected, unwarrantable interventions are avoided and scarce resources are allocated efficiently.

Much of the public criticism directed at practitioners, often reinforced and fuelled by the public inquiries themselves and the media, is that tragedies and scandals have arisen because practitioners failed, in part, due to their lack of knowledge about child abuse which a thorough grounding in the research and its findings would have given them. Until recently it was assumed that research has established what the nature of child abuse is, who the actual or potential perpetrators and victims are and hence what are the associated factors which put children at 'high risk'. Thereby child abuse is identifiable, predictable and preventable via the development and application of scientific research. If only social workers and other professionals familiarised themselves with these research findings and integrated them into their everyday practice, tragedies could be avoided.

However, to assume that the messages from research for the policy-maker and practitioner are clear and straightforward is naive. We wish to argue that there has been a failure to recognise the complexity and lacunae of research which attempts to isolate the characteristics associated with 'high risk' and of the difficulties that await those who avail themselves uncritically of its 'findings'. Apart from the difficulty of distilling research findings without distortion for the benefit of practitioners, there are critical methodological loopholes and inconsistencies in the research itself.

The Medico-Scientific Reality of Child Abuse

Up until recent years research and theorising and also policy and practice assumed that we had previously denied and repressed the fact(s) of child abuse and that children had suffered as a result. It was assumed that child abuse was a reality which had been hidden in the privacy of the family and hence hidden from public and professional view. Science, particularly medical science, was seen as crucial for establishing the reliable foundations for the generalisable knowledge of child abuse and hence informing policy and practice. It was believed that the deep structures and realities of child abuse were knowable and that it was intellectually, culturally and strategically possible to do something about it. What was needed was research to uncover this reality and rip away the layers of disguise. The development of scientific and objective knowledge would allow professionals to identify abuse and intervene benignly on behalf of children. The model was based on what one of us has called elsewhere (Parton, 1985) the disease or public health model of child abuse, and developed from the approach articulated by Henry Kempe and his colleagues (1962) in Denver in terms of the 'battered child syndrome'. While child abuse referred to a wide variety of situations that varied in form and degree of harm, the notion of the battered child syndrome, until recent years, remained the root metaphor.

As Giovannoni (1982) demonstrated, the model originated in the late 19th century when public health developed a methodology and terminology for mounting programmes and interventions to control and eliminate acute infectious diseases (Armstrong, 1983). Such an approach assumes that the disease is attributable to a particular virus or bacteria which can be clearly demonstrated and which hence constitutes the essential causes of the disease. Not only can its causal links be shown, but its habits, strengths and weaknesses can be determined so that ultimately the disease may be tackled. Other facts about the disease can be established with regard to its point of onset, duration, symptoms, impact on other parts of the body and ultimate outcomes, ranging from minor discomforts to death.

Having established the knowledge and facts, a system of ideas is formulated for intervening and hence preventing the disease or problem. Most crucially it means identifying the population which is at risk of being exposed to the noxious or infectious agent via proximity or because of certain characteristics which make them more vulnerable. When applied to child abuse it is assumed that if we can identify the characteristics associated with actual or potential abuse, we will be able to identify and hence predict and prevent it. The crucial role for the researcher thus becomes one of establishing the characteristics associated with actual or potential abuse, while the role of the practitioners is concerned with learning these facts or indicators so that they can then identify cases of actual or potential abuse.

In order to assess the approach it is important to address a number of questions. How far does the phenomenon of child abuse approximate to this model? Is there agreement amongst researchers about the nature of child abuse and how it is defined? What are the characteristics or factors that have been associated with child abuse whereby it can be identified? How far can it be predicted, prevented and treated in the way suggested?

Clearly an unambiguous definition of what constitutes child abuse is fundamental for the efficacy and utility of the model. However, the definition varies amongst professional groups, across cultural, ethnic and religious groups, and by geographical location (Korbin, 1981; Gelles, 1982; Giovannoni and Beccera, 1979; Starr, 1982; Valentine et al., 1984). There is no standardised definition of child abuse that has been developed by researchers and accepted and operationalised by practitioners. As we have already seen, the definitional boundaries of the problem have broadened. While Henry Kempe defined the problem in 1962 as 'the battered child syndrome', by 1976 he had abandoned the concept in favour of the more all-inclusive term 'child abuse and neglect,' which referred to 'the permanent adverse effects on the developmental process and the child's emotional well-being' (Helfer and Kempe, 1976, Introduction). It is not simply that the definition of the problem has undergone considerable 'diagnostic inflation' (Dingwall, 1989, p. 29) but that, despite vigorous debate over the last two decades, little progress has been made in constructing a clear, reliable, valid and agreed definition of child abuse (National Research Council, 1993, p. 57).

This lack of a definition is the most telling indicator that most research in the area of child abuse is at a very rudimentary level. Without a standardised definition, research findings can be misleading and confusing. It creates a fundamental problem when attempts are made to judge its existence, prevalence, size and significance. If researchers are unable to agree about what constitutes child abuse it, potentially, puts policy-makers and practioners in an invidious position of trying to identify, prevent and treat a problem whose nature and magnitude remain undefined. Nowhere is this more evident than in relation to sexual abuse, as recently dramatically illustrated in relation to a study carried out for the NSPCC (Brindle, 1995). The problem prompted the Cleveland inquiry to note that 'it has been impossible from the evidence provided to the Inquiry to arrive at any consensus or to obtain any reliable figures of the general prevalence of sexual abuse of children in the country or in Cleveland' (Secretary of State, 1988, p. 4). It also commented that 'we are strongly of the opinion that great caution should be exercised at the present time in accepting percentages as to the prevalence and incidence of sexual abuse. We received from published articles and oral evidence figures of 5%, 10% and upwards. Such figures depend on what is meant by sexual abuse' (p. 5).

These comments reflected a review completed at that time of eight research studies on the frequency of childhood sexual abuse in the UK (Markowe, 1988). The prevalence of sexual abuse in the studies varied from 3 per cent (BBC, 1986) to 90 per cent (BBC, 1987). A major reason for such variation was that the studies used quite different case definitions of sexual abuse, many of which included a number of elements. For example, the often quoted MORI survey (Baker and Duncan, 1985) considered:

> A child (anyone under 16 years) is sexually abused when another person, who is sexually mature, involves the child in any activity which the other person expects to lead to their sexual arousal. This might involve intercourse, touching, exposure of the sexual organs, showing pornographic material or talking about things in an erotic way. (p. 458)

The interviews with a nationally representative sample of adults about their childhood yielded a figure of 10 per cent who reported being sexually abused. Of these, 51 per cent of the experiences reported as abusive involved no physical contact, 44 per cent involved physical contact but not sexual intercourse and 5 per cent reported full sexual intercourse. It is important that when statistics on incidence enter the public and professional domains we are clear about what is being referred to and what is included in the definition. The wide variation reported in research concerning the incidence and prevalence of child abuse in part reflects the very different definitions of the problem used (Wyatt and Peters, 1986). As La Fontaine (1990) has argued, 'figures depend very much on the way they are produced: they are affected by the definition of abuse but they are also affected by the sources of information and the methods of research used. The difficulties of establishing anything like an accurate assessment are seldom given serious consideration and they are formidable' (p. 45). So not all the discrepancies can be ascribed to definitions alone. A number of other aspects of research design, such as the type of sample, the number and nature of questions asked to elicit details of sexual abuse, and the mode of administration have all been shown to influence the estimates of prevalence identified. As Ghate and Spencer (1995) have demonstrated, there are a whole range of methodological and ethical issues which have to be considered before carrying out any study of the prevalence of sexual abuse.

While these issues of definition, incidence and prevalence are sharply illustrated in relation to sexual abuse, they pervade the whole area of child abuse. As a consequence they pose real problems for the policy-maker, practitioner and manager, who are expected to respond to a problem whose magnitude and significance are open to wide and sometimes conflicting interpretations. Brian Roycroft, President of the Association of Directors of Social Services in 1987, answered the question 'what is the incidence of child abuse and child sexual abuse?' in his evidence to the Cleveland inquiry by stating: 'we don't know .... There are no firm statistics available at either national or local level to determine the incidence of child abuse.'

These issues have recently been starkly highlighted in a debate concerning the number of suspicious child deaths in England and Wales as an indication of the performance of child protection services. While Colin Pritchard claims that between 1973 and 1988 there was a substantial reduction in baby homicides, equivalent to a fall of 61 per cent in England and Wales and 57 per cent in Scotland (Pritchard, 1992; 1993), Sue Creighton (1993) has argued that there have been no such reductions – the changes simply reflect different recording practices. We do not even seem to have any agreement on the number of children who die as a result of child abuse.

Factors Associated with Child Abuse

However, these definitional and methodological issues are not only of significance for debates about incidence and prevalence. They also influence the factors and characteristics which are identified as being particularly associated with child abuse itself. These in turn have implications for attempts to identify, predict and prevent the problem and particularly which children, families and sections of the population are seen as 'high risk'.

Central to the concept of prevention in the medico-scientific model is the idea of cause. In the case of acute infectious diseases, attempts are made to isolate a single identifiable organism. How has such an approach been operationalised in child abuse research and how appropriate is it? Essentially the approach has been to try to identify the factors or characteristics that are associated with cases or situations of abuse, to assume that these are qualitatively different from the rest of the population and finally to hypothesise that these factors or characteristics in some way relate to the basic cause(s) of the problem. As a consequence, these factors or characteristics should direct attempts to identify and predict, and hence prevent.

The first difficulty is, as we have seen, that the term 'child abuse' covers a range of behaviours and problems, so that a search for a single or even a cluster of 'causes' is likely to be in vain.

The vast majority of research in the 1960s in America and the 1970s in Britain was based on relatively small-scale, retrospective clinical studies of cases that had come to the attention of health and welfare professionals. Essentially, the cases and their history were studied to establish what factors or characteristics they had in common. They suffered from two fundamental problems. First, they used variable and often vague definitions of abuse, so that in many cases it was not clear that they were dealing with established cases of abuse. Invariably the cases studied had been referred because of a variety of concerns and worries about the children but there was no unequivocal evidence that the children had been abused – according to any definition. Second, such studies rarely used any matched control groups. As a consequence we have no evidence to suggest that the factors identified as associated with abuse were in any way specific to this group (Spinetta and Rigler, 1972). They may simply have reflected the population from which they were drawn. In 1978 Allan concluded her survey of such research by writing:

> The quality of research in the area of child abuse still leaves much to be desired. There has been little attempt to review previous research with a view to formulating and testing specific hypotheses ... frequently studies seem to start and finish with relatively untested common sense assumptions. Much of our existing knowledge has been gathered from descriptive studies which lack controls and proper sampling procedures. This has enabled authors to make claims and counter claims about the importance of different variables in the absence of any sustained efforts to discover which are directly and which are artefactually related to abuse. (Allan, 1978, p. 59)

As a result, different research came up with different findings so that the policy-maker and practitioner ended up with long lists of poorly defined and sometimes contradictory characteristics.

The primary focus for research has been the identification of the characteristics of the adults and children which are associated with child abuse. However, the findings have proved inconsistent and often contradictory. Early studies assumed that a distinct psychiatric disorder could be found to differentiate parents or other caretakers who abused their children. Although a small percentage of parents were diagnosed with a psychiatric disorder, most individuals were simply identified as troubled or anxious and rarely exhibited extreme psychopathology (Steele and Pollock, 1968). A consistent profile of parental psychopathology or mental disturbance has not been established (Melnick and Hurley, 1969; Spinetta and Rigler, 1972; Polansky et al., 1992). These early studies stimulated research on parental characteristics more generally and attempts to identify the personality profile of abusing parents (Milner and Chilamkurti, 1991). Recent *prospective studies* have identified a set of parental personality attributes associated with child maltreatment in terms of low self-esteem, external locus of control, poor impulse control, negative affectivity and antisocial behaviour, including aggression and substance abuse. Central is a triad of highly correlated personality characteristics involving depression, anxiety and antisocial behaviour (see National Research Council, 1993) which are themselves associated with disrupted social relations, social isolation, poor support systems and inability to cope with stress (Crittenden, 1985; Wolfe, 1985).

The research on adult personality characteristics associated with child sexual abuse is more extensive than that on other forms of child abuse since the primary cause of sexual abuse has been sought in the profile of the adult offender. No specific diagnostic category has been identified. While some molesters are reported to be timid, unassertive and awkward, others are said to exhibit conduct disorders and poor impulse control; others, however, have achieved professional respect and are successful community leaders. Psychiatric profiles used to classify sex offenders report the presence of an antisocial personality disorder, but there is a wide variety of psychopathology and an accepted system of sexual offence classification and the contribution of perpetrator characteristics has not been established (Hartmann and Burgess, 1989).

The problems associated with attempts to establish the characteristics of adults who abuse are exemplified in the research on alcohol and drugs, for the often noted association between substance abuse and aggression has suggested that the use of alcohol and drugs may be a significant risk factor in abusive families. What quickly becomes apparent is that the associations between alcoholism, drug abuse and child abuse are not well understood.

Studies of alcoholism amongst abusing parents have considerable methodological problems resulting from sample selection and research design. Hamilton and Collins (1982) concluded that the results were contradictory with some studies finding a significant relationship while others did not. Similarly Orme and Rimmer (1981) found no empirical data to support an association between alcoholism and child abuse. More recent studies are based on improved methodologies, but their results continue to be contradictory and only one study has offered strong evidence of a connection between child abuse and alcohol use (Famularo et al., 1986), but again the researchers noted that limitations in the study design may have affected the incidence of reported alcoholism in their groups. One prospective study that compared matched groups of sons of alcoholic and non-alcoholic fathers found no significant differences in the extent of child physical abuse (Pollock et al., 1990). Thus, while alcohol and drug abuse are often cited as principal risk factors in child abuse, the evidence is very uncertain.

Risk factors associated with the children themselves have also been studied. Retrospective research has suggested that factors such as prematurity, low birth-weight and illness or handicapping conditions in the infant or child interfere with attachment making the child more vulnerable to maltreatment (Lynch and Roberts, 1977; Oates et al., 1979). However, others have argued that this is not the case and suggest that such findings result from a variety of flaws in the research methodology (Dingwall, 1989). The identification of child risk factors associated with abuse has generated controversy as to whether such child behaviours and characteristics contribute to or are consequences of the abuse. Researchers have also sought to distinguish between child characteristics that may be causal and those that maintain or perpetuate abuse (Ammerman, 1991; Drotar, 1992). In general, however, little is known about the processes and interaction through which child characteristics and behaviours become risk factors, either by contributing to or maintaining abusive situations.

Thus attempts to identify key risk factors associated with child abuse have failed to establish any clear causal relationships or sequences between the variables. Crucially they have failed to differentiate between what constitutes 'high risk' and the rest. More recently studies have attempted to refine their research methodologies and tried to be much clearer about what we can claim to know and not know about child abuse, recognising that it is a much more complex problem than was first thought. It is now suggested that it is more appropriate to see child abuse as a result of multiple interacting factors, including the parents' and children's psychological traits, the family's place in the larger social and economic structure, and the balance of external supports and stresses, both interpersonal and material. The role of the different health and welfare services are also seen as crucial in this process. Not only will the balance of factors vary depending on the severity and type of abuse being analysed, but there appears to be no uniformity in the association found between different sets of factors and different types of abuse. It is also recognised that even where there may be some correlation between certain factors and certain forms of abuse, it is inappropriate to assume that the one causes the other; both may be linked to a third but unseen set of structures and mechanisms.

The emerging social interactional models emphasise the importance of viewing child maltreatment in the context of the family, community and wider society, rather than emphasising only individual characteristics and stresses

(Belsky, 1980; Garbarino and Gilliam, 1980; Parke and Collmer, 1975; Wolfe, 1991). The phenomenon of child abuse has thus moved away from the conception of a symptom of an individual disorder or psychological disturbance towards seeing it as an extreme disturbance of childrearing which itself is part of a wider context of other serious family problems, such as poverty and antisocial behaviour.

Interactive models generally build on a probabilistic risk assessment process, assuming that child abuse occurs when multiple risk factors outweigh protective, compensatory factors – some of which may be enduring and others transient (Ciccheti and Carlson, 1989). Again some may be more important in instigating abuse while others support its endurance. Risk does not arise from a single causal factor but a combination of multiple interacting elements located at the individual, family, community and societal levels. Not only does the significance of factors vary over time and space, but there are a variety of pathways to abuse. Abnormality is a relative phenomenon. Clearly, however, the complexity of such an approach cannot be reduced to a checklist of factors which can be used in any clear or categorical sense to identify and predict abuse. While methodologically and theoretically much more sophisticated, the direct implications for policy and practice are far from straightforward.

So while we may know something about who is *more likely* to abuse and who is *more likely* to be a victim, we do not know why, when, how often and with what degree of certainty abuse will take place, nor what the consequences for the child will be.

When analysing the factors associated with abuse it is, however, important to differentiate between 'what we know' about physical abuse and neglect and 'what we know' about sexual abuse. In many aspects all children are at risk since being a child is itself a socially and biologically vulnerable state.

As far as physical abuse and neglect is concerned a variety of factors have been identified which may put children in certain families at risk. Anne Cohn, from her exhaustive review of the research, summarises these factors as follows:

Larger families, families with closely spaced children, families with young children, and single-parent families are at greater risk. Also vulnerable are families under great stress, which may result from financial difficulties, marital discord, social isolation, or poor health. Parents' child management and social skills, as well as their self-esteem, help to define who is at risk. Certain characteristics or traits of the child, including low birth-weight, prematurity, illness in infancy, and impediments to attachment and bonding may also be factors. (1983, p. 171)

Research specifically concerned with sexual abuse has identified risk factors which, while similar in some respects, include important differences. David Finkelhor has reviewed a variety of American surveys of adults in order to assess the information provided about the relative risk of children from different backgrounds experiencing sexual abuse (Finkelhor, 1986; Finkelhor and Barron, 1986). Significantly the surveys were consistent in failing to find differences in rates according to social class or race. This is an important difference as physical abuse and neglect does seem to be associated with social, material and environmental stress and hence with social class and social deprivation.

In Finkelhor's review, several factors emerged as being consistently associated with a higher risk of sexual abuse: when the mother is unavailable to the child either as a result of employment outside the home or disability or illness; when the child lives without one of the biological parents; when a child reports that the parents' marriage is unhappy or conflictual; when the child reports having a poor relationship with the parents or being subject to extremely punitive discipline or child abuse; when the child reports having a stepfather. While girls are at higher risk than boys, increasingly research is suggesting more boys experience sexual abuse than was at first thought. Pre-adolescents appear to be more at risk than either younger or older children. Girls with few friends in childhood report more abuse, though this may be an effect of abuse and not a risk factor. Perpetrators are at present almost exclusively male, though increasingly a few women are reported, particularly in retrospective studies. La Fontaine (1990) has identified similar factors in the pattern of sexual abuse in British surveys.

More generally it seems that discussions and explanations of physical abuse and neglect may be seen most productively as a problem relating to parenting, which in turn needs to be located in an understanding of social class and the gendered divisions of child care, while sexual abuse, to a much greater extent, needs to be understood more explicitly in relation to male power and masculine socialisation. However, the divisions are far from clear-cut or straightforward as we will argue later.

Prediction and the Identification of High Risk

Embedded in the notion of high risk is not simply that cases of actual child abuse can be separated from the rest but that certain factors, characteristics or signs point to the potential for such abuse in the future. The science and technology of risk assessment are crucially based on the assumption that *future* harm can be prevented and predicted and thereby modified and controlled. However, as we will argue, such an approach is fundamentally misconceived. For while the various associated risk factors may help in informing more general preventive strategies and overall policies concerning priorities and resource allocation, because child abuse is such a complex issue we have not developed the skills, techniques or understanding for successful prediction. We are unable to predict with any accuracy who will or will not abuse. In particular, such attempts at prediction are bedevilled by what Dingwall (1989) has called the 'definitional fallacy' and the 'statistical fallacy'.

First, the 'definitional fallacy'. Essentially this relates to the earlier discussion of the failure by researchers, policymakers and practitioners to operationalise a clear and agreed definition of what constitutes child abuse. As Dingwall (1989) has argued, the definition of the problem has broadened considerably and the growth of research 'reflects the transformation of original concerns to embrace virtually any problem which may have an adverse impact on a child and can possibly be attributed to some act of commission or omission by an adult' (p. 29). He quotes a number of examples in illustration which include: the administration of cannabis by teenage babysitters

(Schwartz et al., 1986); the keeping of household pets where a child has asthma (Franklin and Kahn, 1987); child labour in Nigeria (Asogwa, 1986); and the mistaken diagnosis of abuse seen in itself as a form of abuse (Kirschner and Stein, 1985). This process of 'diagnostic inflation' has arisen in major part because the term has proved symbolically so powerful in drawing attention to a series of adult–child issues and legitimating them as a social problem. Research has invariably failed to recognise this and as a consequence has often failed to approach its task in a neutral way by trying to account for the nature and the incidence of particular forms of adult–child interactions and their consequences. It is then a subsequent and essentially a political/moral question as to whether and which of these should then constitute child abuse.

This failure to address seriously what constitutes child abuse has led to some strange lacunae. In particular other more general social scientific studies of children, child care and family life have rarely been drawn upon to inform and clarify what is known about child abuse. For example, during the 1970s the Department of Health and Social Security and the Social Science Research Council funded a number of studies concerned with the nature, causes and outcomes of deprivation and disadvantages in families. This initiative arose out of the then Secretary of State Sir Keith Joseph's interest in the 'cycle of deprivation' (for a comprehensive review see Brown and Madge, 1982). From these studies an attempt was then made to identify 'families in difficulty'. What is apparent is that the risk factors identified run parallel to and in many respects are very similar to those already noted in relation to child abuse and neglect. It was argued that whether problems stem from personal shortcomings, from the structure of society or from some combination of these two influences, the focus should be on the family and on signs that something is likely to be 'wrong':

> Certain areas of family functioning are particularly useful for predictions of this kind. These features of family life – which it should be re-emphasised are indicators of, rather than the reasons for, problems – include the age and maturity of the parents, burdens carried by a family, consistency and change

in the lives of children, dynamics and support within the family, and the experiences and characteristics of individual family members. (Madge, 1983, p. 201)

While Madge does not claim that the guide is infallible nor that the list of risk factors is complete, she does argue that the items – 'an alphabet of risk' – both singly and cumulatively help to establish the probability that individual families will be under stress. This is claimed as a major contribution to identifying and predicting 'families in difficulty'. Clearly, however, the moral, legal, policy and practice connotations and implications associated with 'families in difficulty' are qualitatively very different from those associated with child abuse. The crucial questions that this raises are simply: what are predictive studies claiming to predict and what is the nature of the risk which is being identified?

Second, the 'statistical fallacy' which draws attention to another, related, set of problems. Whatever method of screening or identification is used, prediction rates rise no higher than two wrong judgements for every right judgement. Empirical support for the prediction of future harm is very small. Research on prediction falls down in terms of both its reliability and its validity.

This arises from the statistical problems of 'false negatives' and 'false positives'. If the rate of child abuse amongst families in the population is relatively low, and we have noted that the incidence of sexual abuse may be around 10 per cent (Baher and Duncan, 1985) while the incidence of serious physical abuse may be 3–4 per cent (see Straus et al., 1980; Gelles and Straus, 1987; Schene, 1987), and the accuracy of the prediction technique is relatively weak, there is considerable potential for wrongly identifying some who will never be abused (false positive) and missing others who will be abused (false negative). If the criterion to predict abuse is 80 per cent accurate (and no technique(s) have developed such high levels of accuracy) and if the rate of abuse in the population is 10 in 100, then if 1,000 people/families are screened, 80 out of the 100 will be correctly identified while 20 will be missed (false negative). However, we will also incorrectly identify 20 per cent, or 200 of the original 1,000 screened. Thus, for

every 80 correctly predicated we will have 20 false negatives and 200 false positives.

Work by Kevin Browne clearly demonstrates the problems involved. He has prospectively evaluated a typical
checklist completed by midwives and health visitors
around the time of birth (1993). The checklist was developed from a number of demographic and epidemiological
studies he had previously carried out in the UK with
special reference to non-accidental injury to children
(Browne and Saqi, 1988). There were 12 items on the checklist: history of family violence; parent indifferent, intoler-
ant or over-anxious towards child; single or separated
parent; socio-economic problems such as unemployment;
history of mental illness, drug or alcohol addiction; parent
abused or neglected as a child; infant premature, low birth-
weight; infant separated from mother for more than
24 hours post delivery; mother less than 21 years old at the
time of birth; step-parent or cohabitee present; less than
18 months between birth of children; infant mentally or
physically handicapped. Health visitors in conjunction
with professional colleagues completed the checklist on all
children born in 1985 and 1986 in three health districts
in Surrey, England. In total, 14,252 births were screened
for the potential of child abuse and neglect and 964
(7 per cent) were identified as "high risk".

The full population of 14,252 children was then followed
up for five years and, in 1991, 106 families had been subject
to a case conference for suspected or actual abuse of their
newborn child, giving an incidence of seven children in
every thousand. Fully completed checklists, with the relative weighting for each factor taken into account, could
correctly classify 86 per cent of potential cases. The screening procedure was sensitive to 68 per cent of abusing families and correctly specified 94 per cent of the non-abusing
families. However, nearly a third of the abusing families
had few risk factors and were incorrectly identified as 'low
risk'. Similarly 6 per cent of the non-abusing families were
incorrectly identified as 'high risk'. As Browne (1993, p. 29)
points out, 'the checklist detection rate would mean that
for every 14,252 births screened it would be necessary to
distinguish between 72 true risk cases and 892 false positives in the 964 cases identified as "high risk". He goes on

to argue the importance therefore of a second screening process to be carried out with the high risk families based on the significant differences between abusing and non-abusing parent–child relationships (Browne and Saqi, 1987).

These problems of identification and prediction related to the definitional fallacy and the statistical fallacy have become evident in a number of public inquiry reports which have attempted to address the issue of high risk. The Beckford Report (London Borough of Brent, 1985) was very critical of the social workers' failure to use such predictive research. However, while the report argues that it is crucial that social workers identify 'high risk', it comments that 'we do not define "high risk", mainly because we think that it is not susceptible of definition' (p. 288). Drawing upon the research presented to it by Professor Cyril Greenland, and reported in full in Greenland (1987), the report asserts that:

> the proportion of 'high risk' cases out of all proved cases of persistent child abuse will be small, and the task of identifying may not be easy. But the attempt to isolate such cases from the majority of child abuse cases must always be made. In answer to the question, can 'high risk' situations be identified in advance, Professor Greenland told us that he could give an answer, 'a cautious yes – in some cases'. He went on to say that it seemed prudent to classify all non-accidental injuries to young children as 'high risk' cases, since 80% of all children unlawfully killed by their parents had been previously abused. (p. 288)

Thus we are not given a definition of high risk. More significantly, however, we are not given any indication, from all the allegations and referrals that come to official notice, of how we are to sift out the high risk cases. By implication they are all high risk cases. The Beckford Report completely fails to address the problems arising from both the definitional fallacy and the statistical fallacy.

In contrast, the Cleveland Report (Secretary of State, 1988) was very aware of the issues in relation to sexual abuse and spent considerable time trying to weigh the often contradictory evidence presented to it concerning identification and assessment. It was particularly concerned that assessments should not accuse parents and families on the basis of unproven diagnostic and predictive techniques.

Much of this was concerned with the significance of the anal dilation test as a sign or indication of sexual abuse. The report concludes that 'we are satisfied from the evidence that the consensus is that the sign of anal dilation is abnormal and suspicious and requires further investigation. *It is not in itself evidence of anal abuse*' (p. 193, our emphasis). More generally, 'it was accepted that anal abuse may cause a range of signs, from surface skin damage, fissures, defects of anal verge, to severe lacerations, but that *in our present state of knowledge*, none of these in themselves, or in various clusters, establish with reasonable certainty that anal abuse has occurred. *All are, or may be, open to alternative explanations*' (p. 189, our emphasis). The Cleveland Report is not simply commenting on the current state of knowledge in terms of the ability of certain signs or characteristics of 'high risk' to predict abuse in the future. Crucially it is pointing to the contested level of knowledge for using certain signs or symptoms as indicating the presence of abuse at all.

In commenting on the nature of the social work processes and practices following a medical diagnosis of sexual abuse, the report comments that 'it requires cautious measured intervention which will allow *the risks of a false positive finding to be balanced against those of a false negative*' (p. 85, our emphasis). The report is pointing to a crucial issue, for if we do not have the skills or technologies to correctly identify and predict actual or potential cases of child abuse with any precision, what is the balance to be struck between missing some (false negatives) and falsely labelling others (false positives)? For attempts to keep false negatives to a minimum may increase the likelihood of false positives, while attempts to reduce false positives will increase the likelihood of tragic false negatives. While research can perhaps clarify and sharpen such issues, how they are resolved is essentially a political and moral question. The debates have been most sharply demonstrated and played out in relation to sexual abuse, but they are not exclusive to sexual abuse alone. They permeate and in many ways lie at the heart of our contradic-

responses to child abuse and thereby encapsulate the uncertainties of child protection work. It is inherently risky in a way which is quite different to the way risk was originally conceptualised and operationalised. It is only now that the full significance of this, the fundamental problems it poses for the medico-scientific approach and its implications for research, policy and practice are becoming apparent.

Medico-Scientific Realism

Increasingly it has been recognised that there have been a whole range of problems with research and explanations of child abuse based on the medico-scientific approach and that these have encompassed both the definitional and the methodological. Neither the way we have defined child abuse *nor* the way we have researched it has been able to represent the true nature of the phenomenon or its many forms, characteristics and causes. The difficulties, however, have until recently been seen to reside with the researchers and practitioners themselves, for only now are we coming to terms with the problem together with the difficulties involved in responding appropriately. The definitional problems have been viewed essentially as a remedial matter, as if it were only a case of obtaining agreement within the scientific and professional communities about the definition(s) and that the task(s) of studying child abuse and establishing risk factors for the purposes of identification and intervention would then be simplified. It is taken as given that child abuse has an objective, often hidden, reality in its own right. It *exists* and constitutes a problem by virtue of causing harm or disturbance to a significant number of children and young people. The poor level of research, policy and practice is seen as simply a reflection of the fact that we are only just beginning to recognise and come to terms with the fact(s) of child abuse. It has taken time for its *true* nature to be *discovered* – professionally, scientifically and epistemologically. Only now are we beginning to *believe* such abuse is a reality instead of *denying* its existence. Science, particularly medical science, has been crucial to this discovery, and the application of certain technologies such as the use of X-rays, anatomically correct dolls, the anal dilation test and the disclosure interview have proved crucial to this unmasking.

Henry Kempe (1979) was quite explicit in describing a specific sequence of *developing stages* in the way society recognises the *existence* of abuse. Certainly his formulation was significant in informing the way child abuse was thought about and responded to during the late 1970s and early 1980s in Britain. It was particularly important in framing the CIBA Foundation Report on *Child Sexual Abuse Within the Family* (1984) which was to prove influential in the development of policy and practice in Britain in the mid 1980s in relation to sexual abuse (see Parton, 1991, pp. 84–91). Kempe identified six stages.

Stage one: denial that either physical or sexual abuse exists to a significant extent. Abuse that is seen is felt to be due to psychotic, drunken or drugged parents, or foreign guests, and nothing to do with the community as a whole.

Stage two: the community pays attention to the more lurid forms of abuse – the battered child – and begins to find ways of coping more effectively with severe physical abuse and, through early recognition and intervention, with less severe abuse.

Stage three: physical abuse is better handled and attention is now beginning to be paid to the infant who fails to thrive and is neglected physically. More subtle forms of abuse, such as poisoning, are recognised.

Stage four: the community recognises emotional abuse and neglect and patterns of severe rejection, scapegoating and emotional deprivation.

Stage five: the community pays attention to the serious plight of the sexually abused child.

Stage six: the guaranteeing that each child is truly wanted and provided with loving care, decent shelter and food, and first class preventive and curative health.

In many respects changes in policy and practice until the mid 1980s can be seen to have followed this developmental model. While few would agree we have seriously addressed stage six and responses to and recognition of the other stages are patchy and inconsistent we can be seen to have travelled from stages one to five over the last 25 years. Certainly, the way the problem is officially defined has moved from 'the battered baby' in the 1960s and early 1970s to 'non-accidental injury to children' in the 1970s and 'child abuse' in the mid 1980s.

Thus, while the critical empirical evidence severely questions the traditional medico-scientific approach to child abuse in its own terms, attempts to develop and rework the model, particularly in terms of the more interactional approaches suggest that the realities of child abuse can be identified. While much more sophisticated and complex explanations and approaches have been developed, the emphasis on trying to develop and identify risk factors has become even more central.

Conclusions

At the conceptual and theoretical levels, however, even more fundamental problems and criticisms become evident. The approach and its proposals for action are heavily dependent on the conceptual apparatus of *positivism*. Positivism's essential assumption concerns the unity of the scientific method, so that the premises and approach(es) of the physical and natural sciences are applied to human action and society. Although there are many varieties of positivism, the main concern has been with individual positivism where it is admitted that while different influences might contribute to the creation of the problem, it is in the individual that the crucial predisposition is situated.

The approach takes for granted a scientific, neutral stance whereby society and human action are comparable to a natural organism. It is assumed that human action is determined or caused by clearly identifiable factors. As a result, the study of child abuse becomes the examination of antecedent factors or their indicators and correlates. If we can then identify, stop and/or modify the antecedent factors, we can stop or modify the problem. We need therefore to discover the laws and regularities which cause the problem which can then be applied in everyday practice so that we can identify, predict and prevent in a rational way. In the process, the objectivity of the scientist and the neutrality of the professional are acclaimed and there is an attempt to analyse and present findings in a scientific, perhaps quantified, way.

There are two essential problems with such approaches. First is the assumption that there is a moral consensus in society and everyone agrees not just that child abuse is a problem but also on what the nature and dimensions of the problem are. While appreciating that we have not yet arrived at such a situation, it is assumed that, with increased knowledge and greater attempts at inter-professional and multi-agency approaches, such a consensus will emerge. Also, while the complexities and difficulties associated with child abuse are now recognised, invariably it is assumed that there is an underlying reality of child abuse which is objectively given but which is often hidden. For example, although the Department of Health *Guide for Social Workers Undertaking a Comprehensive Assessment in Cases of Child Protection* (DoH, 1988) sees checklists of risk factors as potentially dangerous, it does assert that 'practitioners should be aware of the constellation of factors often associated with dangerous families' (p. 12). The guide provides 167 detailed questions which social workers should explore. As Hallett and Birchall argue, there is 'a disconcerting implication that collecting the data will automatically provide the necessary judgement' (1992, p. 183). The signs of child abuse may not be clear but its underlying objective reality will emerge. Clearly, however, child abuse is a highly contested area and a very wide range of events are encapsulated under the blanket label.

The problems we have seen with the definition of child abuse cannot be reduced to the technical or the methodological. The definitional category of child abuse is not naturally given, for over the past 30 years the issue has become politically and symbolically very powerful. As a consequence, scientific research is far from neutral and value-free. In fact the literature has paraded extraordinary value positions under the guise of objectivity. Highly evaluative terms such as 'immaturity', 'disordered', 'disorganised', 'undersocialised' have been common. Child abuse was launched as a public issue out of a variety of different moral, professional and personal interests, and these and many others have continued to influence its subsequent development (Nelson, 1987; Parton, 1985). Child abuse is a deeply contested category. Not only is it multi-faceted, but increasingly, it is argued, it is socially constructed (Dartington Social Research Unit, 1995). According to Howitt 'the clear message emerging from the lack of absolutist definitions of "child abuse" concerns the impossibility of separating abuse from the social system which identifies it, regulates it and policies it' (1992, p. 5).

This takes us to the second major problem. Approaches drawing on positivism present and analyse the social world as if it were a reified laboratory 'out there' in which individuals can be manoeuvred according to their best interests in some detached way. In treating human beings as a neutral medium through which antecedent factors come to expression, the issue of meaning is ignored. It reifies social phenomena without reference to their meaning for those who are party in some way to the processes involved. But human action takes place in a context which is interpreted by all concerned. Human beings are not simply determined but actively construct their world and make sense of it. An 'abusing mother' or a 'child sexual abuse victim' may not define themselves as such.

What is considered child abuse for the purposes of child protection policy and practice is much better characterised as a product of social negotiation between different values and beliefs, different social norms and professional knowledges and perspectives about children, child development and parenting. Far from being a medico-scientific reality, it is a phenomenon where moral reasoning and moral judgements are central. As Dingwall, Eekelaar and Murray argued in 1983:

> Practitioners are asked to solve problems every day that philosophers have argued about for the last two thousand years and will probably debate for the next two thousand.

Inevitably, arbitrary lines have to be drawn and hard cases decided. These difficulties, however, are not a justification for avoiding judgements. Moral evaluations can and must be made if children's lives and well-being are to be secured. What matters is that we should not disguise this and pretend it is all a matter of finding better checklists or new models of psychopathology – technical fixes when the proper decision is a decision about what constitutes a good society. (1983, p. 244)

4
Deconstructing Child Protection: Some Methodological Choices

All of the research associated with the orthodox approach to child abuse can be loosely framed as positivist. It assumes the respectable cloak of scientific inquiry and we refer to it as orthodox because, by and large, it contributes to the authoritative version of child abuse and it has largely gone unchallenged (Hughes, 1990).[1] As we argued in Chapter 3, it has been perpetuated by the adoption of certain accepted methods of scientific inquiry, largely drawn from a positivist position, and including most of the qualitative research, which frame the social problem of child harm and injury as something which can be remedially resolved and thus open to this line of inquiry. It is not by accident that the beginnings of the current phase can be attributed to the discovery made by paediatric radiologists in the late 1950s of the 'battered baby syndrome' (Parton, 1985; Pfohl, 1977). Prior to this 'discovery', child harm and injury was something responded to by child welfare agencies, the law, the police and the public (Parton, 1985; Corby, 1993). Significantly, it was not responded to by a research community. The (scientific) discovery of the 'battered baby' initiated a research programme, strongly imbued with the values of medical research, which branched into the social domain without reflection on the tortuous philosophical issues which dogged the social sciences (Winch, 1991). These issues, which could be broadly grouped under the question of whether the study of social phenomena could be conducted by the same methods as the physical sciences, passed by largely unnoticed. More specifically, this paradigm, and most of the literature as a consequence, pays no attention to the way in which knowledge about child abuse, child harm and injury, its victims, perpetrators and participants, are shaped, constructed, maintained and used.

What is Child Abuse?

Child abuse is a highly contentious and contested area in terms of theory, research, policy and practice. Issues and tensions which permeate and characterise debates at the wider policy level also, and perhaps more sharply, permeate and characterise practice at the micro day-to-day level. An example of the first would be the public debates that raged around the issue of 'ritual' or 'satanic' abuse (La Fontaine, 1994) – what sort of a problem was it? An example of the second could be the case of Simon, aged eight, who was forced to beat his drunken father who sat in a chair naked every night until he was too weak to beat him any further. Was this, or was it not, child abuse, or was it, as a court official commented, 'father abuse'? Reduced to its essentials the *truth* or *reality* of child abuse is continually being addressed, publicly and professionally, both in terms of the individual referral or case – is this a case of child abuse? – and in terms of wider policy debates – how big a problem is it, what priority should it be accorded, and crucially, as a moral issue, what should be done about it?

In many respects these issues touch the heart of some central questions which have concerned social theorists in relation to social phenomena for many years. How far does child abuse have an objective reality in its own right or how far is it primarily in the eye of the beholder? Put briefly, most of the conventional literature, such as that reviewed in the previous chapter, accepts that child abuse exists. The role of the social scientist and practitioner, as we have shown, is to gauge the size, dimensions and characteristics of the problem, to explore its roots and causes and to investigate solutions whereby it can be modified or removed altogether. In contrast, there is a position which is broadly associated with social constructionism which is not concerned with whether child abuse exists or not but how and why the condition comes to be viewed as child abuse in the first place. Constructionists are concerned with trying to account for the emergence, maintenance, history and conceptualisation of what is defined as child abuse and what is defined as child protection work.

For some it would be objectionable to consider child abuse as anything other than a real problem. Within this view the social constructionist can be accused of rendering the world meaningless – if everything is a social construction then it suggests that nothing 'really' exists, it just depends on how we wish to label it. This position is stated thus:

> no behaviour is necessarily child abuse.... Some sets of facts come to be labelled as cases of child abuse because they go beyond the limits of what is now considered to be acceptable conduct towards a child. These standards change over time and also vary, not only between cultures, but also between different members of the same culture. Child abuse is thus a social construction whose meaning arises from the value structure of a social group and the ways in which these values are interpreted and negotiated in real situations. (Taylor, 1989, p. 46)

The implication is that because child abuse varies from one place to another, and can be defined differently by different people, it is a relative problem. This position has recently been reinforced by the Department of Health (Dartington Social Research Unit, 1995) who share Jane Gibbon's view that, 'as a phenomenon, child maltreatment is more like pornography than whooping cough. It is a socially constructed phenomenon which reflects values and opinions of a particular culture at a particular time' (quoted in Dartington Social Research Unit, 1995, p. 14).

To say that no behaviour is necessarily child abuse or (to use the increasingly interchangeable term) maltreatment, or to suggest that child abuse reflects values and opinions of a particular culture, is an analytic choice. For the victims, perpetrators and families involved an experience which they choose to call abuse clearly does exist, although its meaning may be contested. Children use the term 'abuse', parents use it and practitioners use it. However, noting that child abuse is the subject of relative definition is a part of the problem of child abuse. That is, the fact that in everyday life child abuse is open to definition – in a way that whooping cough is not – makes the claiming of child abuse a contestable matter. The fact that it can be said of child abuse that it is defined relatively, that it depends on how it is labelled (and who does the labelling), is a symptom of its *socially organised character*, and it is the *social organisation* of child abuse which forms a central theme of this book. Viewing social phenomena as socially constructed does not mean that they are subject to relative definitions (*per se*). It means that definitions must be *achieved* on each and every occasion of practical application, wherever it is necessary to consider what is, or whether it is, in this case child abuse.

We have already noted that child abuse does not necessarily have to have overt signs. Unlike whooping cough it doesn't have a unifying symptomology; rather the signs commonly associated with 'abuse' are signs which could signify many things. This makes the context of allegations and behaviour important. The Department of Health (Dartington Social Research Unit, 1995) suggests that understanding the importance of context helps to define abuse. This is to state what people do to help define the almost indefinable – they look for other factors which could be associated with it. What is interesting for us is not whether this is wrong or right, but *how* they do it and *what becomes relevant* – how are abuse and maltreatment *signified*?

The Social Construction of Child Abuse

The principles behind a social constructionist approach were outlined by Berger and Luckman (1984). Their work was focused on the social construction of knowledge, and the sociology of knowledge. Their proposal was to substitute 'knowledge' in inverted commas for knowledge – for a sociological study of 'what passes for knowledge in society' (Sharrock and Coleman, in press). As Sharrock and Coleman point out, the advantage of the idea of the social construction of reality could have been to elaborate on the socially organised ways in which (what Schutz termed) 'the accent of reality' (1964–7) was bestowed from within social settings. The aim was not to 'rubbish' different points of view, nor to expose the world as something that doesn't really exist, although it has been used in this way. They suggest that there is a slippage between sociological and epistemological issues which we find is very much in evidence in recent child protection research. It involves no more than the supposition that to speak of 'what passes for knowledge in society is to give an account of the nature of knowledge' (Sharrock and Coleman, in press).

This is the danger for those who suggest that child abuse is no more than an issue of labelling; that to speak of what is labelled as child abuse in society is to give an account of the nature of child abuse. For example, the Department of Health proposes that the amount of abuse in society alters according to a 'threshold': thus, 'the amount of abuse in society depends upon the point at which thresholds are drawn. Move the dividing line upwards and the amount of abuse in society diminishes; a downward movement has the opposite effect' (Dartington Social Research Unit, 1995, p. 13). This is a clear example of the very slippage to which we refer. The interest and importance of a social constructionist approach is (broadly) sociological. It is not just to say that there is something labelled 'abuse' and that the label changes between time/culture/place; rather it is to keep a clear methodological position which directs attention onto how the term 'abuse' works in a given culture. Thus it is not possible for us (as analysts) to say that any behaviour is abusive, but that is not to say it is not possible at all. Quite the contrary, it is a term which is now ubiquitously available to all, very few people in the Western world would not be aware of the term 'child abuse' and many use it. Thus, as a social phenomenon it exists, and understanding how it exists, how people choose to use it and when, is of some importance in displaying just what sort of a social phenomenon it is. Deconstructing its use enables us to question how it is useful, and how it is used. The end result of this method of enquiry is not to say that child abuse is relative but to say how it *works*.

Deconstruction and Social Construction

We are interested in how child abuse as a socially constructed phenomenon can be seen, and what this methodological choice implies for practice. If child abuse can be viewed as 'that which passes for child abuse in society', then one way to understand how it comes to 'pass for child abuse' is to identify the mechanisms which give rise to such passing. Our attempt to observe and report upon such mechanisms is what we refer to as deconstruction. It is not about 'deconstructing' as in breaking down different versions of a phenomenon and ironicising one version over another (Fuchs and Ward, 1994); rather it is about identifying the methods by which child abuse gets recognised in an organisational setting, that of child protection work. We do not, and cannot, adopt a 'realist' or a 'relativist' position. This problematic and artificial distinction is not of concern to us here, or to thousands of children, their families, social work practitioners, police officers and courts. Instead we are interested in the mechanisms of 'passing' something off as child abuse, or not, which is an everyday phenomenon.[2]

Our interest derives from an assumption that this 'passing' can render much useful information about the social organisation of child abuse. Useful, because whilst this quality of social phenomena has not been recognised in the conventional child abuse literature, its consequences are strongly felt and themselves cause problems. For example, child protection practitioners have a problem, often articulated as the 'damned if you do, damned if you don't' problem (Dingwall et al., 1983), which comes down to moral dilemmas about how best to intervene. Recent pressure to focus on tighter gatekeeping and switch to assisting children 'in need' does not necessarily help. How are social workers to know which children are the right ones? By treating the work of child abuse intervention as a socially organised phenomenon it is possible to identify some of the methods that practitioners use to decide on which children warrant intervention and which do not. Whilst not providing 'correct' answers to the question, we can show how the answers have been found, and open up some questions about how these methods might impact on child welfare intervention if services were oriented towards children 'in need'.

Some sites of 'passing' something off as child abuse are organisational – social work offices, classrooms, health clinics, interviewing suites, courts and police stations. The actions which constitute the 'passing' (or not, as we shall go on to explore) are situated in these places, and in the homes of children who are reported to statutory and voluntary agencies. One area of interest in the literature has been about how these locally situated actions are related to, effected by, or otherwise conditional on the wider social, political and moral environment, and what this environment might be (Gil, 1979; Parton, 1985; Ferguson, 1990; Parton, 1991; Wise, 1991). For example, following Foucault (1972), Donzelot (1980), Philp (1979) and Rose (1985; 1989), Stenson argues that the role of social work is one of mediation between stigmatised minorities and the 'mass of established citizens ... both monitoring and judging the lives of clients and attempting to equip clients with the knowledge and skills for a self regulating citizenship' (1993, p. 42). Stenson attempts to display this 'mediation' through the discourses he claims to have observed in social work interviews: 'citizen exchange discourse' or talking as if equals, and 'hierarchical, normalising discourse' which has as one component 'educative' or 'self regulating' aspects. This notion that social work is regulative is not new (Parton, 1994a; 1994b), but the observation of the work of social work to display the discourse in action can empirically back up what have hitherto been seen as marginalised politically motivated claims. Shifting from notions of state control to the concepts of 'normalising' and regulation, not by the state but through locally situated interchanges, begins to highlight the complexities of child protection work. Social workers are never simply, and only, state agents, and clients are not empty, manipulable vehicles for social work practices.

From the outset we would suggest that we do not see the relationship between locally situated action and social structural considerations as a simple one. Our approach will only begin to explore it. Others have attempted to do the same, particularly in looking at the state (and its laws) as powerful factors in intervention, and suggesting that practices reflect those forces (Parton, 1985; Frost and Stein, 1989; Ferguson, 1990; Parton, 1991). A further dimension has been explored by feminist theorists who locate child abuse in the moral, social and political environment of patriarchy (Gordon, 1988; Driver and Droison, 1989; Campbell, 1988; Wise, 1991). What all of these analyses seem to fail to do (with the exception of Wise, 1991) is treat the definition of child abuse a priori as practically problematic. For example, whilst many texts on the subject (see, for example, Parton, 1985 and Finkelhor, 1986) show that there are various definitions of child abuse, they all characteristically arrive at a definition for their practical purposes (of theorising, or researching the problem they subsequently define). The sources of these different definitions are various researchers, practitioners, clinicians and victims. What they show is that there are competing definitions. One aim of this book is to seek out the ways in which the work of child protection agents becomes defined as child protection. It is from this starting point that, we believe, we can identify some of the social features of the setting which bear some relationship to the constitution of child abuse and its contemporary remedies. We will, there-fore, not be offering a definition; rather we will show what the work of defining child harm/injury/maltreatment/abuse consists of, for those who are culturally sanctioned to judge.

Child Protection as Situated Action

Without wishing to get drawn into some major theoretical debates in the social sciences – the macro/micro distinc-tion, modern/post-modern frameworks, state and agency debates – we are strongly aware that our work is written and will be reviewed in this context. Our position there-fore needs some clarification. Put briefly, it is that what goes on between individuals is 'situated action' (Suchman, 1987). That is, the meaning of interaction is achieved in, and situated in, a local setting, and that setting is achieved by the situated action. Suchman introduces the term 'situ-ated action' to describe workplace behaviour. She states that the 'term underscores the view that every course of action depends in essential ways upon its material and social circumstances' (1987, p. 54).

This does not deny the presence of culture or normative rules of conduct; rather it acknowledges the actors' achievements as more or less proficient members of pro-fessional, organisational and social cultures who use nor-mative rules of conduct to produce the outcomes available to observation, on each and every occasion. This view of action requires a different approach, so that 'instead of looking for a structure that is invariant across situations,

we look for processes whereby particular, uniquely constituted circumstances are systematically interpreted so as to
render meaning shared and action accountably rational'
(Suchman, 1987, p. 67).

This pertains to the notion of 'reflexivity' which
Garfinkel (1992) provides in that the setting is itself socially
constituted. Thus child protection agents, like anyone else,
systematically interpret the unique circumstances they find
themselves in to make them sense-able to themselves and
their clients, who do the same. They do this by making a
purchase on what is known to be shared and in sharing
what is known to be (accountably) rational. What is known
and made to be shared, or share-able information, and how
it is known and shared has to do with the social and organisational culture in which child protection is practised.
Because the subject of child protection is part of one of the
most basic components of our culture – childrearing practices – the study of it reflects not only a professional organisational interest, but all the things that are relevant to it in
our culture. This is no more, or less, than saying that
culture plays its part.

Records as Data

Drawing on this and the work of others, particularly Sacks
(1992), we begin to get a clearer idea of the impact of
culture and social group on the way in which life is
defined for and by society's participants. Our participants
are child protection agents who articulate the world of the
people they interact with in their files, and it is these files
which have provided our main data source. This may seem
like taking a 'one-sided' view, and possibly a collection of
idiosyncratic ones at that. However, two important observations need to be borne in mind. First, child protection,
as we have said, is situated in the culture in which it is
practised (we will defer for the moment considering what
'culture' might mean here: that is the subject of empirical
investigation). Individual practitioners may have 'individual' traits and practices but they must draw on certain
shared assumptions, and it is the shared assumptions that
interest us. Second, in relation to our main data source,
that of file records, it should be clear what these constitute.

It is known that records do not represent a complete version of the events they describe. They record only relevant aspects at the time the record was compiled, aspects which in the light of future events may be reappraised. But what do we mean by relevant here? Files have an unfolding retro- and pro-spective character to them. One aspect of the job of opening a new case is to see what relevant information is previously recorded. For example, is there a 'social history' on the family? The task is then to make this pool of relevant information more complete, but only in so far as that is relevant to the job at hand. If there is not a 'social history' for example, and it is considered that for the purposes of the current intervention there should be, then one would be completed. Thus, files are constructed for and by organisationally relevant concerns. They provide us with information on what is accountable (to supervisors, clients, colleagues and other practitioners), on what it is important to account for in making decisions about child protection matters. This has implications for the present study. Garfinkel (1992) stated that any investigator would encounter 'troubles' in reading the files if they are asked to answer questions which differ from the organisationally relevant purposes and routines under which the contents of the files are assembled in the first place. These are very different troubles from those that concern practitioners, such as when files are incomplete, incorrectly completed or 'badly' kept. The fact that files do not tell the full story is essential to their validity as a data source. What they tell is the story that child protection workers know is relevant for organisational purposes, relevant in the work of protecting children. 'When ... records are looked at in this way the least interesting thing one can say about them is that they are "carelessly" kept. The crux of the phenomenon lies elsewhere, namely in the ties between records and the social system that services and is serviced by these records' (Garfinkel, 1992, p. 192).

The files of child protection workers are no different from the files of any other organisation – they are replete with text which concerns the 'organisationally relevant purposes and routines' of child protection social workers. Whilst, officially, child protection workers are mandated to detect and prevent significant harm or injury to children, the files tell their own story of what are organisationally relevant actions and reports. It is the story of the files which we report on in this book. Their significance should be clear. They represent what is organisationally accountable, what the proper work intendedly consists in. They tell us how, under a child protection mandate, social workers account for that mandate for organisational purposes. They therefore tell us how decisions are accountably arrived at, what is important, appropriate, adequate for practical purposes to say, and not say, to orient to and to leave, to make judgement about and not to judge at all – for organisational (child protection) purposes.

Some Implications of Organisational Methods for Inquiring into Child Protection Work

Previously, public inquiries and inspections about how child protection social work is conducted have tended to be for organisational purposes themselves. These inquiries are situated within the work and do not at any time treat the topic of the work – detecting child abuse – as problematic. Rather, they treat its policies, procedures and rules as the subject of proper interpretation, and endeavour to show whether the right rules have been applied (see, for example, DHSS, 1982; DoH, 1991). If, however, the problem of child abuse (or a child's death or significant harm or injury) is inquired into without treating the making of claims about child abuse as problematic, the inquiry is likely to miss an essential point: that a central part of the trouble of defining a case is based on situated action, on the ways that practitioners and, crucially, parents, referees and children make sense of presenting information at any given time. This has less to do with policies and procedures or even risk assessment factors, and more to do with culturally bound methods for interaction, conversation and the interpretation of claims in local settings.

The most recent review of inquiry reports (DoH, 1991) identifies a number of features which are relevant to this observation. It was suggested that key factors identified in relation to the handling of cases which led to child abuse deaths had to do with information and the way in which it was interpreted. Observations were made about how some information was 'known' but did not seem to be fully appreciated and that there was a need to identify what is important from a 'flood of relevant data'; that there appeared to be a failure to distinguish fact from opinion and that social workers were too trusting and uncritical. Some data was unappreciated, particularly if it had come from a source which was itself distrusted, and there was the 'decoy of dual pathology', missing the relevance of information if decoyed by a different problem. 'The inquiries are full of instances where, having identified one problem, professionals fail to appreciate another' (DoH, 1991, p. 59).

It was also noted that information could be held but not pieced together with the rest, and that the current mode of understanding a case was important. For example, 'the principles of clients' self determination, working through parents, keeping families together, on the one hand and pessimistic perception of alternatives to care within the family on the other, influence understanding and action' (p. 60). Social workers were criticised for their 'loss of objectivity' and for having 'long standing blocks' where assumptions made at an early stage influenced later inter-pretation of information. Finally, the study of the inquiries endorsed the Beckford inquiry report in finding that 'high risk' is difficult to define, and stated that it is not possible 'confidently to predict who will be an abuser, for the potential for abuse is widespread and often triggered by the particular conjunction of circumstances which is unpre-dictable' (p. 63). How then should child protection workers assess risk of future significant harm – the task to which they are directed by *Working Together* (Home Office et al., 1991)? From the files we begin to see some of the ways in which they do assess risk, reflecting the practical resolu-tion of attempting to do what is officially recognised as not possible, yet has to be done, somehow, for practical purposes.

Child Protection and Practical Reasoning

The review of inquiries noted these relevant features of decision-making about child abuse cases as criticisms in handling the specific cases under inquiry. We would suggest, however, that these features are expectable products of practical reasoning processes and act as much to inhibit recognition of child abuse as they do to predict it and to achieve a child protection 'case'. In relation to prediction, for example, Howitt (1992) suggests ways in which practitioners' reasoning may lead to 'errors'. Such errors refer to the way that cases of child abuse may be either wrongly detected or maintained in an over-intrusive fashion. Howitt identifies three principles which operate in relation to them: 'templating', 'justificatory theorizing' and 'ratcheting'. 'Templating' refers to a process whereby social workers match presenting clients against a 'social template'. The 'template' is a culturally informed prototype against which workers assess the client – how far do they match it, and how far removed from it are they? 'Justificatory theorizing' refers to the way in which theories justify the decisions made. While Howitt's use of the term 'theory' is somewhat loose, he claims that the 'classic example' of this in his research was something termed 'contrition theory'. 'This assumes that in order for a family or a family member to be "treatable" (i.e. "they can be worked with" in the professional parlance), evidence has to be shown that the full implications of what has happened are understood and acceptance of responsibility confirmed' (1992, p. 355). Finally, 'ratcheting' refers to the way in which the child protection system 'moves in a single direction'. Once in the system the reason for entry becomes secondary to the existing circumstances, and 'unwinding' or going back tends not to happen. Thus it becomes quite difficult to get out. Howitt uses children taken into care as his example, and there is some empirical support for this (Thorpe, 1994). Ratcheting is the same process (though reversely applied) as having 'long standing blocks', referred to by the DoH. It is similar to saying that once a decision has been made, a categorisation, the case is oriented in this way (Wattam, 1992). The mistake is to think that because all the processes have been observed of social workers, they are unique to child protection. Whilst 'dominant mode of understanding' and 'contrition theory' and the like are drawn from a particular child protection knowledge base, many of the features described are shared by all of us as methods of practical decision-making.

These processes and others which we go on to describe in this book are not easily resolved by changes in law, policy or procedures. We suggest that they are the products of ordinary social interaction and the culturally bound information-processing features referred to earlier. To propose that they should be remedied is to propose that social workers should 'think' differently from the rest of society – that they should treat all information, for example, with a sceptical stance and suspend the 'rule of doubt' (Shutz, 1964–7), that they must develop different, that is different from mundane, criteria for establishing the relevance of information, or that all information should be treated as of equal relevance. But this recommendation denies what has to be 'taken for granted' to get the job done. Information must be made sense of somehow, and meaning is achieved in and through the situation in which that information is found and used. As Garfinkel points out, 'with respect to the problematic character of practical actions and to the practical adequacy of their inquiries, members take for granted that a member must at the outset "know" the settings in which he is to operate if his practices are to serve as measures to bring particular, located features of these settings to recognizable account' (Garfinkel, 1992, p. 8). The remainder of this book is concerned with what child protection workers accountably take for granted in order to do their work, the processes they must use and the accountable sense they make of the information presented to them.

Moving from Child Abuse to Risk Insurance

While it is clear from literature and research in this field that the terms 'abuse', 'maltreatment' and more recently 'significant harm and injury' have become almost interchangeable, what they all have in common is a consensus that they should be the concern of child protection workers. When we refer to the story the files tell us, and we know that files (at the very least) must account for organisational concerns, we might expect to find accounts of what is or is not child abuse in each particular case. In fact, as we go on to show in Chapter 8, defining whether or not a child is 'abused' is a rare occurrence. The term 'abuse' is used occasionally, quite often when reported by referees, and the terms 'maltreatment', 'harm' and 'injury' are rarely found. What are the implications of this? Some years ago Sacks commented that he got fed up listening to hours of conversation (much as one would reading thick piles of files) and he recalled the following point:

> There's a classic story about Malinowsky going into the field, wanting to find out about genealogy. He would talk to the natives about genealogy, and he found out that each native would talk for an hour before giving him any genealogy, in just bragging about them, and he'd have to go through a whole big thing. Then at one point he remarks that he really became an anthropologist when he could realise that genealogies were irrelevant, and it was the talk, the bragging, etc., which was crucial. (Sacks, 1992, p. 179)

In much the same way, and following Garfinkel above, consulting the files to find out about what is child abuse is very difficult. Rather than accounts of what is or is not abuse, we find vast amounts of text about whether a specifically alleged event occurred, about the behaviours of mothers and occasionally fathers and children, about home life (washing, cleaning, tidiness and so forth) and about what other people (particularly other professionals) say. Like Malinowsky we came to understand what was important – it is not whether a child is 'abused' but, significantly, whether the material and emotional circumstances of a child are acceptable to child protection workers. Given that child abuse does not necessarily require signs or symptoms, and given that very few reported cases present with actual harms and injuries, child protection workers do the only thing available to them – they assess the 'snapshot' of the child and his or her relevant family to decide on whether the child is safe. This is something slightly different from *risk assessment*. It might be more appropriately termed *risk insurance* – making sure by the means available (and we go on to describe what these means are) that for practical purposes a child is 'all right'.

The Construction of Clients

In adopting the files as our primary data source we have clearly taken a methodological decision which may appear to exclude certain parties to the child protection process. Other actors in the settings, such as parents and children, may make different sense of the situations described in the files. For example, in a study which examined the views of the worker, parent and child in a set of cases, one mother described her response in relation to her expectations about intervention:

> You expect them to sort of come round ... trip the kids off and sort of check 'em, from head to toe for bruises and whatever ... at one time I used to explain how [the child] got that bruise, how [the child] got that bruise, but they didn't want to know ... they don't check on them, I think it's bad ... you can give them a right sob story and they'd just accept it. (Westcott, 1995, p. 56)

Attention has recently turned to parental perspectives because, post Cleveland and with the advent of parental rights groups, it was considered that they had been ignored. Related to this is the scant attention paid to social work as an achieved activity, based on the situated practical accomplishments of (at least) two people interacting with each other. There has been criticism that previous studies of social welfare decontextualise the social worker/client relationship. Clients, where they are subjects at all, are viewed as 'being of a substantially discrete nature' which 'denies the relational pairing of categories (social worker/practitioner–client) from which the term "client" derives its meaning' (Lightup, 1982). What has been ignored is the way in which parties to intervention construct the outcomes they do on each occasion. A recent study by Cleaver and Freeman (1995), for example, suggests that 'faced with an accusation of child abuse, irrespective of its gravity or the weight of the evidence, parents devise coping strategies, which, as far as possible, will accommodate the accusation and its implications' (p. 95). This is described as the 'operational perspective' of the parent, which may not match the operational perspective of the investigator. The study suggests that parents and professionals are unlikely to share similar 'operational perspectives' at the beginning of an inquiry. Parents may feel angry, resentful and violated, and worry about prosecution or removal of the child, whatever may have happened.

Westcott noted that coordinating the materials from interviews was difficult and stated that 'it often appeared that clients and child protection officers could not possibly be discussing the same process' (1995, p. 45). Parents who felt negatively about the service commented on a lack of 'mutual understanding' and it was clear that relationships did not carry the same meaning for workers and parents. For the child protection officers the quality of relationship had more to do with 'acknowledging their problem', whereas parents appreciated someone who was 'friendly', 'easy to talk to' and 'a good listener'. When asked what they did with their social worker, parents were hard pressed to answer and generally stated 'nothing much'. Mothers in particular felt that the child protection officer was 'for the child' and hostile or disinterested towards themselves. They felt excluded and some felt that their 'needs and views were directly opposed to their children's and that CPOs took the child's "side"'.

This difficult position is endorsed by a study of mothers whose children were victims of sexual assault (Hooper, 1992). In relation to statutory help and intervention mothers generally described some negative responses including blame and disbelief, being held 'in abeyance' as objects of professional intervention rather than people trying to get on with their lives. Some felt that adjustments were happening too fast: for example, having to make decisions about prosecution within a few days whilst still trying to come to terms with 'finding out'. From the agency side, Hooper notes that confusion could be viewed as an unsatisfactory 'non-safe' response and thus prejudice the mother and child's position.

However, whilst we consider the parent, child and others as equally important in a moral sense, we were interested to know what was their importance, or what was their nature, in an organisationally accountable sense. Starting from the point that decision-making is a locally situated action involving all those present, we asked how parents and victims feature in the claims-making activities in dealing with an allegation. We opted to treat this aspect as a discoverable matter, and, as we shall go on to show, one which became of central importance. The subjects of the files are the parents and children, but they are articulated in very specific ways, which might account for the troubles they define when interviewed in studies such as those above. However, we do not, once again, want to suggest that they are being wrongly (or rightly) represented. Rather we seek to depict how they are represented for organisational purposes, for the purposes of doing child protection work.

Situated Moral Reasoning in Child Protection Work

Some previous ethnographic studies have enabled an examination of the child protection process in greater detail. For example, Lightup (1982) included observations of a case where a child had been hit by his father as punishment: 'what was involved was not just the negotiation of a "picture of events" but also a "moral profile" of the people involved in an attempt to establish some sort of fit on a moral dimension between what was seen as "acceptable behaviour" and what was seen as "sanctionable behaviour" (p. 169).

Lightup then goes on to describe how practitioners picked up on the absence of any concern over what had happened and related this to reports of a previous 'incident' two years before as well as problems with non-school attendance. He notes that this was then interpreted as documenting the underlying pattern of a typical case of non-accidental injury. 'The contextual features of a previous example of the use of "excessive" punishment and a neglect of school were the vital factors involved in making this decision. This "documentary method of interpretation", involving as it may do either the redefinition or the confirmation of the original definition of "what the situation on any particular occasion is understood to have been … in the light of later events", led the conference to categorise these previous incidents as being indicative of problems within the family the nature of which required them to take action at that time in an attempt to prevent further difficulties arising' (p. 170).[3]

Lightup regards this as an example of 'a competing moral profile'. He suggests that if the father had shown respect and regret the outcome may not have been taking all the children into care and that what is at issue is re-entry to a 'moral community'. This research reinforces the point that child protection work involves making moral judgements about people as parents and about normal behaviour (Dingwall et al., 1983; Thorpe, 1994; Dartington Social Research Unit, 1995).

Our analysis of file texts showed that much of the reported work in child protection was concerned with descriptions of parents and that an activity characteristic of child protection was 'situated moral reasoning'. This term describes the way in which social workers articulated expectable features of parenting and utilised them in their judgements of child abuse claims. Parents (and more specifically mothers) did not necessarily feature in the files by warrant of descriptions of their presence or of what they said or did, as, for example, a reporter might record who was present at a scene. These things were written about in terms of their relevance to deciding on whether further action following a report was required. Thus parents were articulated in a certain way and, as we go on to show in the following chapters, mothers in particular were written about in relation to their protective behaviour, in effect as indicators of the level of future risk. This finding, that deciding on a case is, in part, related to judgements about competing maternal or, more rarely paternal, profiles is important. It shows, as we have already indicated, one of the key criteria in the practical activity of risk assessment. A recognition of how risk assessment works in practice provides not only a quite different approach to understanding and analysing risk, but also quite different insights into the orthodox literature on risk assessment.

Risk Assessment as a Moral Enterprise

In a comprehensive review, Pecora and Martin (1989) proposed that the central focus of risk assessment is on the likelihood of maltreatment, not on the severity of the child's injuries. They gave the example of an 11-year-old boy who suffered from concussion and head lacerations because he fell accidentally after his father pushed him whilst punishing him 'during a heated argument over his first curfew violation'. At other times the family is described as functioning 'normally'. This case is compared to a young mother aged 19 with a one-year-old child, living in a caravan in an isolated area. The child is spanked 'over 4 times a day' but there are no bruises. The father is away a lot, and the mother has expressed anger and frustration at her situation. Pecora and Martin ask which child is more at risk? They do not answer this question; for them the answer is implicit in the initial observation that the severity of injury does not have to match the risk level. Thus, the second child is, by implication, more at risk. However, in these examples there is one distinction between the two cases: in the first an injury has occurred, and in the second it has not. Might it also be possible to say that prior to the injury the child in the first case was more at risk (because the injury did in fact occur), or that, in the second case, if the mother did over-discipline her child one day that would put the child at less risk because the mother would appreciate the seriousness of her actions, as happened with the father in the first example? None of this is discussed. What is of note is that the information the investigators find relevant to risk assessment is the behaviour of fathers, notions of family functioning and the expressions and responses of mothers, but without qualifying how these factors might systematically be broken down, or be assessed as risk criteria.

The only way in which the second example stands as a candidate version of 'high risk' is in its purchase on certain 'moral reasoning' about young parents, coping alone, with very young children in difficult financial situations, all of which, as we have stated previously, are not necessarily 'risk' factors. A similar conclusion can be drawn by examining the 'critical path' analysis advocated by Roberts (1988). 'Gerry', aged seven, was found to have serious bruises at school. A critical path of Gerry's family is displayed, which identifies 43 factors or events going back to the childhood of both parents which are seen as relevant in some way to the outcome – Gerry's bruising. These include parents' family size, 'strict upbringing with physical punishment', 'forced marriage', 'away with forces' and so forth. We do not know the 'critical' factors in Pecora and Martin's first example since the case is not analysed in that way. However, the outcomes are very similar. That is, two children were beaten in families which exercised severe physical discipline techniques when the child misbehaved in ways which would be culturally acknowledged as negative: i.e. breaking a curfew and stealing. Risk assessment is clearly a moral enterprise. This is not to decry it, or to minimise the work that has been done. Rather it is to recognise moral enterprise as a significant feature of child protection work, and not to 'scientificise' it out. What we want to do is bring it up front, as it were, and ask how it is operating for the worker, children and families involved.

In the early 1980s Dingwall, Eekelaar and Murray conducted an ethnographic study which aimed to show 'what the relevant agency staff consider to be mistreatment' (1983, p. 20). Data was collected through direct observation and questioning. The researchers found that most agency staff drew upon two types of evidence: 'clinical' evidence, i.e. physical symptoms and signs on the body, and 'social' evidence, i.e. that to do with the child's environment, relationships and material conditions. They discovered agreement amongst practitioners that both were needed, although a minority of medical staff thought that clinical evidence was sufficient. From this research Dingwall et al. suggest two models of discovery:

a) Find signs – conclude abuse or neglect
b) Find signs – consider context – infer responsibility – conclude abuse or neglect, or conclude other cause (p. 36)

As we demonstrated in Chapter 3, there is now some consensus in the conventional literature that there are few definitive physical signs of child harm or injury. Furthermore, no signs are free from their social context (Baccus, 1986) and the assessment of signs involves the making of judgements. The physicians who thought they could just use 'clinical evidence' were using the same methods we have outlined in the previous chapter, that suggest child abuse is something which can be unproblematically defined and identified. The second model includes consideration of context and inferring responsibility, and it is these activities which predispose the decision-making process towards situated moral reasoning.

It is, however, not just parents who are under scrutiny. Children too are articulated in certain ways. There has been some attention paid to the notion of the 'ideal victim' (Blagg, 1989) and the way in which children are categorised for child protection purposes as plausible or 'telling the truth' (Wattam, 1990; 1992). It has also been found that one of the 'methods' that people use to decide on whether to report harms or injuries is to determine the culpability of the child. Reporting a child is less likely if the child is viewed as being at fault, or to blame, in the reporting behaviour of physicians (Warner and Hansen, 1994), undergraduates (Dukes and Kean, 1989) and teachers (Tite, 1993). Children, as we will go on to show, are no less victims of situated moral reasoning than their parents, caretakers and the family childrearing practices.

Risk and Normality

On this last point, there seems to be some purchase made by investigators on what are considered to be 'normal' childrearing practices. The research on what happens in 'normal' families is limited. However, research suggests that some physical injury to children is acceptable, an observation reinforced by studies of normal parental discipline. A national study of violence towards children in America (Wolfner and Gelles, 1993) revealed that the base rate for minor violence (physical punishment) was 619/1,000, and for severe violence (abusive violence) was 110/1,000. This picture, recently reinforced by British research (Dartington Social Research Unit, 1995), would appear to be one where corporal punishment of children is practised by the majority of respondents. A similar position holds for allegations of sexual assault. With reference to normal childhood sexual activity, Kinsey et al., (1948; 1953) found that 57 per cent of men and 48 per cent of women recalled some type of sexual play before adolescence. Friedrich et al. (1991) found that 2–12-year-old children exhibit a wide variety of sexual behaviours, but the 'more aggressive behaviours and behaviours that imitated adult sexual activity were among the most rare' (Lamb and Coakley, 1993, p. 516). In Britain, Smith and Grocke (1995) found that parents who reported that their child had definitely or probably bathed with parents, been seen masturbating and touched mother's breasts were in the majority. A question arising from this is that, given the 'normality' of corporal punishment and sexual play for children, the observation that many of the harms and injuries reported can be quite minor in nature (Thorpe, 1994; Warner and Hansen, 1994) and that the majority of allegations made to statutory agencies consist in vague information reporting either general concerns or low levels of intrusion (Wattam, 1991), how is it that some children are brought to the attention of statutory agencies and not others? Furthermore, given the prevalence of potentially abusive signs in normal families (bruising from punishment, masturbating etc.), how are children at risk to be identified? Once again, and to reinforce the point, what we find in practice as a practical resolution of this unsolvable problem, is the work of 'risk insurance' – rather than identifying abuse (or risk), practitioners look for criteria which cushion, protect or act to prevent anything happening again, whether or not it happened in the first place, in the vast majority of cases.

It has been suggested that frontline workers use 'concepts of "normal" family life as a way of identifying deviance and, hence, considering the possibility of abuse or neglect' (Dingwall et al., 1983, p. 55). Taking as our starting point the idea that child protection work is a locally situated activity and that situated action is our concern, we would suggest that this conclusion is inadequate in describing current practice. Whilst concepts of 'normal' family life are not irrelevant to the decision-making process in child protection, we want to suggest from our deconstruction that the use of normality is complex. There is, for example, a time–space dimension, which enables assessments of 'normal' behaviour to occur on each occasion. Furthermore, to talk of 'normal' suggests there is agreement about what that might be, when theoretically and practically there is known to be disagreement about what is 'normal' and what is not.

Categorisation and Corroboration as Methods for Deciding on Normality and Risk

In the late 1960s Harvey Sacks (1992) identified what he called 'some very central machinery of social organisation'. Sacks went on to define this machinery as 'Membership Categorisation Devices' (MCDs), by which he referred to the way in which people used 'category sets' to classify a population. The names of the sets included such things as sex, age and religion, and they were reported by Sacks to be 'inference-rich'. One of their important characteristics was not that they identified any actual groups or organisations (although they might have done), but that people utilised the quality of 'presumptive membership' and all entailed therein when interacting with others. One of the interesting questions in child protection work is how people referred to the service are categorised and, as a consequence, oriented to. Categorisation should not be confused with stereotyping, role ascription, or other such terms. It is an activity which allows for the complexity, the unfolding nature, the retrospective–prospective quality of interaction referred to by Lightup above, and also allows for changes in categorisation over time. As any social worker knows, people are not just categorised as 'clients' and oriented as such, although that might be part of what goes on between social workers and service users. What is more helpful, in terms of understanding what child protection work consists in, is to look at categorisation activity. Because categorisation devices are inference-rich, they operate to 'orientate' interaction. As Jayyusi notes,

> the selection of a membership category by any member to refer to or characterise any other member (or even herself) could not be understood simply in terms of criteria of 'correctness'. Rather, it involves considerations of much greater analytical complexity, such as 'apropriateness', 'recipient design/recognitionality', 'implicativeness', 'orientation to already used categories in the discourse so far', and so on. (1984, p. 213)

Deciding on whether a client is a client, a case a case, or a piece of evidence is a piece of evidence, and what sort of 'client', 'case' or 'evidence' they are, involves a categorisation process from the very beginning of contact (Wattam, 1992). But because of the way in which categorisation orientates the search for further information, it is also implicative in the construction of clients, cases and evidence. What we begin to see in observations of the work and its recordings and texts are the ways in which one piece of information leads to another, the way that grounds for suspicion become warrants for action, and the way that warrants for action result in the outcomes they do. It would appear that it is not just a case of matching a parent or caretaker to a 'template' and seeing if they fit, nor asking whether (however inadvertently) they are 'normal'. Deciding on 'normal' is a moving, and negotiated, feast between practitioner, the subject(s) of reports and any other relevant people on any relevant occasion.

Dingwall et al. point out seven grounds for suspicion in relation to one case: lack of explanation, vagueness about what happened, delay in presentation, injury type, apparent lack of affection, submissiveness of child and lack of information. Similar criteria have been identified by subsequent studies. Examples include delay in bringing the child to attention or the explanation for injury changes, does not match the injury or cannot be provided (Hammond et al., 1991; Hight et al., 1979; Ledbetter et al., 1988; Warner and Hansen, 1994). Dingwall et al. (1983) suggest that grounds for suspicion can be grouped into three basic categories of evidence: 'the injury', 'the account offered' and 'the demeanour of parent and child' which all appear to be located in a 'structure of mutual corroboration'. More recent reviews of practice in relation to grounds for suspicion in allegations of child sexual assault (Wattam, 1991), and validity of report (Wattam, 1992), identify the structure of corroboration as central to decision-making in cases. Child protection practice appears to be centrally concerned with corroboration. Traditionally, the term tends to be associated with legal practice. While its meaning is not that different, the tests of the strength of evidence used in legal corroboration work are different from those used in everyday life. What we are referring to here is the use of corroboration as a common-sense reasoning device: how information is used to stand for, signify or otherwise validate an allegation of mistreatment, and/or the possibility that a child may be in danger of mistreatment in the future.

Conclusion

The position we take is more than a critique of a methodology underpinning the findings, statistics and claims made by positivist inquiries into child abuse. Such a critique is already in evidence, although it has gone largely unheeded by official child protection statisticians and, as a consequence, the local authorities whose job it is to compile, collate and contribute to such statistics. Such a critique generally takes the view – as we stated at the beginning of this chapter – that child abuse is a social construction. However, it is not enough to say only that child abuse is a social construction, or that it is a problem of contested definition. All the (social) world (including whooping cough) could be viewed in this way. It is to take a methodological choice which enables us to see how social phenomena are constructed, not just what their construction consists in. It is important to know how these things work, what methods are used, 'rules' acted upon, and criteria operated.

Our questions, arising from the data we report on here, are: what enables child protection workers to make claims of child abuse, and, perhaps more importantly, is that what child protection work consists in? We used the files of child protection workers because they contain accountable, organisationally important features of the work. Their validity comes not from the individual writers, but from their organisational value – what is contained within them must be available to any entitled reader in order that others can see that the work has been done (even if they are never read). We noted that, in answer to the first question, it was not possible to find definitions, or even records of the act of defining child abuse in the files. What we find is a wide range of text about mothers, houses, children's behaviour and the like. We go on in subsequent chapters to lay out precisely what these are and how they appear to be operating.

One of the issues we begin to draw out, however, is that, because no behaviour is necessarily abusive (and an unspecifiable amount could be potentially abusive), social workers are faced with a very practical problem – how do they do the job of protecting children in a very uncertain world? What we suggest is that they do not detect (except in a minority of cases) actual harm or injury, nor do they assess risk of harm or injury. What they do is use the situation to do the next best thing – assess whether a child is adequately cared for, an activity we describe as risk insurance.

5
Finding the Child in Child Protection

It has been noted that 'egocentrism' was one of Piaget's most misunderstood concepts (Flavell, 1963). We do not wish to add to the misunderstanding, but rather to use the term to make a point. By 'egocentrism' Piaget referred to a stage in a child's life where they were unable to see things from another's point of view, because they had no conception of the notion that other points of view existed. Piaget proposed that children develop out of egocentricity by acquiring the ability to 'decentre'. Thus it can be anticipated that most adults are not egocentric in the strict sense of the word. However, there is a sense in which the way adults view children could be termed 'adultcentric' (Wattam, 1990; Kitzinger, 1990). By this we refer to the way that interpretations of children's behaviour, their rights to a perspective or point of view, are achieved through the entitlement of adults to construct notions of 'child', 'childhood' and children themselves. In the previous chapter we attempted to draw out some of the issues around the position of social construction and identified the implications of viewing child protection as situated action. Our intended focus was on the social organisation of child protection and the detection of child abuse. In this chapter we begin that process by suggesting that child protection depends a great deal on the social construction of children and the ways in which children subject to child protection intervention are seen as cultural products and become objects of organisational interest.

The idea that childhood is a social construction is now generally accepted (Butler and Williamson, 1994). The case for the social construction of childhood is made through historical analyses, which depict the ways that childhood has been variously viewed over time (Aries, 1973; De

Mause, 1974; Stainton Rogers and Stainton Rogers, 1992). Such analyses, though different, tend to give broad-ranging 'brush stroke' images of children and talk about the way that different cultures and epochs represent childhood, through literature, paintings and reports from the time studied. A fundamental premise for establishing a case of child abuse is to determine that it is a child who is the object of scrutiny. Being a child, as much of the literature on the social construction of childhood attests, is more than being of a certain age. What comes along with the category of 'child' is a host of expectable features – which have been said to include vulnerability, innocence and a lack of mastery of adult skills.

The 'Silent Child'

Kitzinger (1990) suggests that implicit in the publicity surrounding child sexual assault is 'an assertion of what childhood "really" is, or should be'. A dominant construct in the literature is the notion of childhood innocence, which Kitzinger states is problematic and counterproductive for three reasons. These are that innocence is a source of 'titillation' for abusers, that notions of innocence 'stigmatize' the knowing child, and that it presents an ideology of childhood which is used to deny children power. A second dominant construct is the 'passive victim', a 'silent sufferer of victimization'. From her own research, Kitzinger suggests that many children are actually anything but passive in their response to sexual abuse, that 'although such tactics are rarely recognized by adults, children seek to evade abuse with all the resources they have of cunning, manipulativeness, energy, anger and fear' (1990, p. 162).

As a result, key constructs of childhood may feature in defining 'abused children'. Constructs such as the 'knowing child' and being a certain type of (passive) victim echo the idea of the 'ideal victim'. Blagg (1989) proposed that notions of deserving and undeserving victims operate within the child protection process, for children as well as adults, and that these influence the treatment they receive from state agencies. He also suggests that there appears to be widespread 'blindness' when it comes to seeing child victimisation, and an incapacity to read the messages that children give. The ultimate point is that children who do not fit the stereotype do not get 'seen'. Blagg was referring to the ways in which children become, or crucially do not become, recognised as 'victims'. Kitzinger goes a step further by suggesting that, once recognised as victims, constructions of childhood produce a certain type of response – one which reinforces aberrant behaviour as deviant, rather than 'normal'.

> Activities that could be recognized as attempts to resist, or cope with abuse are, instead, labelled 'post-traumatic stress syndrome' or cited as evidence of deep psychic scarring. Such disease terminology obscures the child actively negotiating her way through the dangers of childhood. She is recast as a submissive object of victimization even by the process of intervention and treatment. (Kitzinger, 1990, p. 166)

The idea of absent and present children, which we introduce in this chapter, relates in some ways to these ideas – that children are articulated and represented in specific ways, and that it is only certain children who 'speak' in the files. However, we will suggest that rather than obscuring the seeing of child 'victims', which it is not possible from our data to make empirical statements about, the rationale for the way in which children are present in the files has to do with supporting the child protection task, of justifying actions taken and beliefs held. From our own materials we would suggest that the 'child' is not recast as a submissive object in obvious ways, that is, they are not described as submissive objects *per se* in the files that we looked at. However, what we did find is the 'silent' child. By this we mean that certain aspects of children are largely 'missing' in the files – which could be best described as the child's voice. If we want to find the child's perspective in the text it is conspicuous by its absence – accounting for the child's feelings and wishes, or even presence, in anything other than a descriptive way is not an organisationally relevant matter (Wattam, 1991). The following referral (drawn at random from the same 100 per cent sample of child protection reports in Western Australia outlined at the beginning of Chapter 5[1] demonstrates this silence.

Hannah is mother of baby Richard, aged approx. 8 mos, and is Mrs Benson's sister. Hannah is 16 y.o. and currently lives in her parents' house in [place] while her parents are in [town]. Mrs Benson concerned about Hannah's capacity to care for Rick, she has been on her own looking after baby for about 3 mos. Mrs Benson has been concerned for some time and visited Hannah, Sunday. According to her description, the baby sleeps in a drawer, is often seen dressed in nappy with no top even at night, is left in wet nappies, sleeps on a filthy sheepskin rug and gets bathed once per week. The house in which Hannah lives is also very dirty. Mrs Benson said her sister (not Hannah) can confirm story and she has notified Hannah's mother in [town]. Apparently mother said leave it until they return from [town] shortly. Hannah apparently has lived in [place] for a while (1 yr) and attended Smith High School for a short period. In reply to my question if Hannah had any friends in [place] Mrs Benson stated that the father of Rick, Tom (doesn't know surname) sometimes stays with Hannah, he is believed to be aged 18/19 yrs and a bit 'slow'. Hannah is also described as 'not very bright' by Mrs Benson. She also indicated that it is unlikely that Hannah has taken the baby to the clinic and that he has only had 1 of triple antigen injections. Mrs Benson described the problem as that of Hannah not knowing how to manage a baby, as she has enough trouble caring for herself.

I advised Mrs Benson that an officer would contact Hannah ASAP. Suggest that contact should be made soon as child/mother in need of assessment/support. Mrs Benson said she had often thought of taking Rick and caring for him, but she works 6 days per week, and is married with 2 children of her own which leaves her little time.

Jane – for your urgent attention please.

Assessment

From what was observed and discussed today, it is apparent that Rick is not being cared for at (minimum) level and Hannah's ability to provide a clean home was not evident today. Hannah's attitude was one of passive defiance, she answered our questions in monosyllables, was evasive, avoided eye contact; she didn't attempt to play with Rick during the time we were there, nor did she offer any information; when she carried him, she had him so his back was against her side, and where she could not interact with him. Hannah was observed to try to make him sit alone, but he was unable to remain sitting alone. It was also apparent that Hannah tried to mislead us on a number of occasions, including a statement to the effect that she hadn't seen her sister who lives in [place] since last year, yet her sister stated that she had visited Hannah last Sunday.

Hannah stated that her sister Bea (20 years) could come down and assist Hannah with household work and the care of Rick. [Hannah's mother] also indicated that she would be returning to [place] shortly. However, it seems that Rick's development has lagged while he has been living with the other (maternal) family members since his birth. [Health visitor] confirms that Rick's lack of development has not occurred as a result of Hannah moving down from [town] some three/four weeks ago. From our observation it seems that Hannah has needs far beyond those which may be supported by the inclusion of homemaker skills in the house; it seems that Hannah has little knowledge of caring for a baby and his/her development stages, which has not been provided by members of her family or outside networks to date.

Plan: In view of the above it seems that Rick is not able to develop optimally in the above environment without intensive input. Hannah has been advised that she has until Monday to make some attempt to clean the house and that Steven and myself will visit on Monday. In the meantime, I am making enquiries re. obtaining a cot for Rick and checking if there are any vacancies at [place] for Hannah and Rick to be admitted for intense assessment, support and tuition.

Within a short period the baby ended up in substitute care (alone) with the prospects of rehabilitation being discussed at some point in the future. This referral, like all the others we saw, constitutes one version of events – in this case, the sister's version as reported by the social worker. It is the referrer's version which becomes the 'credentialled' version (Pollner, 1975). By this we mean that her account of events is taken as the correct version until information comes along to disprove it. There is no question in the file text that the referrer might be lying, attempting to mislead or be manipulative. Rather these qualities are attributed to Hannah, who has been referred because what she says does not fit with the referral information. This may be wrong or right; it does not matter. What matters is the way the initial version is given precedence. One version is taken as a marker, with which to match, to *corroborate*, any further information.

Within this first version Hannah and her baby are described as if they were objects. Any contribution that they make to the version is by way of the referrer's interpretation of their actions and behaviour. What Hannah has said, how she describes their situation, is not part of it. In this way the subjects of the referral are silent. Their representation is done by selecting behaviour, characteristics and circumstances about them which are of concern. The fact that Hannah herself is a child chronologically is completely bypassed, for example. Although the most available descriptors for children are drawn on (age, school attendance, 'not very bright', reference to mother – see categorisations of children below), the fact that she might be a child is not referenced: the orientation is to her as a mother and the focus is on her capacity as a mother. This is quite common in the files. A second bench-mark for defining risk is the maternal characteristics, without comment on how these too are culturally bound and constructed. The father of Rick is equally silent, and the same observations apply, yet he too might in other circumstances be reframed as a child (such as provision for leaving care, for example). Thus, and to reinforce Kitzinger's claim that the fate of children and their mothers are inextricably tied, we find that only specific children are accorded childhood status in the files.

Our subject 'child' is also 'silent'. His behaviour is always described in relation to his mother's actions. These actions are given as grounds for concern and thus could be said to be 'protection' relevant – i.e. candidates for 'abuse'. This may be hard to grasp given the fact that Rick is only eight months old. Yet eight-month-old babies can be very active contributors to their environment. During the course of the visit it is likely that Rick's presence contributed more than his ability to sit, or rest on his mother's hip. Anyone with experience of eight-month-old babies will know that, unless asleep, they can be quite vociferous, eat, maintain eye contact, cry, reach for objects etc. None of these contributions are, however, commented on: the image gained from a reading of the text is of a silent baby. Rick's status as a child at risk depends on his being an object of observation *in relation* to his mother and his (sleeping and hygiene) environment. The social workers have constructed this version as an account of a child requiring (urgent, intense) intervention. It can, however, be suggested that Rick was not silent throughout since a completely unresponsive baby would constitute further grounds for concern and would be accountable. Thus, the mother's actions and inability to provide were the rationale for intervention on behalf of a child 'at risk' – not the current state of the baby.

Transitions from Ordinary Child to the Child of Concern

One form of social organisation which makes ascriptions of child abuse possible is the differentiation between adult and child. The first premise for child abuse is that it must be children, and not adults, who are the subject of concern. What is clear, even from this first example, is that adults have an entitlement to judge a child's situation and to give the 'credentialled' version of the child to other adults. This entitlement over children is variously socially organised, according to whether children are one's own or others', older or younger, behaving in a way which might endanger their life or the lives of others, and many other considerations. The work of child protection is centrally concerned with making judgements and assessments about children which derives partly from this generic entitlement of adults over any child, and partly from the specific organisational entitlement to decide upon whether a referred child has been harmed or injured, or is at risk of future harm or injury. These two entitlements inevitably overlap so that we find, in the files, things that any adult might say about any child, and things that a child protection worker might say about a child who is a candidate for abuse, as all part of the same process of judgement and assessment. This point has major consequences for children who become the subject of child protection work. This is because what might ordinarily be said about them, by a friend, neighbour, parent, teacher or other adult are things said in a specific setting – that of child protection work. In this chapter we consider some of the consequences of this transition from the ordinary to the specialist setting.

Categorisations of Children in the Files

In the previous chapter we introduced the notion of categorisation, a term developed by the late Harvey Sacks (1992) to demonstrate some of the prevailing, and commonly held, methods that people use to make sense of their world. There are three essential points about categorisation that are relevant here.

First, categorisation is an activity, undertaken by each and every one of us, in our day-to-day lives. In order to categorise, people make use of categorisation devices. To acknowledge someone as a 'mother' we make use of the device 'family', or to see someone as a 'woman' we deploy the device 'gender'. Some categories and devices are more obvious than others, such as gender, age, skin colour, people who wear uniforms and so forth. These categories are available on sight. Thus, it is possible to see at a glance who is an adult, and who is a child. There are of course provisos to this statement – is a 17-year-old who looks 20 an adult, for example? Nevertheless, in a great many situations the categorisation is available.

Second, categorisations are not fixed or unalterable, but they are, nevertheless, applied. In making use of categories, any person can be viewed as a category incumbent. That is, they can achieve membership of any given category, as it is relevant, and until such time as it becomes either altered or irrelevant. Thus we can categorise another person as a 'friend' when introducing them to someone else, when trying to work out who our friends are and so on, as and when it becomes relevant. However, we might go on to categorise them variously as a 'woman', 'school teacher' (or whatever their occupation happens to be), 'no longer a friend' and so forth. Whilst some categorisations apply to both children and adults – friend would be one – the available categorisations for the majority of children are less than those for adults. For example, occupational status would be excluded, as would a variety of adult-related action categories (drink-driver, house-owner, tenant, darts-team member and so forth). Many action categories could also apply to children, including all of those just offered, but we would not expect them to. A wide choice of categories has some bearing on category selection and thus the way someone is oriented to. For example, we may meet a person who talks about her job and her children. Immediately we have three category options (woman, worker, mother) which can be taken up in the ensuing conversation or transfer of information. If, however, we meet a child who talks about her mother and her school we obtain a different set of category relevances, all of which maintain her status as a child. A restriction on available categories makes their deployment more permanent, less open to reorientation and change.

Third, category incumbents can also be categorised by devices which contain expectable behaviours. Thus, if we see someone giving mouth-to-mouth resuscitation, we might categorise them as a 'first aider' or, if they are wearing a white coat and carrying out the activity next to an ambulance, a 'para-medic' or 'doctor'. This does not mean that everyone thus categorised behaves in a certain way, merely that certain behaviours are available for expectation to other people. This is more clearly demonstrated when expected behaviours do not occur, such as where someone has had an accident and a person claims they are a doctor then fails to give mouth-to-mouth resuscitation, or whatever the appropriate, immediate treatment might be (Jayyusi, 1984). This becomes significant in the categorisation of children partly in the way that certain behaviours implicitly become expectable, and also in the way that the absence of expectable behaviours becomes an accountable matter in assessing whether a child has been abused. It is particularly relevant to judgements about children at risk, since these judgements depend on available expectations of behaviour and circumstances.

Categorisation is a culturally bound activity. It depends on shared cultural knowledge and cannot be done without it. Thus, when children are categorised it is within the confines of the particular culture in which that activity is conducted. It both draws on the culture and reinforces the culture. Kitzinger refers to the way in which children are controlled. Whilst this can be quite overt in terms of adults' entitlements to discipline children and tell them what to do, control can be taken for granted. It is not always in any concerted intentional effort that children might be controlled by child protection agents (or their teachers, parents and other significant adults) but by the reinforcement of the culture which we can see operating in categorisations and category bound activities, one which (Kitzinger suggests) is disempowering for children.

These three claims become useful analytic devices in the examination of texts and records written about children. They shed light on how information about children is oriented to – that is, what categorisations are used. Furthermore, we can monitor how the categorisations become altered, when it is relevant to alter them and for what purposes, and finally, in orienting towards child-category-incumbent behaviours, it is possible to see what behaviours become relevant, and what happens when they are breached.

An overview of the files reveals that one feature of them is the character of categorisations of children. Amongst these, age and gender were the only variables it was possible to enter for all the cases studied. An overview of statistics in relation to child abuse reveals that these are the only characteristics that are easily retrievable about children themselves.[2] James and Prout (1990) note that age has a particular significance in childhood. 'For example, adults on first getting to know children frequently ask their age, parents are asked how old their children are and children themselves often state their ages with formidable accuracy: six and a half, ten and three quarters. Such an expressed interest in a person's "age" during adulthood would be considered at best rude and at worst intrusive' (p. 221).

James and Prout maintain that this focus on age rests on a set of 'implicit constructions of the position of children in the life course'. There is an assumption by social analysts that age, in comparison to ethnicity and class, plays a minimal role in stratification. However, it is suggested that 'far from being absent from social structure, concepts of age are the main scaffolding around which western conceptions of childhood are built and it is through reference to concepts of age that the daily life experiences of children are *produced and controlled*' (James and Prout, 1990, p. 222, our emphasis).

The fact that age was ubiquitously reported in the files relates in some way to this proposition – though how is not so clear. Is age stratification a means of producing and controlling children in child protection work? Well, certainly not in an intentional way. Rather age appears to act as a marker, a way of knowing children: how else can they be known (which, of course, is Prout and James' point)? Age and gender are both based on biology, and are the most available categories apart from skin colour (which interestingly was not reported), but they tell us little about social organisation. The way in which age is situated in the files is in relation to the kind of things identified in the case above – supervision, schooling, in fact all the things it is considered relevant to report on in the files. Because age is always a first marker, all these things are commented on in relation to age, as they are above. Thus age acts as an important definer of whether anything is amiss, 'age inappropriate', and as such acts as a key variable in defining whether a child should be of concern to the agency, i.e. in need of protection. Whilst this is, in a sense, no great discovery, it points to the intrinsic and taken-for-granted nature of culturally bound practices in relation to children. Age and children are intrinsically associated with each other in every file. Something as innocuous as age may not be problematic – but other, equally embedded constructs may be.

For example, elsewhere in the files children's intellectual and emotional attributes are often accounted, such as in 'a bright girl', 'a slow girl', 'not a very capable child', 'a happy outgoing little boy', 'a mature child', and so on. It would seem that there are a set of characteristics that are linked to children as descriptions of them which contribute to the work of defining whether a child has been abused or is 'at risk'. As we have just suggested, the category 'adult' has limited usefulness with regard to expectable behaviours. If an attempt is made to predict the actions of a person aged 30, 'adult' would not be the first categorisation we would draw on in order to do so. Others might be more relevant depending on the presenting information, such as 'barrister', 'animal lover', 'policewoman', 'teacher', 'alcoholic' and so on. We would not routinely expect to see descriptions such as 'a bright adult', 'a mature adult', a 'happy, outgoing, big adult' – the routine descriptors of children. These categorisations do more than just describe – they make the child available for assessments in ways which are not used for adults (unless they are particular adults, for example with challenging behaviour).

Developing Grounds for Concern

The category 'adult' is of primary relevance only on particular occasions: for example, when one goes to the cinema and asks for tickets for 'two adults and one child', or where behaviour is being criticised and the adult category is deployed in the criticism, such as 'you are not behaving like an adult'. In this usage, 'adult' is part of a 'relational pair' (Sacks, 1992) of 'adult–child': 'adult' can be used in the context of 'child', as opposed to 'child'. Thus 'you are not behaving like an adult' could have a similar sense as 'you are behaving like a child'. 'Adult' needs its relational pair of 'child' to complete its sense, and vice versa. Categories are, to coin Sacks' term, 'inference-rich'.

The opportunity to make use of inferences has a particular significance in 'relational pairs'. The inferences that can be made expand such that the other pair does not necessarily have to be stated to do some work – to make inferences available to decision-making. The terms 'adult' and 'child' are frequently found in the files, and on some occasions they are explicitly paired. The following is an example of this pairing, in this case of 'adults' and 'boys': 'It is also possible that they have seen such pornographic video material in the company of adults, and that the same adults behaved, with the boys present, in a similar way to that enacted on the video.'

Starting from the premise that adult–child is a pair, we can begin to see some of the work that pairing does. The substantive content of the extract refers to the pornographic video material, something which 'adults' are allowed access to. By using 'adult' as a description of a person who has (legal) access to such material, the relational pair 'child' (legally someone who does not have access) is immediately invoked as a moral identity – someone who *should not* have access. The extract then describes a situation where, in fact, the 'boys' are alleged to have had access. This use of language establishes the alleged incident as something that should not happen. The work that 'adult' does is, quite briefly, to state (without stating – through the work of relational pairing) that children are being talked about with a negative connotation. The pairing gives an entirely different sense than if we substituted names, for example: 'It is also possible that they have seen such pornographic video material in the company of Sheila and Dave, and that the same Sheila and Dave behaved, with Bob and Alan present, in a similar way to that enacted on the video.'

Notwithstanding the continuing negative connotations produced by the word 'pornographic' in connection with a male and female acting in front of two males in a pornographic way, the substitution of names takes something away from the meaning of the original text. The meanings, which derive from the category-incumbent behaviours and expectations of the membership category device 'childhood' and the category 'boys', are missing. Essentially it is the negative, 'not allowed' sense attached to children that is missing, rather than one of just social disapproval. In the files there is a routine use of categories such as 'child', 'boy', 'girl', 'toddler', 'baby' and so forth, which invoke a whole set of expectable behaviours associated with these categories.[3] Along with them, there is a sense that what a category-incumbent of 'childhood' should, or should not, be doing is taken for granted as knowledge shared in common. Because it is taken for granted, and because the construction of 'child' is not explicitly negotiated (unless relevant, such as when a subject is 16), then this use of 'child' and other related categories does work (which it is intended to do) but without being made explicit. It would be impossible, on each and every occasion, to specify what we mean (entirely) by particular words used (Garfinkel,

1992). Thus we are not criticising the use of moral categories. What we wish to draw attention to is the work they
do, on each and every occasion of their use, to construct
children, and subsequently child abuse.

All children reported to child protection agencies stand
as candidates for possible harm or injury. In order to decide
just what sort of a candidate they are, practitioners use category-incumbent behaviours. Breaches of expectable 'child'
behaviours are accountable, and are of relevance to child
protection work. Thus, what is accounted in the files gives
us some idea of what is 'normally' expected of children in
these particular circumstances. Non-breaches are similarly
accountable and are of relevance to assess non-candidacy.
Examples of this work can be seen in the following: 'the
boys had spent very little time with their father'; 'he has
tantrums and neither parent makes any attempt to correct
the children'; 'developmentally both children would seem
to have accomplished most of the developmental task
expected of, and commensurate with, their age'.

From these examples we can begin to gauge what is
expectable about children, and how that expectable quality
of behaviour is used to make assessments. In the situations
described it was taken as expectable that children spend a
(canonically unspecifiable) amount of time with their
fathers, that they require correction (which was accountably not being given) and 'develop'.[4] These are just a few
of the category-incumbent behaviours to be found. Their
relevance for the practitioner lies in their availability – how
else could children be written about and judged?

This returns to our earlier point that there are consequences of a transition from the ordinary to the specialist
setting. Each of these statements could be made ordinarily
outside a child protection setting with little consequence.
The removal of ordinary taken-for-granted observations
about children from the realm of what any (entitled) adult
can say in any situation into a child protection setting also
removes the meaning of these observations into a specialist
arena. So that rather than invoking categorisations of
'child' in a general sense, they become devices for invoking
'child' who is also a candidate for the agency concerned, a
child who may have been or who is at risk of being
harmed or injured. By virtue of a referral or report to the

agency the child is already pre-categorised as a possible cause for concern. For example, if we take the first entry above, 'The boys had spent very little time with their father', this could be construed in another setting as an observation, a minor complaint from perhaps a niggling relative. Situated in a child protection setting with a cause for concern about the children already stated (as it is in every case), it becomes more than a minor complaint. It provides candidate behaviour on which to judge a child protection complaint.

The presence of this pre-categorisation, and the work that it subsequently does, is entirely glossed over. Thus in a specialist setting a child who could be judged ordinarily is judged after having his or her candidacy proposed, but is judged as if ordinarily. In the previous chapter we referred to the way that social work reasoning depended in the most part on 'common sense'. The instances given above are an example of such reasoning. A crucial point is that, because child abuse does not necessarily have to have signs or symptoms, all children are potential candidates, and many of the observations made of child protection candidates could be made of all children. However, it is social workers, in a child protection setting, that are doing the reasoning and the outcomes are therefore different than they would be in another setting, although the methods may remain the same. The outcomes of judgements are the subject of child protection policies and procedures. The shift from one setting to another, the ordinary to the specialist, is not commented on in the file texts. Much as the meaning of each and every word must be taken for granted in order to get the work done, so must this shift.

When we state that the categories are inference-rich and infer expectable behaviours, there is a danger that this process gets simplified. It has been suggested that practitioners are imputing their own standards, suppositions and assumptions about what is right, proper and normal for children in the form of value judgements (Higginson, 1990). While this could be said to happen at any particular time in a case, at a case conference for example, this does not reflect the richness and complexity of decision-making. When we follow the career of a case we find that while such judgements may be made on one occasion, they are not always made, nor are they always retained. We are not talking about value judgements here, but the way that children are routinely categorised, which reflects the moral order invoked to make the judgement, commenting on, talking about and acting upon children.

Absent and Present Children

A further point in relation to 'finding the child' and the way that children are represented in child protection work has to do with what we have termed 'absent' and 'present' children. We have already noted how some children are 'silent'; their presence is as objects of description with no report of any contribution they may have made. This quality takes on different dimensions in the 'absent' child. Despite the fact that Rick is only described, we do learn something of his situation, to do with where he sleeps, how he is dressed and so forth. In other cases the information about the child is minimal – the child is almost 'absent'. This is illustrated by the following case which concerns a Vietnamese child aged nine. The referral was recorded as:

> J is urgently seeking services of a Vietnamese social worker to assist in apprehending a door-to-door 'Christian' preacher who is at present sexually interfering with one of her nine-year-old-pupils. The mother is not fully aware of what is happening and is refusing to take any action. [The only other information on file was a note.]

> The above nine-year-old girl was referred to the Department in May this year following disclosure to the Social Worker at — primary school that a [description] man has sexually interfered with her when her mother was working night shift.
> Through contact with the Department, the mother has realized the dangers of leaving [the child] unsupervised, and since then has stayed home to look after [the child]. The department has also helped the mother to be transferred on to special benefit, attend English classes and sewing classes to improve her work experience while [the child] is at school.

As there are no other existing problems, I would recommend closure of this case.

Whilst we learn that the child is nine years old, at school
and has made a 'disclosure', that is all we learn about her.
The other information concerns the mother – an issue we
explore further in Chapter 8. There are no character ascriptions, observations of intelligence or behaviours – merely
that the girl is 'at school'. How is it that some categorisation work is relevant in one case and not another? In this
case the allegation concerned an act that had taken place,
which the child had given an account of. The attention in
this case is to work with the mother to prevent any future
recurrence.

Now consider a case of two sisters in which the allegation was less clear. One sister alleged digital penetration of
the other sister by the stepfather, but the sister in question
refused to endorse the allegation. Thus there was some
ambiguity – had the alleged incident occurred or not? The
case record concludes with the following:

> I arranged for [the sister] to come in with [the social
> worker] to discuss the statements made by M. She
> should call today [date]. Even with an attempt to keep a
> clear mind on this matter there seems to be some smoke
> – [the sister] is most anxious to get out of home and live
> at [the hostel] with M.
>
> Spoke to M again, is reluctant to help to get sister to
> speak to us. [The hostel] have rung again re. payment of
> board – told not our province – Mum still trying to get M
> home as now separated from [the father]. I don't believe
> we can proceed further without their cooperation and
> feel that reluctance to cooperate may indicate there is
> more to this than meets the eye.

The file text in this case is characteristically different from
the other two cases we have used so far. It contains
descriptions of the child's state at the time (anxious to get
out of home, reluctant to help to get sister to speak). This
child is both present and given a voice. We found that in
cases where social workers were not sure of what might
have happened, as in this case, the behaviour of the sub-

jects becomes relevant to record in the context of assessing whether anything has happened. Thus, and to reinforce the point, category-incumbent behaviour is accountable, is relevant, when what has happened to the child is open to question. In answer to the question 'where do we find children in the files?', it is generally where what has happened to them is in dispute. In the minority of cases where it is not in dispute their input is absent, and the text concerns their parents, environment, school and so forth.

Distinctions between Knowledge and Belief: Developing Frameworks for Assessing Risk

Jayyusi (1984) makes a distinction between category-organised belief and category-organised knowledge. She states that

> the distinction here between category-organized belief and knowledge is that the former can be identified as that set of substantive features that are (loosely) perceivable as category-bound, but whose use thus in talk by a speaker is treatable as a display (or implication) of *belief* as opposed to knowledge (even if claimed to be knowledge by the speaker). In other words, they have, strictly, the status of a *belief*: so that, for example, we may *believe* that women cry easily, that politicians are devious, that young boys are unruly. We cannot, however, be said to *know* such things in general. Although some persons may claim for them the status of knowledge, they remain the sort of things that *are treatable as beliefs* by other members, so that, routinely, knowledge-claim/belief-claim disjunctions may arise for them.' (p. 146, original emphasis)

Thus, the line between knowledge and belief is a tenuous one. As researchers and observers, ours is an analytic interest in the ways in which knowledge and belief are played out in the texts and practices of social workers. Before doing so it is worth clarifying the following: first, that certain features of claims must be perceivable (by some others, though not necessarily the person making the claim) as belief, and secondly, that disjunction or lack of agreement could arise from the claim as to whether it is knowledge, or whether it is belief. These two points have profound implications for social workers dealing with allegations of child abuse. It is this very disjunction between knowledge and belief that is a source of trouble. At one level it could be that a claim is made that a child has been abused, that a parent believes this is not so, but the social worker knows that it is. Similarly the inverse could hold, the parent knows, but the social worker believes. Such a disjunction is the root of a good deal of disagreement between social workers and parents. However, there is a second level at which category-organised belief becomes of crucial importance. It could be that in the context of something as vaguely defined as abuse, belief has to be the primary operating feature of claims about it, rather than knowledge, which, as we have previously stated, is rare. Practice oriented by belief, rather than knowledge, is not only open to dispute from a range of quarters, but it also becomes more inclusive.

A case (drawn from a UK sample)[5] concerning a ten-year-old boy, Andrew, exemplifies how the line between knowledge and belief is often glossed over. In addition, this case shows something quite interesting about a shift which we found in records of cases, one which could be said to be characterised by a shift from category-organised knowledge to category-organised belief. The first report comes in May, 1986, when we learn that Andrew's mother was

> finding it impossible to control Andrew in the home. Requesting help with this.

Two days later a second report states that the mother

> can't cope with Andrew. Set fire to book and dropped it on carpet on Saturday, set fire at — Primary School, broke window and lit fire in book cupboard …. Would like RIC asap.[6]

Andrew was received into care and returned three months later. The case is closed with the entry:

> family life appears reasonably settled: parents are happy Andrew is back home, and their management and coping capacity appears good; and Andrew appears

happy and less disruptive/destructive (no sign of interest in fire!!).

It is reopened on the 10 May 1988 when the mother phoned social services and reported that:

> [The mother] left matrimonial home at [address] about one month ago – she says it was because of problems with Andrew. Husband willing to have her & daughter back but not Andrew – he wants him in care. Andrew is becoming increasingly difficult at [the hostel] & has run away 4 times since he has been there. Ran away 7.30 a.m. & arrived at school at 11 a.m. [The mother] says she has been advised by Mr P, Educ. Psychologist, to put Andrew into voluntary care; also says staff at school are concerned about him. [The mother] concluded that it probably wasn't best for Andrew. Spoke to Andrew, he hates being at [the hostel] but wants to stay with mother. Could SW visit & offer support & advice re. rehousing or moving back to matrimonial home.

The social worker visited and confirmed the referral information. At this point the intended mode of intervention was practical to do with housing and support in child management. He

> told her I would keep the case open and offer support when necessary.

He then arranged for the old file to be sent to his office and contacted the educational psychologist who told him that the mother

> was a Schedule 1 offender – having spent a period in prison in 1982 for sexual offences against school boys.

The social worker then

> discussed this fact with [the team officer] expressing the fact that this mother was now living with her children in a hotel room. It was decided to hold a Child Protection Case Conference.

In 1986, when the child was referred for behavioural problems, the issue of the mother being a Schedule 1 sex offender
was not recorded or reported on as being relevant in the files.
At some point in the previous handling of the case
this information would have been known, because
the same social worker who dealt with the case then gives
the information now. In 1986 the problem was framed as one
of troublesome behaviour. The same problem re-referred two
years later was reviewed in the light of the mother's previous offences in 1982, some six years earlier. In the initial case
conference minutes it is stated that a social worker

> informed Conference that, whilst there is no clear
> evidence, Andrew's present behaviour meets the criteria
> for possible sexual abuse, and that agencies should be
> aware of our concerns.

Various social workers reported on their contact with the
family and the school confirmed Andrew's behavioural
problems. Then,

> a general discussion regarding the family and its prob-
> lems followed, focusing on [the mother's] offences; the
> risks she presents to Andrew, and to a lesser extent [his
> sister]; on her frequent threats to place Andrew in care,
> and on the family dynamics which appear to have led to
> her leaving the matrimonial home.
>
> In view of these factors, it was decided to place both
> children's names on the Child Protection Register... .

In 1986 we have a child whose behaviour is depicted as
what could be described in terms of category-organised
knowledge – setting fire to carpets, books and so forth.
These are framed as 'disruptive/destructive', but the
actions which lead to this categorisation are not in dispute.
The notion of belief or possibility is not invoked in the category of disruptive/destructive. It is taken as an adequate
description of the child's behaviour, and does not require
further justification in the file. However, in 1988, the
picture is somewhat different. Initially the reported behaviour was again framed as troublesome, and the response
was to offer practical advice – 'rehousing or moving back

to the matrimonial home'. Shortly afterwards the mother's Schedule 1 offence[7] is pointed out. This initiates child protection procedures and a case conference is convened. The child becomes categorised as a child at risk, rather than a child who is disruptive or destructive. What we see is a shift, from category-organised knowledge (accompanied by descriptions of acts) to category-organised belief (categorisations based on 'no clear evidence' and behaviour which meet the criteria for 'possible sexual abuse'). We suggested earlier that category membership remains until it ceases to become relevant. What happens here is that the child's behaviour is still relevant to his categorisation as 'becoming increasingly difficult' but that this behaviour is reframed as 'meets the criteria for possible sexual abuse'. The knowledge of a previous sexual offence invokes a possibility, a belief, and it is this belief which invokes child protection procedures. On both occasions the presenting behaviour was similar, and the mother's offences were known about. What is new in the second episode is the introduction of being 'at risk'. The result is an expansion of agency intervention – knowledge of acts retained the focus on the acts. *Belief* in abuse allows the focus to broaden. In this case the expansion resulted in Andrew's sister being placed on the child protection register. Her behaviour was not treated as problematic in any of the reports, but the introduction of category-organised belief, and the notion of risk, makes her presence in the home problematic.

The files show this feature of belief as a warrant for child protection intervention operating in many cases. In Andrew's case the process was to alter the type of intervention from child care or welfare to child protection. A second type of case is almost the inverse of this, where child protection is invoked and the child-care concerns which are exposed warrant case closure. Here a belief about 'possible' sexual abuse is the warrant for intervention, and knowledge of actual incidents of harm or injury are reported but effectively end the intervention. This case concerns Joy, a 12-year-old girl. The initial referral was made after her stepmother

> presented to school with concerns re. child's behaviour – lying, stealing (from shops) recently lifted up shirt to

show workmen her breasts. Previous incident of Joy caught playing with penis of 9 yr step-bro.

The referral was made by the education social worker who expressed concern about the family relationships and finally 'possible sex abuse'. Just over a month later a second referral was made which begins

ESW previously approached department re. concern about possible sexual abuse of Joy.

The previous referral had not been activated so this second categorisation was based only on the first report. No action was recorded for the second report. A third referral was made seven months later which reads:

previous query of sexual abuse. Joy has been upset & sad at school for a long time, today is very upset – crying. Doesn't want to go home, says her stepmother beats her. Hit her twice this morning... .

A visit was arranged.

Visited 09.30 with Mrs Smith. Had friendly chat with Joy to get to know her before she went off with rest of school to Adventure World. What came through is that she is unhappy at home – mainly with stepmother. [Stepmother] continually picking on her. Dad is OK but likes to go to Grandma's best. Grandparents live at [place]. Joy visits quite often – goes to grandma's if she has problems – would like [stepmother] to change – to treat her as a person & not keep putting her down. Told Joy we would visit tomorrow to talk with her again.

[next day] Mrs Smith & I had long chat with Joy – seems unhappiness stems from the treatment by [the stepmother]. Also told us [one of the half sisters] was sexually assaulted by her father when she was younger. Joy doesn't get on with any of her step-sibs. When she told Dad she wanted to go to Grandma Dad heaped guilt & sympathy on her – 'You don't love me anymore'. Although we asked a number of questions on sex abuse she said nothing had happened to her. She said there were no secrets & could always tell her Grandma if anything was bothering her. Although Joy says no about sexual abuse I don't believe all has been disclosed as yet.

A week later Joy arrived at the office with the mother of a friend. She had run away from home. She again showed the bruise inflicted by her stepmother a week earlier, saying she'd tried to run away a week ago but didn't know where to go. At this point the bruise was checked and a meeting held with the family to discuss family 'dynamics' and ways of resolving some of the conflict. Some five months later a note is recorded on the file:

I saw Joy recently at McDonalds in [town] – She recognised me & said hello. She looked fine and happy.

Recommendation: NFA [no further action].

Ironically Joy asks to be treated as a person, yet the intervention is almost entirely focused around the possibility of sexual abuse. Even after Joy presents the social workers with a bruise and clearly states that she has not been sexually abused in a context which suggests that she knows what the term means and that she could say if she wanted to, the social workers retain that orientation. Finally, Joy presents them with the bruise again and, after a talk with the family about ways of resolving conflict, the case is effectively closed. Whilst this is only one case and may have been differently handled elsewhere, we want to stress the strength of the orientation towards a 'belief' in sexual abuse over and above knowledge about actual incidents, which seems to characterise a great number of cases. This belief can serve to reorientate previous intervention and lead to inclusive practices with regard to the rest of the family (as in the first case), or it can act as a filter for all other information which is seen as secondary to it (as in the second).

This process is underpinned by the introduction of sexual abuse as a child protection concern. Attention paid to sexual abuse from the mid 1980s onwards has had a tremendous impact on practice, the dynamics of which are exemplified both here and in the increasing number of reports of possible child abuse to agencies. Essentially it introduces the notion of abuse which does not necessarily have to have signs or symptoms, so there will always be a 'risk' that the child is a possible victim. Thus, social workers now appear to be operating in the context of risk (as opposed to actual harms and injuries) and must show in their records that they have done their work, that they have oriented their inquiries towards possible sources of harm and accounted for them.

Conclusions

Categorisations of children are culturally bound to categorisations of parents, which themselves reflect cultural expectations. As Kitzinger observed, and as we have seen above, mothers are often blamed, censured for not being protective and available to the child at all (relevant) times. Furthermore, 'The fate of women and children are intimately intertwined – not only because women (and men) spend many years being children but because women take responsibility for all types of child-care' (Kitzinger, 1990, p. 167).

Viewing social phenomena as social constructions is (as we noted in Chapter 4) a methodological choice which attempts to detect the ways in which the social construction of situations and persons is achieved in local settings. This allows for children participating as social actors, but not in the sense that they haven't been (or have been) properly heard. Rather it is about how their actions and their categorisation (by others) operate and act to achieve the meaning that 'child' and 'childhood' variously have in the conduct of child protection investigations. What we find is that children are categorised as objects – they are what we have termed largely silent. Second, we find that this way of describing children alters when what is alleged to have happened is in dispute. This is particularly relevant to sexual abuse allegations. However, their voices are only present as they become relevant to the allegation. Social workers seek reasons within their accounts to corroborate or verify the allegation being made. Third, we noted a developing shift in categorisations of children which move from a knowledge of actual incidents to concerns about possibilities of incidents – from responding to harms or injuries to anticipating risk of abuse.

Whilst children must be seen as active in their own construction, they are active as part of a socially organised process which comprises other components which achieve that construction. It is important to tease out this issue since how children and their circumstances are seen (and judged) has much to do with how they are constructed and what it is about them that becomes important in that construction. Clearly, from the above example, and generally from the files, a key factor in categorising children is their mother. Now, to some this may seem like a long-winded way of making an obvious point, that the welfare of children is inextricably tied to the attributes, attitudes and abilities of their mothers. This notion, however, brings out the way in which decision-making practices are culturally bound. This is more than saying that attention needs to be paid to different ways of bringing up children (with or without parents), such as when an Aboriginal child is being considered and her care is the responsibility of the wider extended kin network. It is less about 'cultural relativism' (Dingwall et al., 1983) and more about how certain fea-tures of our own culture are reinforced by child protection intervention.

Recent social policy in the UK emphasises the importance of 'listening to children', attending to their 'feelings and wishes', treating them as persons and not objects of concern. In order to do so it may be necessary to reconstruct perceptions, categorisations and constructions of children in day-to-day child welfare practice. Not just to look at alternative childhoods across cultures, but to look at alternative constructions within our own cultures. Thus, noting that child well-being is culturally bound to maternal constructs and behaviour may be contradictory to reconstructing children as persons. In addition, a reconstruction of children who have hitherto been constructed in terms of their mothers may involve reconstructing notions of motherhood (Kitzinger, 1990), parenthood and parental responsibilities,[8] something which we turn to in the next chapter.

6
Identifying Some Risk Assessment Criteria

We now move to a central issue in child protection work. This chapter is concerned with issues surrounding the investigation of child maltreatment allegations as they are recorded by social workers in child protection case records. Particular attention will be paid to those matters which the social workers consider to be of importance during the inquiry process. The questions will be asked: What are the factors which workers write about and choose to draw to formal and official attention when investigating an allegation of child abuse? How do social workers achieve some resolution to issues which often seem irresolvable but which are key to operationalising child protection?

The data used in the analysis, consisting of the case record text of 30 investigations, was selected at random from 655 child protection investigations undertaken by the Department of Community Services, Western Australia, between 1 March and 30 June 1987. This data was collected as part of a research project used in the design of a computerised Child Protection Information System (Thorpe, 1994). The 655 investigations constituted a 100 per cent sample. Each one of these cases was allocated a number from 1 to 655 and the 655 numbers were fed into a pseudo random numbers generator using the GLIM statistical package. The first 30 numbers generated were used to form the sample: it is therefore an approximate 5 per cent random sample.

The major purpose of the original research project was to develop a range of outcome measures so that the Child Protection Information System could be used to routinely monitor and evaluate child protection work in Australian state child welfare agencies. One of the perspectives used to identify different patterns of outcome was that of the 'career heuristic' (Goffman, 1961) so that both quantitative and qualitative measures could be combined in order to ascertain the contingencies which created different career types in child protection. This chapter is concerned primarily with events at the very beginning of case careers, namely the referral and investigatory processes.

Table 6.1 enables a brief comparison to be made on a number of selected data fields between the original 665 case records and the randomly selected 30 case files used in this chapter.

The randomly selected 30 cases differ from the sample from which they were extracted in a number of ways. Aboriginal people, neglect allegations, serviced cases and 'at risk' classifications are all over-represented in comparison with the original sample, while physical abuse and sexual abuse allegations are comparatively under-represented. Overall, however, Table 6.1 suggests that if anything the random sample offers a higher proportion of *more serious* cases than did the original, since significantly more were kept open for child protection intervention than was the case in the original sample. Moreover, in the origi-

Table 6.1   Some comparisons between the original 655 records and the randomly selected 30 records

	655 records (100% sample)	30 records (4.7% sample)
% Single parents	49	50
% Aboriginal	23	33
% No services[*]	63	53.3
% Receiving services[**]	37	46.7
% Neglect allegations	47.1	66.6
% Physical abuse allegations	22.5	6.6
% Sexual abuse allegations	22	16.6
% Classified as 'At risk'	16.6	23.3

[*] Includes 'not substantiated', 'no investigation' and 'substantiated' or 'at risk' cases which were closed without any service.
[**] Includes all 'substantiated' and 'at risk' cases which received a service.

nal sample, only 94 (14 per cent) of the 655 children were harmed or injured in identifiable ways. In contrast, of the 30 allegations analysed in the random sample, ten children (33.3 per cent) were harmed or injured.

Seven of these ten cases were 'neglected' children and three were children who had been victims of sexual assaults. A further seven children were judged to be 'at risk', while in eleven cases there was no further action, no investigation was possible (one case) and in another case the result of the investigation was not recorded on the file. It is worth noting that in this sample, two children were subjects of allegations of physical assault. In the original study from which these cases were extracted, physical assaults were 22.5 per cent of allegations and 8 per cent of further action cases (Thorpe, 1994).

Table 6.2 is a frequency distribution of the care-giver family structures of the children whose circumstances were investigated.

Half of the allegations were concerned with children living in single-parent households – 14 in single female parent families and one in a single male parent family. Eight children were living with both biological parents and five with families which had two parents but which were reconstituting. The care-giver family structure context of the allegations suggests here that non-standard family types (single parents, reconstituting families) provide two thirds of child protection allegations.

Two thirds of the children living in single care-giver families were removed from home and placed in substitute

Table 6.2   Care-giver family structure of referred children

Care-giver family structure	No.	%
Both biological parents	8	26.7
Reconstituting family	5	16.7
Single female parent	14	46.7
Single male parent	1	3.3
Unknown	2	6.7
Total	30	100.1

care. The initial classification of these cases after investigation was confined entirely to the 'at risk' and 'neglect' categories.

In contrast to the single parents, two-parent families were more likely to receive home-based services (50 per cent) and the chances of case closure with no further action were also much higher. Three of these cases involved sexual assaults on children and, even then, one was closed without service.

The overall picture presented by these 30 cases suggests that non-standard single-parent families are over-represented at referral, more likely to be categorised as 'at risk' or 'neglect' after investigation and more likely to receive services which involve the most intensive and intrusive forms of intervention – removal from home.

The original research, which was undertaken in Western Australia, showed that the child protection system in that state netted a substantial number of Aboriginal children. Table 6.3 is a frequency distribution of the ethnicity of children within the sample of 30 cases used in this chapter.

One third of the referred children were of Aboriginal descent. Aboriginal people constitute approximately 3–4 per cent of Western Australia's population. Therefore, in this sample they are over-represented by a factor of ten.

Social Workers Investigating

This chapter will now move from the exploration of the statistical aspects of the sample and look at the ways in

Table 6.3 Ethnicity of children about whom child protection allegations were made

Ethnicity	No.	%
Aboriginal	10	33
Non-Aboriginal	14	47
Unknown	6	20
Total	30	100

which the investigating social workers described their tasks after they had received the initial referrals.

In this section, details from the records of five investigations will be presented and analysed to reveal the factors taken into account by investigators after allegations were made about the care of children. These five records have been chosen for two reasons. First, they exhibit progressively greater degrees of divergence from a set of inter-linked characteristics (which will be demonstrated by using text from Case 167). Second, they also exhibit progressively greater degrees of 'protective intervention'. Case 167, for example (the first of the five cases), was closed immediately after the investigation and categorised as 'not substantiated'. In contrast, Case 441 (the last of the five cases) was subject to very high levels of intervention including a police arrest and prosecution, medical attention and the temporary physical relocation of the child along with a non-offending care-giver.

The original study of the 655 cases was completed in 1988. Since that time, textual analysis of these cases has been used in several different publications (Thorpe, 1989, 1991; 1994; Thorpe and Thorpe, 1992). However, these analyses have hitherto been confined entirely to substanti-ated and 'at risk' cases and no attempt has been made to explore the nature of the 'substantiation' process itself or the 'not substantiated' child protection cases in that original study. In the original study (Thorpe, 1994), the 'not substantiated' cases consisted of 330 records, or 50.4 per cent of the original 100 per cent sample of 655 cases. Table 6.1 shows that, of the 30 cases selected for textual analysis, 53.3 per cent (16 cases) did not receive a service. In 13 of these situations, cases were placed in the category 'not sub-stantiated' after investigation. Thus, for the first time, 'not substantiated' cases have been subject to detailed exami-nation. They reveal that investigators focus on a number of key factors when attempting to make judgements and that these approximate to a set of norms about family life and childrearing practices. Again our concern is not to decide whether social workers made the right or wrong judgement but to try to make transparent the criteria they used for carrying out this central task of child protection work precisely because the case was not substantiated.

Case 167

One case in particular, Case 167, is of special interest precisely because the case was 'not substantiated'. The case
concerned allegations about a three-month-old baby. It was
opened as a child protection matter when a duty social
worker in a local child welfare office received a telephone
call from a neighbour of the family in question. The record
gives the following account of the telephone conversation
and the ensuing investigation:

> Phone call from [a neighbour] who has concerns about a
> young infant [under 9 months] who cries 'day and
> night'. She doesn't know name of family – says that they
> are young with maybe another child (toddler).
>
> [The neighbour] is being 'driven mad' by the infant's
> continual crying – feels that the baby is either sick or 'not
> being fed'.
>
> [The neighbour] hasn't had a decent night's sleep for
> weeks and has resorted to taking sleeping pills. Can't
> give any more info. except that a friend of young mother
> visits with other children. [The neighbour] wishes to
> remain ANON.
>
> [The neighbour] has flat on same landing opposite the
> young family's flat. There is a father around the place
> somewhere – [the neighbour] doesn't think that young
> mother is single.
>
> Recommendation: Home visit to investigate p.m. today,
> as there is a baby involved.

Action:
A home visit was made to the [referred] family by myself
and [another Social Worker] on [date]. On our arrival, we
found [the mother] hanging out washing on the line.
[The toddler] was with her while [the baby] was asleep
in the flat.

[The mother] did not seem unduly worried or defensive about our visit, but expressed surprise at our concerns. She said that [the baby] was a fairly good baby
who she felt did not cry excessively. She said that [the
toddler] was a noisy child who screamed a lot to go

outside. [She] said that [the toddler] couldn't be left
unattended in the downstairs play area, as the area was
not properly fenced off or safe. The family flat being on
the first floor made this more difficult.

In more general terms, both children were appropriately dressed, the flat was in good order, clean and tidy.
[The mother] herself presented as being tidy and as a
person who cared about her appearance. [The father]
(who we did not meet) is currently unemployed but
attending a [Further Education] Course at the time of
our visit.

[Both parents] have extended family living nearby.
[The mother] has a sister, who has three children who
she says she visits often. She said that [the toddler] loves
to play with the other children in the garden. [She] said
that she took the children to see [a child health centre
sister] for their 6 monthly check-up and that there had
been no problems. She showed us her clinic attendance
card and suggested we contact [the sister].

I contacted [the sister] who said that both children
were thriving, and, if anything, they were developmentally advanced. She said that both parents attended the
clinic with the children, and that they presented as being
very caring and concerned.

The agency's account of receiving a child protection referral and the subsequent investigation begins with a telephone call from a neighbour whose reaction to a baby's
perceived distress has become so extreme that she has had
to resort to sleeping pills. The worker makes a note of this,
since it provides an indication of the extent to which the
referrer is alarmed and disturbed by the baby. The baby's
crying does not appear to be normal; the expression 'day
and night' is repeated twice and this behaviour is held to
be symptomatic of abnormal parenting, the baby being ill
or 'not being fed'. Connected with this, we have an image
of the mother as someone who is 'young' – again the social
worker who records the telephone call uses that word to
describe the mother or family four times on the referral
sheet suggesting that the mother is inexperienced, immature or simply cannot cope with the demands of the baby.

An external factor is noted in terms of a visitor who has children, and whose influence is not specified. The final issue raised by the telephone call is concerned with an actual or possible partner of the carer – 'there is a father around the place somewhere'. Where he is located physically is another uncertainty in the situation. This record of the telephone call contains features which validate concern through four areas:

1. The degree of alarm created in the referring neighbour in response to her perceptions of the baby's distress.
2. The child's behaviour: continuous crying is not normal and may be a symptom of neglect.
3. The external influence exerted by a visitor is not known: it may be positive or negative.
4. There is a father, but his physical presence cannot be specified in time or space. His role in the household is uncertain. He, too, may be a positive or a negative influence.

The social workers visit, the investigation gets underway and the first image recorded by the investigator could have come straight from a television washing powder commercial: 'We found [the mother] hanging out washing on the line. [The toddler] was with her while [the baby] was asleep in the flat.' What is important here is not simply the image of an apparently normal mother in a normal family doing normal domestic work (supervising children, doing the washing), but the scene setting for what is to follow in the rest of the report. The mother in this account is not a working mother, she stays at home and is available to her children, a point to which we return in relation to the construction of maternal identity in Chapter 8.

The mother's reaction to the investigators is important: she is neither 'worried' nor 'defensive' but is surprised. She does not give the impression of someone who is hiding something but is surprised that someone might consider her an unfit or neglectful mother. In this reaction, her character continues to stand up to scrutiny. Her description of her children's behaviour portrays them as normal: the baby does cry, but not excessively, the toddler is 'noisy', he wants 'to go outside'. The mother demonstrates her capacity to provide adequate supervision for him by pointing out the dangers of an unfenced play area.

The investigator's report moves on to describe the physical condition of the children who are 'appropriately dressed': this expression could encompass the physical state of the clothing as well as its adequacy in terms of climatic considerations. Domestic conditions are at an acceptable standard: 'the flat was in good order, clean and tidy'. The mother's apparent competence is reinforced by the quality of her appearance: she 'presented as being tidy and as a person who cared about her appearance'. The maternal identity is sustained; the mother 'presented' well.

Although the father was not present and was unemployed, and therefore not able to support his family as breadwinner, his response to this misfortune was distinctly positive: he was re-training and re-skilling. He was improving himself.

The proximity of relatives for both parents leads us into an image of a past romantically and idealistically peopled by families living close to supportive kin and the toddler playing safely outside in the fresh air with his cousins.

In this account, not only did the mother freely cooperate with the investigators by answering their questions and showing them her house, but she went a step further and actively volunteered information about attendance at the local child health clinic. She showed them her appointment card and invited them to contact the clinic sister.

In completing this investigation, the worker telephoned the sister who observed that 'both children were thriving, and, if anything, they were developmentally advanced'. We discover here that the children are actually exceeding the norm, a testament to the perceived 'model' parenting they are receiving. Finally, the sister's comment that 'both parents attended the clinic with the children' provides concrete evidence that they are able to move with the times. An unemployed father, like many in his situation, is using it as an opportunity for self-improvement and he is also involved in childrearing: he shows signs of being a 'new man'.

We are provided with a number of criteria which were drawn on by the child protection workers in this case in the process of coming to a judgement and making decisions. What we suggest, however, is that Case 167 provides a series of definitions as to what child protection workers more generally regard as relevant in their decision-making. In all, there are 12 factors in this account:

1. The reaction of others in terms of how they view the scale of deviations from a norm (the neighbour's emotional state).
2. The child's behaviour (crying 'day and night').
3. The moral character of the carer (the 'young' mother, being tidy and caring about her appearance).
4. The influence of others (visitors).
5. The role of the carer/partner (the absent father).
6. The specific/non-specific nature of the time/space dimension (father is 'around the place somewhere'; without him the 'snapshot' of family life is incomplete and, if the family is mobile, it may not be easily available for surveillance or disciplinary intervention).
7. The overall image of family life.
8. Reactions by carers to investigators (the mother was 'surprised' but not 'worried').
9. The supervision of children (safe play).
10. The nature of the distribution of roles and responsibilities in the family (mother hanging out the washing; father away on a training course).
11. The proximity and nature of interaction with extended family (the sister lives nearby and 'visits often').
12. The views of other state agents (the child health clinic sister).

It is interesting to note that the investigators' report makes no mention of them having looked at the baby during their time in the flat. They might have seen it while they were looking around, but the baby's physical person does not feature in the account. Like the cases explored in Chapter 5, the baby is 'absent'. The assessment is articulated primarily in terms of the maternal identity and behaviour, the state of the house and the father's role. We now draw upon these 12 criteria to see how far and in what ways they are used in other cases.

Case 37

Case 37 represents an investigation in which an allegation
of neglect was substantiated by an investigating child protection worker. It can be seen from a reading of the text
that the investigation was not simply about establishing
whether or not an alleged act of neglect had taken place; it
was primarily concerned with the range of factors
identified in Case 167. It was the consideration of these
matters which led the investigator to make a judgement on
the situation and a firm recommendation to his manager
as to how the agency should deal with it.

[The caravan park owner] reports that two women by
the name of — are in a rented caravan in his park, with a
total of 5 young children. They have recently arrived
from [another state].

It appears that on numerous occasions recently the
children have been left alone in the caravan or in the care
of one of the women, who absents herself – effectively
leaving them on their own.

Last night [date] at about 2.00 a.m. one of the children,
an 18 month old, appeared wandering around the park,
unable to find his way back to the caravan. None of the
women could be located. The child was unkempt and
dirty.

[The caravan park owner] has advised the parents
DCS informed and will investigate.

Make initial contact with [the caravan park owner].

[He] was advised to contact LCU if another problem
arises at night.

Both sister in laws arrived from [another state] about 4
weeks ago. Both leaving their husbands to start a new
life. [Mother A] has changed her mind and has planned
to return to her husband on [date].

Complaints

The complaint was that there were 5 children living in
the caravan, this turned out to be 3.

The children have been left at times in the caravan by
themselves, but both mothers suggested that the next
door neighbour was looking after or keeping an eye on

them. I explained the risks involved with the children being left by themselves, they acknowledged this.

All children presented clean and apparently well cared for. The other complaint re. the young child wandering around the caravan park at 2.00a.m. was true. [Mother B] tried to hide the instance by playing diversions but sister in law [Mother A] said I was in bed with my 2 children, so I knew where they were. I won't tell on anybody, it is up to them to tell you.

It seems [Mother B] was sleeping in another caravan with a man friend and was trying to keep her private life to herself.

[The child] must have gone looking for his mother, he was able to do this by pushing the door open, the latch is broken. I suggested that

(1)   they should ask the manager to fix the catch,
(2)   to be more responsible toward their children in who they ask to care for them,
(3)   gave information to [Mother B] on our Department re. financial and function areas,
(4)   our concerns if further complaints were received,
(5)   legal information to [Mother B] re. custody of children.

I suggest that the issues and the concerns were not major problems with the families, just adjustment issues. Therefore at this time there is no role for the Department.

Recommendation: No further action. Close.

The referring telephone call from the caravan park owner begins with a description of a child who is 'wandering around the park' and his appearance 'unkempt and dirty'. The carers could not be found and they were recent arrivals. These comments cast doubt on their character in two ways: first, they do not supervise the children in their care, and second, they are perceived as mobile, they cannot be fixed easily in time and space.

The investigator begins with their characters: these are single female parents 'leaving their husbands to start a new life', and this event explains the transitory nature of their current lives. One of the women has changed her mind. These are understandable events and they are only *temporary*. The discovery that there were only three children undermines the credibility of the referrer somewhat, but his allegation that the children are left alone is substantiated.

However, the mothers maintain that a neighbour watches the children (a positive) but the investigator explains 'the risks involved with the children left by themselves, they acknowledge this'. The mothers here are seen to be reacting in an acceptable way: they agree with the investigator and his views on the supervision of children.

The report moves on to the appearance of the children, which is satisfactory: they are 'clean and apparently well cared for'. But the observation remains: the child in question *did* wander around the caravan park, and moreover he did so in search of his mother who had not been present to provide supervision. At this stage it emerges that his mother was in another caravan 'trying to keep her private life to herself'. This presents as an ambiguous situation, she deserts her child in order to conduct a sexual relationship. On the other hand she is not exposing her children to this activity and in this sense she is seen to be acting responsibly. At this stage the worker learns of the broken door latch. The caravan site owner, the original referrer, is responsible for this – but it is the mother's responsibility to report the matter to him. The investigator admonishes & the mothers, tells them of the legal powers and responsibilities of the agency and communicates to them some idea of what might happen if further complaints were received. Interestingly, the worker accounts for future recurrence of cause for concern in terms of the issue of further reports – it is the complaint and not just the behaviour which must be stopped.

The final comment, that these were 'just adjustment issues' indicates that the worker judges the difficulties to be *temporary* ones. For this reason, while the allegation of neglect is substantiated, no further action by the Department is firmly and unambiguously recommended.

Of the 12 matters raised in Case 167, 11 emerge again in the report on Case 37:

1. The reaction of others (the referring caravan site owner complaining that 'None of the women could be located. The child was unkempt and dirty').
2. The child's behaviour (wandering around a caravan site in the early hours of the morning).
3. The moral character of the carers (recent arrivals who are mobile, single female parents who have left their husbands and who do not supervise their children).
4. The influence of others (sisters-in-law, both of whom have left husbands).
5. The role of the carer/partner (in another state, not participating in family life at all).
6. The specific/non-specific nature of the time/space dimension (not only are these mothers 'on the move', but the very dwelling in which the families are living is also built to be mobile).
7. The overall image of family life (caravan dwellers leaving the security of permanent homes and husbands/fathers).
8. Reactions by carers to investigators (they acknowledged the risks of leaving neighbours to look after their children, but the mother in question tried to conceal the information that she was sleeping in another caravan).
9. The supervision of children (in this instance, lack of supervision).
10. The nature of the distribution of roles and responsibilities in the family (single female parents).
11. The proximity and nature of interaction with extended family (sisters-in-law not only leaving husbands and travelling together, but also leaving children to be looked after by others).

The 12th matter (the views of state agents) does not appear in this case. It should be remembered that in Case 167 it was the mother herself who drew the investigators' attention to the child health clinic. This indicates that approaches to other professionals may occur as a consequence of the social worker's concern following initial assessment – a kind of norm-referencing and reassurance that the correct assessment has been made. In Case 37 it does not appear relevant to contact other professionals, perhaps because the social worker has made his assessment that the problems are temporary. The conclusions of the investigators in Case 37 are different from those in Case 167 for a number of reasons, all of which relate to a perception that several matters deviated from the normative expectations embedded in the worker's judgements and outlined in the 11 characteristics above. Many of these show greater or lesser deviations from an acceptable level of family functioning. However, some aspects are assessed as adequate and, crucially, the deviations are perceived of as *temporary*. Thus, the investigator concluded that the Department had fulfilled statutory obligations and that no service was requested by those involved.

Case 577

In the next case, Case 577 we see greater levels of deviation which produce a different outcome in terms of decision-making. The referral report begins with an account by a social worker of his meeting with two children who had just appeared in the Children's Court, where they had been charged with minor delinquencies. In this instance, since the referrer was a social worker, the referring event and the ensuing preliminary investigation are one composite report which ends in a recommendation.

> Whilst speaking to [the child] and his half brother, [name], after their appearance in court today I received the following information. They live with parents at [address]. (Mum was in jail overnight for disorderly conduct and appearing in court today.) I questioned their not being at school. The boys said their Mum doesn't wash their clothes and that they have only shorts clean, which is too cold for them to wear. They both had on dirty ripped trousers which they told me they 'feel shamed' to go to school in and that there is often no food in the house. I asked why and [the child] said 'Mum drinks with the money'. [The other child] was in court for 'Receiving' a rug. I asked why and [he] said 'Cause we have no blankets'. Both boys said they had no bedding because the 10

or 12 other adults who stop over drinking at the house took theirs off them and the boys have been sleeping these past cold nights without blankets. They both told me they like living with Mum and 'usually' with Dad but that other people aren't as nice. That Mum's brother Uncle [name] hits them a lot across the head and mouth. They don't like the others because they all drink. I then took the child home to speak to [the father] and stood on the front veranda looking into the house which looked fairly run down, and sounded full of people. I expressed my concerns re. the boys' offending, not going to school, lack of clothing, bedding and food.

[The father] appeared confused and expressed an inability to cope any longer – [the mother], he told me, is drinking heavily all the time and in a drunken state, yelling in the street last night, was arrested. Their 4.5 month old baby was breast fed and [he] was trying to feed it a bottle but was taking the baby to hospital today he said. [The father] agreed the boys blankets had been taken by people and he was afraid to bring meat, he'd bought, home as it would all be eaten by his 'unwanted visitors'. He informed me he'd taken the boys to school but after he'd left they'd taken off. (The boys told me [another boy] persuaded them to leave.) [The father] said he'd had enough and was leaving for [another town] (his home town and family are there) on pension day, Wednesday next week (he's on Invalid Pension) and he's told [the mother] she can come when he gets a house, if she wants to. He told me [the mother] and children would try and get into the Women's Refuge. He told me they wanted rid of their present house because everyone comes there and they feel powerless to stop them. He did not deny the boys' concerns about food and clothing but did not elaborate.

[The father] is appearing in court tomorrow for a charge of drunk.

It would appear a further investigation of the children's living conditions and care is required. Both parents are heavy drinkers.

The court has remanded [the child's] current charge of Enter With Intent for a report, to [date] and requested an assessment of his living conditions, as no parents attended court. [A social worker] has asked that [the boy's] parents be summonsed to court to appear on [date].

This needs to be organised by officer allocated in liaison with [the local child welfare agency manager]. [The other boy's] charge was deferred to Panel (1 x Receiving) as he has a panel coming up.

The referring/investigating social worker begins with a description of two boys. They are contravening certain normative expectations in two ways: their appearance is at odds with the norm (they are wearing 'dirty ripped trousers') and their behaviour is such as to draw comment; these boys are now officially and formally delinquent, and they are also not at school. The character of their mother is immediately called into question: she has spent the night in jail, she reportedly does not wash the boys' clothes and their only clean clothes are not adequate for winter temperatures.

The mother's reported child care standards come into focus. She drinks and does not provide food or blankets. Relatives in this account also feature as a strongly negative influence. Far from providing help and support to the mother, thus addressing some of her perceived shortcomings, they make things worse by drinking at the family home, taking the boys' bedding and even by all accounts physically assaulting them. None of this is anything near normative expectations of child behaviour, parental character, parental behaviour and positively influential relatives detailed previously in Case 167.

In this case, the 12 factors which featured in Case 167 are operating strongly:

1. The referrer's reaction (the situation as described by the boys was not something which, as a social worker, she could leave; she took the children home and challenged the father).
2. The children's behaviour/appearance (complaints about mother not washing clothes, dirty ripped trousers, 'feel shamed' to go to school, no food in the house; the boys were in court for receiving a rug 'because we have no blankets').

3. The moral character of the carer (implicit in the children's complaints; mother drinks with the family's money, she is in prison overnight for disorderly conduct).
4. The influence of others ('unwanted' visitors who all drink, are not nice to the boys, take their blankets, eat all the food in the house; the family is 'powerless' to stop them).
5. Role of the carer/partner (the father is confused, he expresses an inability to cope, he is afraid, he is leaving that day and is also charged with drunkenness).
6. The time/space dimension (the mother can move to live with the father when he gets a house).
7. The overall image of the family (chaotic, alcoholic).
8. The reaction of carers to the investigators (the father says he cannot cope any longer).
9. The supervision of children (the father had taken the boys to school, but after he had gone they left; he did not deny the boys' concerns about food and clothing, but did not elaborate on this; he is trying to feed the baby but is taking it to the hospital that day).
10. The nature of and distribution of roles and responsibilities in the family (mother drinking heavily all the time; father left 'holding the baby').
11. The proximity and nature of interaction with extended family ('Mum's brother hits them a lot'; father is moving back to 'his home town and family are there').
12. The views of other state agents (the referrer is a state agent; the court requires a report giving an assessment of living conditions because neither parent turned up for the boys' hearing).

The visit to the home to see the father reveals domestic conditions at variance with the clean and tidy house described in Case 167: 'the house ... looked fairly run down' and it 'sounded full of people'.

The father's reaction to the investigator was reported as appearing 'confused and expressed an inability to cope any longer'. Very few parents are likely to respond to questioning from a social worker in this manner. In fact the most probable explanation for what appears to be an extraordinary reaction is that the father himself, or certainly one of his close relatives, had been in care. As recently as 1936, all Aboriginal people under the age of 21 years were made state wards in Western Australia and a whole generation of Aboriginal children were removed into various forms of substitute care. This action took place under the auspices of legislative and welfare programmes entitled 'The Protection of Aborigines' (see, for example, Morgan, 1987, and Thorpe, 1994). Experience of direct state welfare intervention and the removal of children from their families is part and parcel of the history of many aboriginal people.

In this case the social worker calls for 'further investigation' and points to an existing channel for potential interventions, namely the possibilities held out by the powers of the Children's Court and the Children's Panel (an institution which delivers the equivalent of formal cautions).

Case 74

A fourth case demonstrates a high level of intervention, not in terms of outcome (such as substitute care) but in terms of level of inquiry. In contrast to the first two cases which involved one interview with a parent, case 74 involved ten interviews during the initial investigation. A headteacher from a special school contacted the department

> asking if we could visit and see [the child] who had been soiling heavily at school the last couple of weeks, as this coincided with his mother being away. The school were suspecting sexual abuse. The school nurse [name] had examined him twice that week and discovered bruising on his buttocks.
>
> EP and I investigated the allegations as follows:
>
> 1.   [date] Interview with [the child], [headteacher] and school teacher.
> 2.   [date] Discussion with school nurse [name] who examined [the child] [1st date] and [2nd date]. [Hospital] doctor who had examined [the child/date], hospital social worker AB and FC.

3. [date] Interview with [the child] and anatomical dolls.
   Interview with JB, Guidance Officer [high school].
   Interview with [the brother] at [high school].
   Interview with [the stepfather] at home.
4. [date] Interview with [the mother and stepfather] at home.
5. [date] Referral to [hospital] for [the child] – seen by Dr T.

In our interviews with [the child] there was no direct statement that [the stepfather] had interfered with him. I do, however, believe that [the stepfather] hit [the child] twice excessively over the two weeks his mother was away. [The child] talked of getting in trouble both times for breaking tapes. This sounded confused particularly as HI [school nurse] said the first pattern of bruising could indicate someone's hands holding open his buttocks. These incidents were further clarified by [the brother] at school. [The brother] told us that [the child] had been in trouble because he had broken one of [his brother's] music tapes on the weekend before and that dad had hit him for this with his hands and later that week [the child] had taken a video tape to pieces and [the stepfather] had again hit him twice with a belt on his buttocks. [The brother] said [the stepfather] had just bought that tape to tape some shows for his mum on her return.

[The child] in his play and talk described everyone touching his willy in the family. He also said he shared a room with [his brother] but sometimes he slept with mum. [His brother] did too. He also said [he] had blood on his willy and that this needed a bandaid. He described the blood as green and the colour of milo. He gave no indication in play that anal intercourse had taken place and was able to talk openly about the anatomical parts of the dolls. He said sometimes dad came to his room at night to give him a kiss good-night. He said dad sometimes got onto the bed if he was scared and then dad left when he went to sleep. He said dad sometimes fell asleep on the toys in the toyroom.

[The brother] was also interviewed regarding possible sexual abuse. He denied that this had ever happened. He said he had slept with mum a couple of times when he was sick and so had [the child]. He said this hadn't happened much. He also confirmed that dad came into the room to say goodnight and would sometimes stay with [the child] for a little while if he was scared of the dark. He said dad slept in his own bed, with mummy when she was there. He said dad had never touched him or showed him his willy. He thought he and [subject child] got on all right with dad and that it had been better with mum away because when she was there she and dad always argued. He also said dad did better cooking than mum and had taken them to the place where he worked.

The school stated that they were concerned about [the child] as his soiling appeared worse in mum's absence and because of [the stepfather's] past record of indecent dealings and intercourse was being questioned as a cause of the soiling. His teacher and nurse described his anus as always large and his walk funny – bum sticking out.

[The stepfather] admitted to punishing [the child] on both occasions and he was worried as to the excessive nature of his punishment. His wife on her return from [place] (away for a holiday with [the stepfather's] parents and stayed longer as [his father] died), was very angry at her husband for his treatment of [the child] and presented as protective of [the child]. She too was concerned about the soiling but felt it was stress related and that [the child] had been missing her. It was suggested that [the child] be medically examined at [the hospital] for any possible medical problems that may be causing [the child] to soil, [the mother] agreed to this.

[The hospital] was contacted and it was arranged for [the child] to be seen by Dr T at the Sexual Abuse Unit. The situation was explained to the Social Work Section there and an interview set up without any reference at this point to possible sexual abuse as this had not been ascertained.

Dr T could find no evidence to suggest any intercourse had taken place and no other medical reasons for soiling. [The mother] and the school both reported decreased soiling on [the mother's] return home and the family commenced a program of praise and reward for [the child] if he didn't soil.

I discussed with [the mother] 'everyone touching his willy'. She explained that [the child] appeared obsessed with his willy at the moment because it had been very sore and red raw at times. They said they had contemplated getting [the child] circumcised recently with their local doctor because of the irritation [the child] was having. [The child] was always asking for bandaids for it and they would often be called to the toilet to help him change his pants.

In conclusion I believe that:

1. [The stepfather] could give excessive punishments to his children. This is more likely to happen in his wife's absence but I believe she is protective of them when she is home.

2. I still question whether [the stepfather] has shown the boys his penis or possibly masturbated in front of them. This plus touching is denied by [the brother]. Anal intercourse does not seem to have taken place.

3. There are relationship problems in this family between [the mother and stepfather]. [The mother] is attempting to have another baby, but doesn't know why. In my discussions with them jointly I have noted lots of friction between the two, and this would appear to be an ongoing and long-term problem.

4. I feel this family needs monitoring. [The school] will do this with [the child] and [his brother] is currently seeing JB at [high school]. I also feel occasional visits to the [family] would be necessary and in particular to offer [the mother] advice and support regarding the boys and the problem of soiling if it continues. According to the school [the child's] soiling has improved a bit but [his mother] reports soiling on the weekend at home.

At my last recent contact [the mother] reported decreased soiling with [the child] and only once at home in four days.

Ten of of the 12 criteria are again present in this case:

1. The reaction of others in relation to scale of deviations from normative expectations (education and health staff reacted strongly to the soiling and suspected sexual abuse).
2. The child's behaviour (soiling, getting into trouble because of breaking tapes, described everyone touching his willy, scared of the dark, getting into bed with mum, walking 'funny').
3. Moral character of the carer, in this case both mother and father: many features of their behaviour in relation to the children are described, particularly the father. For example, he over-disciplines the children, he kisses the children goodnight and comes into their bedrooms, sometimes gets onto the bed, sometimes falls asleep on the toys. He is also a 'better cook' than Mum, and has a past record of 'indecent dealings'. The mother is angry at her husband for his treatment of the child, and is presented as protective. However, we also learn that she is attempting to have another baby but doesn't know why.
4. The time/space dimension (the soiling gets worse when the mother is away).
5. The overall image of family life (lots of friction between the parents, arguing a lot).
6. Reaction of carers to the investigators: they appear to share the investigator's concern about the soiling and the 'sore willy', though differently (somewhat more pragmatically) and not to the same extent.
7. Supervision of the children (the father is noted to over-discipline the children and supervision at bedtime is focused on).
8. The nature and distribution of roles within the family (we learn that 'Dad is a better cook', shares in the child care and takes over the mother's role in her absence).
9. Proximity and nature of interaction with extended family (mother went to visit the grandparents and stayed longer because the grandfather died).
10. Views of other state agents (the referrers were teachers, concern was expressed by the school nurse and school guidance officers will continue to monitor the case).

What begins to be quite interesting when we compare this case to the previous three are the things which become relevant to record. In Cases 167, 37 and 577 there is no description of bedtime behaviour, affection between father and children, or even disciplinary techniques. Is it that these are not relevant to making assessments of children who are alleged to be physically harmed, unspecifiably harmed or neglected? The allegation in Case 74 is suspected sexual abuse, and the focus and level of enquiry is typical. Once categorised in this way the case is oriented to in this way, and behaviours which investigators consider normal are assessed against the behaviours presented – as they relate to suspected sexual abuse. Not only do we see what becomes relevant and how, we also see how normal behaviour, because it becomes relevant to a social work assessment, can be used to interpret whether there is cause for concern. In the other three cases, the fathers (if they had been present) kissing their children at bedtime was not seen as important. We point this out not because it is exceptional or wrong, but to underline that, while there may be a number of criteria, the way these are used and drawn upon varies according to the allegation or cause(s) for concern. In Case 74 it becomes (along with a host of other similar features) part of the assessment. There remains a question in the social worker's report as to whether the father has acted indecently with the boys. However, penetration is ruled out and an alternative solution to the cause for concern about 'soiling' is reached. The case remained open whilst a behavioural programme to deal with the soiling was developed. This required the child (no longer a 'victim') to 'clean himself and take responsibility for rinsing his clothes after having soiled at school'. The parents were to be provided with assistance to 'develop the appropriate skills' by use of a 'social trainer' and holidays were offered to the children.

Case 441

The last case to be discussed in this chapter, Case 441 describes a multi-agency investigation into an allegation of sexual assaults on a female child. In a number of important ways, it departs quite markedly from the aspects of family life and childrearing which have been highlighted by the four cases discussed already in this chapter.

Phone call from [social worker], at [a children's hospital].

[The social worker] advised that a young girl, [name], who is 11 years and 8 months old, disclosed to her mother last night that she had been sexually abused by her step-father. The mother, [name], phoned [the hospital] last night. They were seen by [a doctor] and [the social worker] this morning. It appears that [the child] has been sexually abused for the past 3 years. [The step-father] has been living with [the mother] for the past 5 years. The sexual abuse involved fondling, digital penetration, attempted penile penetration. There was no oral sex, and it appears no sexual intercourse. It was alleged also that other children have been involved as well. [The social worker] reported that it appears that the abuse occurred when [the mother] was out. It appears that it may have been routine and that [the child] was subjected to the abuse whenever [the step-father] had finished showering. [The child] would be required to come in the shower herself. On one occasion it seems [the mother] caught them and he had an erection at the time.

On another occasion, [the mother] was having sexual intercourse with [the step-father] and [the child], came into their bed. He apparently turned his attention onto the child. Although his attention to the child was not sexual, [the mother] thought his reaction to be strange. [The mother], it appears, is demonstrating some ambivalence towards him.

[She] is 45 years of age, or thereabouts, and has a part-time job cleaning caravans. [The step-father] is 35 years of age and is unemployed. Previously he was a truck driver and more recently he has been on sickness benefits.

[The social worker] noted that [the mother] has had a psychiatric history and is presently a patient of [a psychiatrist] at [a psychiatric clinic]. She is not on any regular medication. It is intended that [the children's hospital] would have a follow-up appointment in two weeks time.

The present examination did not provide any medical evidence in respect to the abuse.

Phone call to [the manager of a Women's Refuge].

She advised that the family has not arrived yet. She said that she would leave a message for [the mother] and advise that I would be in touch next week.

Officer's interview with [the mother]:

[She] explained that she had stayed at the Refuge on Friday night only. She moved to stay with her eldest daughter who lives in [a city suburb] on the Saturday. As [the step-father] has admitted the offences, he was taken into custody on Friday. The family moved back to their home on Sunday.

[The mother] explained the events of the last few days:

On [date] in the evening [the child] had disclosed to her about the abuse. [The mother] had phoned [the children's hospital], but was unable to continue conversation on the phone as [the step-father] had returned home. She believed her daughter unreservedly because her daughter had said things that indicated she knew of [the step-father's] preferences in sexual activity. [The mother] did not say anything to [the step-father] that night.

On [date] [the mother] contacted [the children's hospital] again. [A doctor] and [the social worker] interviewed and examined [the child]. They referred [the mother] to the Police. Police Constables [two names] interviewed [the child] and [the mother] and statements were taken. The Police later confronted [the step-father] and 4 charges were laid.

[The mother] explained quite candidly about her history. She suffers nerves and sees [a psychiatrist] at [a psychiatric clinic]. She had already seen [the psychiatrist] in respect to these recent incidents. She is not on any medication, although [the psychiatrist] did prescribe for her sleeping tablets for this last couple of days.

[The mother] said that she was happy with [the step-father], even though she had a very poor sexual relationship with him. She said he always wanted her to shave her pubic hair as he did not like it. She complied with his wishes, until approximately 3 years ago. At that time he went up North to work. When he returned she would no longer comply with his wishes nor his preferences in sexual activities. [The mother] said she did not think that the offences against her daughter were serious. He wouldn't have hurt her and 'anyway it would have stopped when she grew pubic hair'.

[The mother] was still very keen to maintain her relationship with [the step-father], and underplayed the seriousness of the situation for [the child]. She said [the child] will only be with her for a few years anyway. [The mother] was afraid of being alone and felt that there were many positive things about her relationship with [the step-father].

While [the mother] was present, I spoke with [the Police Constable responsible for the police investigation]. He explained that:

1.   [The step-father] has been granted bail, although it seems he was unable at this stage to get someone to go bail for him.
2.   He is due to appear in Court on [date].
3.   He has been charged for two accounts of indecent dealing and two counts of aggravated indecent assault (the latter two charges occurred after April this year at which time the new provisions of the Sexual Assault Laws have taken effect).
4.   The Police are aware there are many other occasions when offences occurred. It would appear that offences occurred at a rate of at least two times per week for a period of 3 years. The incidences recounted in the statements are incidences upon which there is agreement between both [the child] and [the step-father] as to the specific dates and times that these occurred. This is often the case with sexual abuse of children and the charges laid against perpetrators.

Arrangements were made for [the mother] to get clothes, etc. to [the step-father] who is likely to be transferred back to [a local prison] shortly. In respect to the offences, [the Police Constable] explained that some of the offences were accompanied with threats and violence at least on one occasion when he slapped her and made her cry. The threats included with-drawing [the child] from her dancing classes, an activity she very much enjoyed.

Initial assessment
While the mother, [name], has taken all appropriate steps to ensure that her daughter's disclosure has been dealt with properly, she appears truly ambivalent and not understanding of her daughter's difficulties. On the one hand she believes [the step-father] to be very sick and in need of help, but believes this can be solved relatively easily. She believes she has been placed under considerable pressure to choose between her daughter and her partner. She resents this.

[The mother] presents as a very deprived person in terms of her own emotional well being. [She] does not appear to be able to put aside her needs and truly appreciate the extent and seriousness of the harm done to [the child].

[New date]
Interview with [the Police Constable] at [the police station].

Briefly examined the statements given by [the child] and [another girl], born [date]. [The child's] statement indicated that she attended [a primary school] and was in [a year group]. It appears that [the step-father] would slap her if she did not comply with his instructions and wishes. It appears that the abuse started in [a date two or three years earlier] and occurred approximately once a week. The abuse involved digital penetration and [the child] masturbating [the step-father].

The statement by [the other child] related to an incident where both children were in the bedroom with [the step-father]. Apparently [both children] tried to test [the step-father] to see whether the same would happen against [one] if [the other] should leave the room. This was tried and [one child] left the room. [The step-father] tried putting his hand in [the other's] pants.

[Date]
Home visit to [the mother].

Reviewed again with [the mother] what had been happening with the hospital, how [the child] was and what was transpiring for [the step-father]. According to [the mother], [the child] seems to be well and in fact, the abuse doesn't appear to have affected her says [the mother]. She is happy, she is going to school and all is well. I explained to [the mother] that from [the child's] point of view the problem has stopped for the time being. The abuse has stopped and [the step-father] is no longer presenting a threat to her. It appeared that [the mother] was somewhat angry with [the child] because [she] had expressed that she hated [the step-father]. [The mother] did not understand this.

[The mother] is seeing [a social worker] at [the psychiatric clinic]. Made arrangements to be able to see [the child] on [date].

[Date]
Office interview with [the child] and [the mother].

Explained to both the need for me to interview [the child]. I assured [her] that it is not that we need to go over the details of what has happened to her, but rather to be sure that she is OK at home now.

[She] presented as a very bright girl. She is doing well at school and as [the step-father] is no longer at home, says she is quite happy. She appears aware that her mother is strongly bonded to [the step-father]. While sometimes this means that she feels bad because [he] is in jail, she believes that she has done the right thing. There was minimal interaction during this interview and most of [the child's] responses were mono-syllabic.

Assessment
[The child] appears, at least superficially, to be coping well. Unfortunately, I believe [she] is experiencing some dissonance in relation to her mother. While I believe she is aware of this, she is unable at present to be able to express this clearly. It will be some time before [the child] is able to indicate her fears in respect to her mother and in respect to [the step-father].

The report of the social worker begins with a telephone call from another social worker who, along with a doctor, was dealing with a mother and daughter in a local hospital. What follows is a lengthy description of a series of criminal sexual assaults committed by a man on his stepdaughter. This detail, derived from a first-hand account by the child victim, is then succeeded by a very lengthy description of the mother, her past, her accounts of events and her attitudes towards her husband, her daughter and the assaults. Interspersed with them are brief mentions of the progress of police inquiries and activity in respect of the stepfather. The material under the heading 'Initial assessment' is devoted entirely to the mother; it does not deal with either the child victim or the adult offender.

It can be seen that 11 of the elements contained in the four previous reports of allegations and investigations are also present in Case 441:

1. The reaction of referrers (the child has 'disclosed', which triggers both police and medical intervention).
2. The child's behaviour (she has reported assaults, she is 'very bright' and does well at school).
3. The moral character of the carer is reported in interesting ways. The stepfather scarcely bears mention, his actions are criminal, he is arrested and detained by the police. The only behaviours referred to are criminal ones. The situated moral reasoning is different from the other cases – his moral character is not in dispute – he has broken the law and admitted it. The mother, despite the consigning of the stepfather to the criminal category, does not escape blame. Her character is called into doubt by her psychiatric history and, while she does things of which the worker approves (believing her daughter, going to the hospital, temporarily leaving home with her daughter), she 'is demonstrating some ambivalence towards [her husband]'. This theme reappears throughout the account ending in the comment that '[she] does not appear to be able to put aside her needs and truly appreciate the extent and seriousness of the harm done to the [child]'. She is not seen as being truly (and only) maternal. She is also resentful of having to make a choice. She is described

as appearing 'truly ambivalent and not understanding of her daughter's difficulties'.

4. The influence of others consists of the mention of a friend of the child who was also a victim, and whose behaviour was unhelpful in respect of the game played with the stepfather, but helpful with regard to her willingness to give evidence against him.

5. The role of the carer/partner (the person responsible for the assault on the child).

6. The time/space dimension (temporary relocation to a refuge and then a relative; in leaving the home temporarily, we find here an *inversion* of the normal comments on family mobility; the mother and child are actually helped to move).

7. Reactions by carers to investigators (the reactions of the mother to the investigator are not recorded in detail, but it is clear that the mother did cooperate; however, she was described as ambivalent).

8. The supervision of children (the mother's failure to take action in respect of her suspicion of her partner's sexual interest in the child; the offences took place when she was out of the home).

9. The nature and distribution of roles and responsibilities in the family (the mother is a part-time caravan cleaner, the stepfather is unemployed).

10. The proximity and nature of interaction with extended family (the mother and child stayed with the eldest daughter for one night).

11. The views of other state agents (the referral from a social worker in a hospital; the police have made charges and claim they have sufficient evidence for a successful prosecution).

The missing issue in this case is that of the overall image of family life. No mention is made of material domestic conditions; indeed the home isn't even visited. In this type of case the focus is quite explicitly on the mother, her behaviour and her character. The character of the stepfather can be taken for granted; he has admitted the offences. As far as the mother is concerned, however, her ability to protect the child must be spelt out through categorisations of her responses to the child and to the investigator and her psychiatric condition and history. In marked contrast to the other four cases, moral character is central, to the point where material conditions become effectively irrelevant.

Conclusions

The 12 features we have outlined are characteristic of all the cases across the sample. They reflect both what is available to be assessed, and also what is oriented to. They provide almost a pro forma for investigation, yet the areas addressed are not those we could conventionally associate with risk assessment. In addition, it is interesting to note where cases do not include all 12 criteria and which of these features is missing. In doing so we begin to establish what is relevant in relation to different harms and injury allegations. What this begins to point to is the way in which the categorisation of cases, by the original referral information and the matching of that information to the initial visit, becomes crucial in determining which areas are centrally addressed. The child sexual abuse allegations are particularly relevant in exemplifying this, where notions of home life and care by partners become either potentially negative criteria or entirely missing. Yet most referrals arrive as some form of allegation, whether specific or not, and it is difficult to see how practitioners could be encouraged to alter their orientation given that this is the case. In the context of advocating change in decision-making away from investigation into an assessment of needs, this data reveals that there is a prior tendency to focus on certain patterns and areas. Treating a child protection referral as anything else would be very difficult in the current context, and practitioners go about this task with the knowledge, beliefs and resources that are available to them.

Despite the differences in the careers pursued by these five cases, it can be seen that investigating workers consistently compare and contrast the situations they investigate with normative expectations to do with parenting, childrearing practices and how people might be expected to respond and talk in given situations. These normative expectations surface in what becomes accountable, either as a breach of the expectation, such as in Case 577 where the children are noted to be wearing dirty ragged clothes, or as confirmation, as when the mother hangs out the washing in Case 167. Each of the 12 categories uncovered by this analysis has a potential for constructing something as abnormal in *any* childrearing setting. Child protection programmes do not restrict themselves solely to the condition and experiences of children, but exhibit a concern with the totality of the physical and social circumstances of particular childrearing settings, especially the moral character of parents. The definitions of normality which are drawn upon in investigation by child protection workers are illustrated in the account of Case 167, which could be seen to approximate to a television commercial for washing powder. Whether we accept that the decision-making within each of the 12 areas for these cases is wrong or right does not matter. The general orientation to the 12 features remains throughout. It may be that change in orientation is going to prove very difficult to achieve – on what other basis could social workers make decisions? Furthermore, how could questions about help and support have been asked and offered in each of these cases? As it turned out, Case 167 could have been approached in this way, but only in retrospect given the nature of the report. This problem holds for all the cases, the final case raising important issues about help within a legal context. This is not to say that services, help and support are not made available and used, but that in a context of child protection work this takes a particular form. This is the focus of the next chapter.

7
Advice, Guidance and Normalisation

In the previous chapter detailed attention was paid to the issues which investigating social workers took account of after they had received allegations of child neglect or mal-treatment. It was shown that consideration was given to 12 key areas which child protection workers found rele-vant in their decision-making. In this chapter we look at a second major area of child protection work, that of giving advice and guidance to the parents of children where either risk was perceived or neglect and maltreatment had been substantiated. There are two reasons for selecting these particular cases. First, the vast majority of children on child protection caseloads stay at home. Second, the two major aspects of child protection work are investiga-tions and the ongoing work with child protection cases themselves over a period of time. We will suggest that if the former is primarily concerned with the assessment of risk, the latter consists in the *active management* of risk, a process which by definition requires the involvement and cooperation of families and the application of remedial measures designed to provide insurance against risk.

The social work practices involved in child protection are not necessarily the same as those of child welfare. The reason for this is that the core of child protection work is based on the assumption that there is risk of harm or injury to a child, or, in those cases where a child has already been harmed or injured, there is risk of further harm or injury. This means that the work is focused on very specific aspects of family life, namely the provision of remedies for those identified aspects of functioning which are perceived as an immediate or potential threat to the well-being of children. Inevitably this focus places a restriction and boundary around what workers are able to do. In many respects, it can be argued that the child protection agenda focuses and clarifies the social work task because of its increasing proceduralisation (Howe, 1992). It tends to be a very individualised way of working. Issues concerned with wider social disadvantage and misfortune are not pertinent unless they have clear and direct relevance to the risk question.

The Advice and Guidance Sample

The same source of data as that which was used in Chapter 6, the original sample of 655 case records of the 1988/89 research in Western Australia, is used here.

In that original sample a total of 38 children living in 30 families were in receipt of services which were categorised as 'advice and guidance'. This chapter begins with an exploration of some statistical aspects of this 100 per cent sample of 'advice and guidance' cases and then goes on to examine the text of the case records where child protection workers described the nature of their work with the families of these 38 children.

Table 7.1 cross-tabulates care-giver family structure against the classification of 'abuse' type determined by investigating social workers during the initial investigation.

More than half of the children in this sample were living in single-parent families (52.6 per cent), only three of which were headed by males. Nearly one third (31.6 per cent) lived in reconstituting families and approximately one sixth (15.8 per cent) lived with both birth parents. The reasons for intervention in the single-parent families were primarily because of 'risk' or 'neglect', although the single female parent families also feature in the 'physical abuse' and 'sexual abuse' columns. A quarter of the children concerned were victims of physical assaults (26 per cent), less than a fifth victims of sexual assaults (18 per cent) and there were three cases categorised as 'emotional abuse'.

Table 7.2 shows the type of categorisation against ethnicity.

Just over one fifth (21 per cent) of children were of Aboriginal ethnic origin and none of these were victims of sexual assaults. Of the remaining 30 children of non-

Table 7.1 Advice and guidance cases: care-giver family structure and type of abuse

Family structure	At risk	Neglect	Emotional abuse	Physical abuse	Sexual abuse	Total	%
Both biological parents	0	0	1	3	2	5	15.8
Reconstituting family	4	1	2	3	2	12	31.6
Single female parent	5	5	0	4	3	17	44.7
Single male parent	3	0	0	0	0	3	7.9
Total	12	6	3	10	7	37	100
%	32	16	8	26	18	100	100

Table 7.2   Advice and guidance cases: categorisation and ethnicity

Categorisation	Aboriginal	Non-Aboriginal	Unknown	Total	%
At risk	1	10	1	12	32
Neglect	3	3	0	6	16
Emotional abuse	1	2	0	3	8
Physical abuse	3	5	2	10	26
Sexual abuse	0	6	1	7	18
Total	8	26	4	38	100
%	21	68.5	10.5	100	

Aboriginal or unknown ethnic origin, 11 (32 per cent) were placed in the 'at risk' category, 7 in the 'physical abuse' category, 7 in the 'sexual abuse' category and 6 in the 'neglect' category.

While it is clear that at least 12 of these children were not harmed or injured (they were considered to be 'at risk'), it is worth giving consideration at this stage to the actions perpetrated by care-givers which caused children specific harms or injuries. Table 7.3 cross-tabulates the actions of care-givers with resulting harms or injuries to children.

Table 7.3 shows that, despite the categories used by investigators and detailed in Tables 7.1 and 7.2, examination of the case records reveals that 25 (65.8 per cent) of the children suffered no identifiable injury. These 25 cases included all the 'at risk' children (12), all the neglected children (6), two of the 'physically abused' children, two of the 'emotionally abused' children and three of the 'sexually abused' children.

The final piece of statistical evidence used in this chapter relates to the length of time for which cases were kept open.

Table 7.4 shows that just over half (52.7 per cent) of all these cases were closed within three months of the investigation beginning. This included half of the 'at risk' cases (6 out of 12) half of the neglect cases (3 out of 6), two of the three 'emotional abuse' cases, eight out of the ten 'physical abuse' cases but only one out of the seven 'sexual abuse'

Table 7.3   Advice and guidance cases: care-giver actions and resulting harms or injuries to children

Harms/injuries	Excess corporal punishment	Persistent care-giver hostility	Indecent dealings/ molestation	Penetration	Neglect supervision	No identified action	Total	%
Cuts, bruises welts, bites	8	0	0	0	0	0	8	21
Emotional trauma	0	1	3	0	0	0	4	10.5
Vaginal trauma	0	0	0	1	0	0	1	2.7
No harm/injury	0	0	0	0	6	19	25	65.8
Total	8	1	3	1	6	19	38	100
(%)	(21)	(2.7)	(7.8)	(2.7)	(15.8)	(50)	(100)	

Table 7.4 Advice and guidance cases: length of time open and type of abuse categorised

Categorisation	Less than 3 months	3–6 months	7–9 months	10–12 months	More than 12 months	Unknown	Total	%
At risk	6	4	0	0	1	1	12	32
Neglect	3	0	2	1	0	0	6	16
Emotional abuse	2	0	1	0	0	0	3	8
Physical abuse	8	2	0	0	0	0	10	26
Sexual abuse	1	1	1	3	0	1	7	18
Total	20	7	4	4	1	2	38	100
%	52.7	18.4	10.5	10.5	2.6	5.3	100	

cases. This suggests that the most speedily dealt with cases were those involving physical assaults, while those involving sexual assaults were kept open for much longer.

Textual Analysis of the Cases

Our analysis of the case records proceeds in the order of severity of harms and injuries recorded on the computerised database. Accordingly, the first case is the child who suffered vaginal trauma, followed by the eight cases who experienced minor injuries as a result of excessive corporal punishment. Our textual analysis then moves on to deal with the four emotionally traumatised children (three as a result of sexual assaults, one as a result of persistent caregiver hostility) and it concludes by examining child protection interventions in respect of the 19 neglected and 'at risk' children who, according to Table 7.3, had experienced no recordable adverse consequence as a result of parental behaviour.

Case 41 involved a 16-year-old young woman who had been sexually assaulted by her stepfather over a period of 18 months. Although she had been living independently for six months, she had become 'very depressed and weeping at work'; it was her employer who referred her to the child welfare agency. At the first interview the worker elicited from the young woman a full account of the assaults. The discussion included the current poor state of relationships with her parents. Five days later the worker accompanied the young woman for an interview with the police and made a statement. Although the police interviewed her stepfather for five hours, they decided against prosecution because he denied the offence. The worker then advised and supported the young woman in her successful application for a restraining order against her stepfather 'to have a legal way of keeping him away'. The case was then referred to a clinical psychologist who saw the young woman 'on one occasion only. She stated she would re-contact when she was ready'. The psychologist's notes on the interview comment that:

> The anger [the child] experienced towards her stepfather is very dominant, manifesting in images of her

father in dreams coming towards her, grabbing her and throwing her. This happens every night. She can stop her fear and the images through counting, however she cannot handle her anger. This is projected on her boyfriend. ... There have been lots of fights because of this. As a result of the therapy session [the child] recognised this and it upset her deeply, since [her boyfriend] was her main support and first love. We discussed the possibility of her telling [her boyfriend] what was happening to her and having a session together.

The social worker in the meantime had arranged a meeting between the child and her mother who

didn't really want to believe [the child] and stayed with her husband. ... [The child] and her mother contracted to have limited contact via shopping centres.

This work was completed within six months although the case was not formally closed for another five months. In this account we see the social worker successfully enabling the child to achieve a normal and stable life in a situation where the traumas of sexual assaults had caused her to leave home and threatened to destabilise her even further both on an emotional level and in the practicalities of everyday life – those of employment and accommodation. The work consisted of attempts to normalise as far as possible her relationship with her boyfriend and her mother, while limiting the threat posed by the stepfather. This latter action, involving a form of legal intervention in a situation where the police were unwilling to prosecute, can be seen as a form of risk insurance.

Cases 32, 33 and 34 involved two children under the age of four years living with their single mother who was heavily pregnant. Her cohabitee was in prison and the case was referred by the grandmother because the mother 'is threatening to harm the children, that she talks of killing the children'. The investigating social worker reported the mother as being:

very tired, almost to the point of lifelessness ... [she] admitted to loosing her 'cool' with the children and sometimes hitting them too hard leaving bruises. Advised her [the agency] would not tolerate abuse of children, that we were aware of pressures in pregnancy and associated discomfort – toddlers who can climb fences and run onto busy streets.... Recommended strongly that she find alternative care for children, by phoning family [listed the names of three helping agencies]. Advised replay groups etc. [in the neighbourhood].

Letters were then written to the local government housing agency requesting priority in finding accommodation away from a busy main road. The file suggests that the grandmother and an aunt continued to assist in child-care matters.

In this case, the social worker did not dispute the necessity of controlling small children who were exposed to the hazards of traffic; it was the method of control which she pointed out was not acceptable to her agency. All the alternatives suggested were other agents, formal and informal, who presumably could control the children without hitting them. Rehousing, it is suggested, would have the effect of avoiding the necessity of control. In this we see the worker and agency's view of what is regarded as normal modes of control of small children. The mother was acting to protect her children but was not doing so in an acceptable way – by using verbal methods, available child-care facilities or relatives, all limited forms of intervention designed to minimise risk of harm to children.

In Case 38 the text describes a similar situation, only this time the concerns are about an eight-year-old girl who had been hit twice with a stick on her buttocks by her mother's *de facto* partner. Bruising was discovered at school and the matter was reported as physical abuse. The mother's partner admitted he had done this in order to control the child. He was supported by the mother 'who was angry and upset at [the agency's] involvement and said it was lawful for a child to be punished by a parent'; her partner 'took up [the mother's] argument that the only way to gain obedience from [the child] was to physically punish her in the manner described'. The investigating social worker said 'that an assault had been committed, that bruising was evident and that if they refused to co-operate [he] would report the

matter to the police'. This threat eventually brought cooperation and agreement was reached 'to examine ways of intervening' after the worker defined the problem as 'a real need
for you to love your child and treat her with affection'. The
final file comment 20 weeks later says:

> [The child] is much more amenable at home and her
> school work and social behaviour at school present no
> problems. The key to this seems to be that [the mother]
> has now learned to relax a lot more and is not pressurising
> [the child] to behave and perform at a top level continu-
> ously. As a consequence [she] does not now dawdle on the
> way home etc., nor does the need now arise for her to lie
> about why she is late. [The mother] seems to have settled
> happily into her *de facto* marriage [her *de facto*] in turn is
> relating very well to [the child]. He now understands that
> his role of the 'punishing' parent was inappropriate and
> there seem to be no further problems in that area.

Again, the intervention focuses on the question of control
over a child. The matter at issue is not whether or not
control is needed, but rather what is deemed to be a
'normal' method of control (revolving around 'love' and
'affection') and the role of the male. We are left in the end
with an emerging picture of a family about which expressions such as 'relax', 'not pressurising' and 'settled
happily' can be used.

The remaining four cases in this category, Cases 125, 405,
416 and 501, all show similar patterns of referral and intervention. Three of the four involve stressed parents, in these
cases usually mothers.

> [The mother] has seen psychiatrist – assessment is not
> depression but problem with control of anger. ...
> Husband didn't want any children – little support to her
> (Case 125).

> [The mother] presented as a very tired, emotional
> woman. Being a [migrant] she kept apologising for the
> state of the house. ... [She] appears to be on the edge of a
> breakdown (Case 405).

[The mother] was very distressed and admitted she was under a great deal of stress. She has made previous contact with [the Emergency Duty Team] recently when she felt she could no longer cope (Case 416).

The fourth case, like Case 38, involved a father punishing his son for what he perceived as misbehaviour.

[The child] had been hit with the strap by his father the previous night because he had lost his school shoes. ... [He] felt the hitting was justified in the circumstances (Case 501).

A second factor, as suggested above, is the use of physical punishment to control children.

[She] talked about the fact that she is pregnant again ... and how angry and frustrated she gets when [the child] disobeys her (Case 405).

The incident was reported to have occurred the night before at a darts match. [The child] had been pestering his mother for something and in a fit of temper, [she] had picked him up and thrown him heavily onto a table (Case 416).

The response of investigating and servicing social workers was to give clear statements about the *agency's* view of the behaviour of punishing parents. In some cases, the workers do not present it as their own personal view, but rather as a matter for the *state* (see Case 38).

He was advised that smacking his children to the extent that he caused injuries was unacceptable, and that repetition could lead to assault charges via the police and/or ultimate removal of the child/children for their protection (Case 501).

Interestingly, in three of these four cases, the mothers were receiving medical attention as a consequence of reproductive factors. One was experiencing 'gynaecological problems – due to have a hysterectomy', another was described as 'having a termination this week' and one was pregnant.

In all cases social workers emphasised control by means of methods other than physical punishment.

> She feels [the child] is continuously testing her and this wears her down. We decided to look at [his] behaviour in terms of its frequency, [the mother's] reaction and the outcome. I designed a form for [the mother] to complete over period of a week (Case 416).

> Unfortunately, the course she was very keen to attend on stress management was cancelled due to lack of support. … [The mother] was also very keen to attend a course on parenting … but again was cancelled through lack of support. However, she has been very keen to listen to and act on suggestions either from myself or from friends and relatives (Case 125).

> We also discussed alternative methods of controlling his children and offered help should he or his wife wish to discuss child management issues (Case 501).

> I spent a long time discussing alternatives to disciplining [the child] and other ways for [the mother] to vent her anger and frustration (Case 405).

Before these cases were finally closed, social workers checked to see if they had been making proper progress towards the sort of control over the children which had been advised. In one case, the image of the happy ideal family begins to emerge. Uniformly, insurance takes the form of changing one (culturally bound) form of interaction between parents and children. Other potential problems which could have been the focus of social work attention are not on the agenda except by the presentation of pamphlets.

> More importantly she has realised that she really does want to be with and raise her children, and this realisation has enabled her to be freer and much more relaxed with them, and hence enjoy them. … I have provided her

with some literature on parenting, really so as to widen her range of options (Case 405).

We see here the social worker formally advocating a particular and specific view of childrearing as in Case 501 (the courses on parenting). Parenting is projected as something which should be enjoyed.

For others, a promise is sufficient since it conforms to child protection's minimum requirements.

After some discussion [the father] agreed he would avoid using similar severe punishment in the future (Case 501).

In this case, he had been warned of the penalties of non-conformity.

Cases 69, 306 and 313 were children who had been victims of non-penetrative sexual assaults and who had been traumatised by their experiences. All three were adolescent schoolgirls. Case 69 involved assault on three occasions, Case 306 on 'two to three occasions' and Case 313 on only one occasion. Case 69 was open for three weeks, while Cases 306 and 313 remained open for much longer – nearly nine months in both instances. What is interesting about these cases is that they all resisted social work intervention and the advice and guidance offered to them revolved almost entirely around attempts to secure cooperation and thus match the rather restricted menu of help the social workers could offer. This can be seen in both cases where strenuous efforts were made by social workers to get the children and their families to enter into agreements and to conform to a particular client/victim role, whilst simultaneously accepting the *worker's* views of the problem. It would appear from these examples that child protection practices, while attempting to regulate family life, can sometimes even include the disciplining of victims.

It is interesting to note that the victim of sexual assaults discussed earlier in this chapter (Case 41) dropped out of 'therapy' after only one session and that the case was kept open for five months after the social worker had ceased to be of assistance to the child concerned. In varying degrees that also represents the patterns displayed by Cases 69, 306 and 313.

In two of these cases, the first reaction of social workers was to advise mothers to report assaults to the police.

> Saw daughter and mother today encouraging mother to take action (Case 69).

> the Principal of the school, permitted by the teacher to whom the original disclosure was made, to re-question [the child] before the two [child protection workers]. [The child] then made a statement to [the child protection workers] and the police (Case 313).

No mention of reporting to the police is made in Case 306. At initial interview however:

> [The mother] said she would tell [her *de facto* partner] to leave tonight and that she would use the visit of the 'Child Welfare' to frighten him off. She realised she had to make a decision between her boyfriend and her daughter. She said she would need a lot of support and would approach [a family counsellor] who had helped her family before.

While the matter of police involvement is not raised, the mother appears initially at least to be cooperative.

Case 69, however, went wrong right from the beginning; after asking the mother to report the matter, she:

> did not want to. Reluctant to even go to [a voluntary organisation for victims of sexual offences]. Said she and her other daughters would confront [the victim's brother who had allegedly committed the 3 offences] – want to keep it a family problem – could not convince her.

The social worker

> arranged an appointment and contact person at [the voluntary organisation]. [The mother] a few weeks later had not been to [that organisation] nor had she confronted

her son – I could not move her into action – she didn't want [the agency] involved – again warned her of the risks – left her with the opening of either her or [the child] contacting me if they needed assistance.

Here, the worker draws a complete blank and closes the case, a practice which superficially runs completely contrary to accepted child protection procedures which emphasise intervention and action to 'protect'. The suggestion here is that the case was closed because no one in the family would cooperate; it offers an example of how families can act to protect themselves from child protection agencies and that the families which get attention are those which, however reluctantly or aggressively, allow child protection workers in. Even more interestingly it provides some evidence to the effect that some of the families which are 'filtered' out of the child protection system are those which do not want help and voluntarily write themselves out of the script. While, in effect, they filter themselves out, this is not to say that the tensions and difficulties between the various family members have been resolved.

For example, in Case 306, the mother rapidly changes her mind:

Told boyfriend to leave but he said he wasn't going to be pushed around and she decided to let him stay(!).

Further interviews with the child demonstrate her gradual withdrawal:

she said she found talking to us a bit overwhelming and wished we would drop the subject of abuse.

The older sister (who had left home some time before) was then interviewed.

We spent time showing [the sister] how unprotective mother has been (and indeed her grandmother has been).

The round of visits and interviews continued, more extended family members were drawn in by the social workers and the mother was persuaded finally to attend a 'support group'. However, the recommendation for case closure after some nine months had elapsed concluded that

> Mother attended Mother's Group on 2–3 occasions but found it too threatening, [the child] not wanting outside help.

Help of several kinds was offered in this case, but eventually refused. Advice and guidance consisted of attempts to engage the mother, her daughter and several family members into accepting a programme and consequent roles which they ultimately rejected.

In Case 313, the police brought the child's father to court. By that time, however, the child victim and her family had become thoroughly uncooperative even though the father was given conditions of bail removing him from the home.

> [The psychologist] believes children like [the child victim] who are too angry about the department and who are manipulative are unlikely candidates for therapy. It would be better to wait until [the child's] position in the family settles down again when the family is reunited.

Shortly after this comment the father faced a final court hearing:

> At the time of the court hearing the Defence Counsel requested the [child welfare agency] officer to be removed from the court. The Prosecutor agreed as [the child] told the Prosecutor she would not talk in the court with [the agency] present. The Magistrate allowed this and consequently [the agency] had no input to the hearing in spite of our long and intensive involvement. The report handed to the magistrate was not read as the defendant was found 'not guilty'.

A case conference was held shortly after this event, where it was decided to leave the file open in case the family wished to contact the agency. Formal closure took place five months later. The file comments:

> family members manipulative and refused to seek help with problems when offered by [the agency]. Family very *ANTI* [the agency] after police/court involvement.

In this case, the social worker managed to secure cooperation initially, but the case became very convoluted in the lead up to the court appearance when it became clear that the family did not accept the social worker's views on the nature of the problem. Neither, it must be said, did the court. This case provides an example of a family going to extraordinary (legal) lengths to have its case heard without the imposition of the agency's views. There was little evidence of negotiation over the agenda governing attempts to resolve the difficulties of the family.

What is demonstrated is that child protection tends to offer services on a 'take it or leave it' basis. The implications of any switch from child protection to family support services are really quite profound indeed. Will social workers be able to allow family members to articulate and define their needs as they see them or will the highly proceduralised and relatively constrained child protection procedures continue to be imposed? Case 313 provides us with some interesting issues to consider in terms of ethical dilemmas which narrowly focused child protection procedures avoid.

Emotional trauma resulting from persistent care-giver hostility was the major harm cited in Case 373 which was categorised as emotional abuse. In this case, which was open for five weeks, two female children living with their father and stepmother were 'kicked our of their home by step-mother'. After staying late at a disco they were locked out, they spent the night at a friend's house and when they returned home in the morning their possessions had been moved out of the house. The children were interviewed, then the family as a whole was seen two days later, when

> [the child] presented her side of the story but father was adamant about [her] being the problem … [the worker]

requested parents to have one day to think about problems raised and give the girls the same due.

A month later one of the girls left home and returned to the care of her mother, as the stepmother had finally decided she didn't want her. A follow-up visit took place but 'nothing much was forthcoming from mother or [the child]' although it was noted that '[the child] needed to work through her feelings of anger, rejection etc.'.

In this case, the worker was not successful in improving the relationship between a stepmother and her stepdaughter, the conflict could not be contained and the father chose to identify with his wife. The case ended because the child took remedial action and not because of anything which the social workers did. If family support is to become the new focus of child and family services, the question arises, who decides on the agenda and how? Should social workers empower children to make choices even when this might be disruptive for families?

The harms and injuries for two of the seven victims of sexual assaults in the advice and guidance sample were not stated in the records. These two were Cases 194 and 498, involving a girl aged eight years and a boy aged six years. The girl was assaulted once and the boy twice. The person believed responsible for the assault on the girl (Case 194) was a stranger, a door-to-door salesman. The child's single mother was a migrant with a very poor command of English and a request was made for a social worker who spoke a particular foreign language because 'The mother is not fully aware of what is happening and is refusing to take any action'. The implication here (by virtue of refusal) was that the mother was not cooperating. The case stayed open for seven months; the final comment on the record was:

Through contact with the department, the mother has realised the dangers of leaving [the child] unsupervised, and since then has stayed at home to look after [her]. The department has also helped the mother to be transferred on to Special Benefit, attend English classes and sewing classes to improve her work experience while [the child] is at school.

The six-year-old boy (Case 498) was indecently assaulted by a male friend of his mother. The man was prosecuted and the child moved to live with his father because the mother, who was leading a somewhat itinerant lifestyle, decided she wanted a break. The father was contacted and invited to bring his son to see social workers on several occasions. On closure, the file notes that:

> [The father] hasn't kept any of his scheduled appointments with me i.e. on 3 occasions he failed to turn up. Furthermore he has not replied to my last letter dated [date] to contact me. I am therefore closing the file.

This father would appear to be another uncooperative parent who fails to conform to the agency's expectations of the parents of children who are victims of sexual offences and where most of the advice given was concerned primarily with engaging their interest in a specific form of remedial help. The failure to turn up did not result in alternative forms of action being proposed by trying to find out what help the child and his father might have needed.

Cases 489 and 531 involved children who had been excessively physically punished but no harm or injury was detailed on the case records. One child was a 14-year-old boy, the other a 16-year-old girl. In both cases the punishment was carried out by stepfathers and it was the mothers, not the stepfathers, who were initially interviewed. Case 489 was allocated to a student social worker. The work programme was not with the stepfather but the boy. It:

> consisted of eight sessions, six of which were conducted in the office and the other two elsewhere (bowling and fishing). The aim of the contact was to build [the child's] self-esteem and to provide him with some insight into his behaviour, and to look at the way [he] interacts with others around him. The fun sessions were intended to build rapport ... and to enable a strong working relationship to be established. ... During contact [the worker and child] looked at: his life history; self-esteem; characteristics of his friends; feelings and how he expresses his feelings and alternatives to these ways; assertive and

aggressive ways of expressing oneself; and how [the child] sees himself.

The summary report on the file notes that

> [The child] feels that these sessions have been helpful. He said that teachers have been treating him differently at school (giving him more responsibility) and he says it has been helpful looking at his behaviour and how this affects others around him.

The boy had clearly benefited from this attention, but there is no comment at all about the stepfather who wasn't even seen.

The 16-year-old girl was seen twice.

> During [the second] interview, [the mother and her daughter] decided that [she] should stay with her maternal grand-mother whilst she completes year 12 at school, and [the mother] would approach the Family Law Court Counselling service for advice.

As in the previous case, the stepfather was not seen, even though the underlying problem was described as '[the child's] step-father's alcoholism and his conflict with her mother'.

Two children in this sample were listed as victims of 'emotional abuse' who suffered no discernible harm or injury. They were Cases 175 and 409, both boys, aged 11 and 7 respectively. The 11-year-old was referred because he was living with his grandmother in a house which had been condemned by the health department. There were complaints about the boy's behaviour. The file notes that the worker

> called out and saw [the grand-mother] and explained we were under pressure from complaints and that Department wanted her agreement to psychological assessment.

The grandmother agreed and the child was seen by a psychologist on two occasions. The psychologist's report ended with the following comment:

In conclusion, this assessment does not indicate that [the child] is being significantly emotionally damaged by his home environment with his grandmother as caregiver. In many ways he presents merely as a classic example of a child raised by an indulgent grandmother figure. The bond between [the child] and his grandmother is very strong and emotional damage is more likely to occur as a result of removing him from [her] care. I would like to see [the child] encouraged to attend some social or sports activities with peers in his leisure time and to attend some camping activities during school holidays. [The child] does not currently require any psychological input.

The psychologist recommends remedial help by means of the acquisition of sporting skills in leisure time.

Case 409, the seven-year-old boy, lived with his younger brother and parents in a caravan. They were referred by a neighbour because screams were heard at night from the caravan and because the child was not attending school. The investigatory visit revealed that the boy had a black eye.

[The father] said that he was a boxer. He is teaching [the child] boxing. According to [the father] that was how [the child] got the black eye. He said that it got very noisy when they boxed. ... [The worker] pointed out that [the child] was only seven years old and that that should be remembered when they do box ... we verbalised to the family that we were satisfied that everything was OK. However if we received further complaints we would have to come back and see them.

Four days later a return visit took place after some discussion with the local education department, and the worker 'explained the Education Department's stance on the matter and gave the contact number'. The case was closed. The emotional abuse classification arose out of school non-attendance and the parents complied with the legal requirement after being warned.

Six children, living in four families received advice and counselling because their supervision was neglected, although no harm or injury was recorded. Five of these six children were referred because of delinquent behaviour:

> Hyperactivity and difficult to control. Violence towards family members and fights with peers. Verbally abusive. Marijuana user and suspected of 'popping pills'. School truancy (Cases 19 and 20).

> [The police] contacted the office requesting our intervention as the above children had been breaking and entering, stealing and shoplifting in the area (Cases 332 and 333).

> He has also been charged with various offences relating to a stolen bicycle and further charges may follow. The police also believe that he has been smoking marijuana (Case 540).

While the sixth child, a six-year-old girl, was not herself in trouble with the police, her 12-year-old brother 'built himself quite a large court record ... and was a regular truant' (Case 605).

In all cases, investigators judged that the children's deviant behaviour was a direct consequence of inadequate parental supervision; it is not therefore surprising that this matter was the main focus of intervention.

> Following our intervention we were able to assist the mother clarify the issues that led to our involvement. [The mother] has used the rationalisation of the issue to form a constructive plan with [her boyfriend]. This involves moving into [his] home which in effect gives her the support she says she needs and provides a male figure in the boys' lives. Mother sees that this will provide a family environment for the boys and structure that has been lacking (Cases 19 and 20).

> [The resource worker] asked to work with the family and attempt to get [the mother] to take a more responsible parental role and enrol [one child] in a recreational group in the area (Cases 332 and 333).

[The mother] disputed the police account of events but did admit that she leaves [the child] unsupervised for long periods. This is partly due to the nature of her job where she is required to work late several nights a week. She was in the habit of calling in to see her boyfriend on the way home and so would often not get back until late in the evening. She said there were only occasional nights she did not return home at all. Since the involvement of the police she and [her boyfriend] have decided that they will set up home together and that [he] should live with them. [The mother] feels that [her boyfriend] will be able to exert some control over [the child] and will also be there at tea time to ensure that [the child] is fed etc. (Case 540).

Case 605, along with her siblings, became a matter for a Care and Protection Application before the Children's Court. This child, however, unlike her siblings, was left with her parents. The parents agreed to accept changes in their supervision of the children if the applications were withdrawn and that there would be 'regular contact with family and attempts to work on developing consistent behavioural controls'.

It can be seen that in two of these cases (19 and 20) families were attempting to make themselves acceptable by transforming their situations from single female parent families into (patriarchal) two-parent families. For the other two families, one case (540) was closed 'As there have been no further complaints and the children are attending school', and the other transformed itself into a new ideal family:

The family is looking better every week, Mum and Dad don't drink near as much as they did and they appear to have their household under control. They no longer allow people to visit and stay over night. They only drink two days each fortnight which is usually after pension day. The house looked reasonably clean on my recent visits and I have not seen [the parents] drunk yet. We also have not received any reports from the police regarding disturbances etc. (Case 605).

The 'At Risk' Cases

All the remaining 12 cases where advice and guidance was given concerned children who had not been harmed or injured in any way and where there were no care-giver actions which could be identified as 'abuse' or 'neglect'. These cases were all categorised as being 'at risk'. What is interesting about them is the way in which workers' attempts to change parental behaviours into something more approximating to the norm were not generally successful and that this lack of success was caused by a variety of factors including resistance to workers, geographical isolation and mobility. The space/time dimension again emerges as an area for examination. The 'at risk' cases fall into three categories: those which presented because of behavioural abnormalities in the children (six children living in five families), one family where the mother was perceived as potentially neglectful (four children) and two children, in two families, where sexual assaults had or were thought to have taken place. Analysis of text will begin with Cases 264, 351, 386, 423, 506 and 507, all originally referred because of the children's behaviour.

> [The mother] is a young single mother who is experiencing behavioural difficulties with her [8-year-old] daughter. The girl on several occasions has not come home from school 'till 6.45, and is becoming disobedient, aggressive etc. (Case 264).

> [The Aboriginal child] doesn't speak English very much. She understands what you are talking about, but she doesn't talk back. [She] doesn't know how to dress herself! Sometimes she's walking around the Community wearing a T-shirt inside out and back to front. [She] has started her periods, she doesn't know how to look after herself (Case 351).

> [The mother] said she was concerned about [the 16-year-old child's] behaviour whilst she is staying with her father. [The child] has been reported as having been drinking and going to pubs. [The mother] believes this to be a result of [the father's] bad influence (Case 386).

[The children] had told their parents that they were going to look at new shoes for [the boy]. They looked at shoes and then went to the local pinball parlour. While they were in there, their step-father saw them, went into the pinball parlour and ordered them out ....

At a later family discussion on relationships between step-father and children, the stepfather

pre-empted the second half of the discussion by telling me about his sexual feelings towards his daughter (Case 423).

[The older child], a slow child and [his 4-year-old brother] are the subject of a complaint by a neighbour. The boys got out of bed and wandered around in the dark breaking a gnome in the front garden of the neighbour's house. The kids are too young to be charged (Cases 506 and 507).

In these instances we see children violating accepted norms – coming home late from school, wearing a T-shirt wrongly, going into pubs, going into pinball parlours, getting up during the night. There is the suggestion in these cases that these abnormalities are in one way or another a consequence of parents failing to enforce norms. The exception here is Case 423 where the stepfather turned the subject of the discussion (control of two adolescent children) into a 'sexual abuse' investigation which eventually drew a complete blank.

In Case 264 the worker enrolled the mother in a parenting course at her daughter's school and the mother

reported less problems with [the child] and improved relationship with her. Also is letting [the child] sort out her own peer disputes ... she still has unresolved feelings about adopting out her other two kids.

The mother was referred to a psychologist.

The focus of advice for the Aboriginal child was on the local community to act in loco parentis (her mother had died 18 months previously) and the worker was reassured that when drunks enter the community [she] is quickly to someone's house and asked not to go out, until the drunks have straightened up or gone.

The 16-year-old girl who was said to be drinking left her father's home three days after the referral; the worker

discussed with her some of the problems she may encounter through leaving home but continuing to live in [the same town] ... arranged for her to meet with her father so that she could tell him her plans and arrange to get her clothes and other belongings.

Case 423, which concerned a worker's attempts to substantiate 'sexual abuse', consisted of one interview session where the worker

reiterated [his/her own] role. Emphasis was placed upon parental responsibilities in providing protection and care for the children.

The mother of the two boys who allegedly broke a garden gnome

showed some interest in disciplining/managing the children – although she was primarily interested in any child care to get them off her hands.

On a second visit the worker

Provided several leaflets to [the mother] about child management which she seems to be interested in ... and there is some possibility of a Parenting Skills Programme being made available ... – later on there will need to be fairly clear goals and intensive work done with this family to get anywhere with the problem.

The focus of advice and counselling in most of these cases was that of getting parents to exert control over children, and stress 'responsibilities', 'parenting skills' and 'relationships'.

These efforts however did not always meet with success.

I made a couple of appointments which [the mother] didn't keep... . She also didn't follow through the referral to [the clinical psychologist] ... [she] also knows how to seek aid should she need it (Case 264).

[The child] was unable to attend for a review appointment – she spends time between [three different communities], so it is difficult to meet with her ... but it now seems that she has adequate care and protection (Case 351).

This office was about to commence working with the family through regular contacts from a Family Resource Worker. The problems considered as parent–child relationships and schooling. By departing for [another district] the parents effectively stopped intervention which they had readily agreed to earlier (Cases 506 and 507).

The records show that in these cases the families moved within a short time of the files being opened. Ironically the file was closed on Case 386 (the 16-year-old girl who left her father) because the child changed her address, but in this case with the worker's approval and support. The child whose stepfather expressed sexual feelings about her had only very brief contact with the worker. The file was closed on the appearance of familial normality.

Each member indicated that there had been better communication between family members. Tension about clothes, etc. had been resolved (Case 423).

The four children living in a single female parent family who were judged to be 'at risk' of neglect were originally referred by a visitor to the family. The visitor said that the mother was 'on grog', one child had a 'severe nappy rash' and another 'spends most of her time in cot or pram'. The investigating social worker could find no evidence of neglect; she arranged for the six-month-old baby to be medically examined and the doctor

wrote an official report [date] saying, 'Apart from a minor dermatitis [the baby] is a healthy and well cared for baby' (Case 427).

The advice given to the mother in this case was that she accept an offer of child care and support in the home from a family resource worker. However

> [The mother] said she was having no problems coping with her children. She wanted to know who had the big mouth, [she] refused any support of child care from 2–3 hours to days from the Department. She stated again that she was coping with the children (Cases 427 and 430).

The case was closed; nothing had been found during the investigation which supported the allegations and the mother refused to accept that her parenting behaviours required any change. She would not cooperate.

Judging from these cases, rejection of the type of help on offer from child protection is widespread and almost universal. Family support from child welfare agencies is stigmatising and, except in the case of the most vulnerable and inarticulate, it is likely to be refused. Whilst this might resolve potential resource problems (very few people 'in need' of help are likely to accept what is on offer), it suggests that family support will have to be imaginatively devised in order to avoid stigmatisation. What is more likely is that support may be offered but refused.

The last two 'at risk' cases involved one child who had been a victim of a sexual assault by her stepfather (Case 454) and one who was perceived to be 'at risk' of a sexual assault from her father during access visits (Case 491).

The first child's stepfather had been prosecuted, found guilty and imprisoned. The child then left her mother's home and moved into her father's house several hundred miles away. The first visit to the child, newly settled with her father, was reported as follows:

> called to see father and daughter by way of introduction and to clarify the areas of assistance that I might provide. Both [the child] and father painted a very positive picture about how they were going to support each other, and how Dad would assist with school enrolments, introduction to friends etc. (Case 454).

Eleven days later, the social worker dealing with the mother telephoned to say that the girl had been in touch with her mother

> and wanted to come home as she was not getting on with her father. Told NO.

A visit was made to the child and her father the next day: 'Nobody home'. Twelve days later the worker saw them together

> and [the child] was very non-communicative. Dad saying he is sick of [her] sitting around watching T.V. all day and making no attempt to find work or go back to school. [The child] claiming that it's too late to re-enrol at school as she has missed too much and could not catch up ... [the worker] suggested Education Officer may help. [The child] not interested – also does not want to find a job (Case 454).

The child, however, continued to receive counselling from a clinical psychologist and two months later she was reportedly 'working toward independent living' and continued to stay with her father.

Case 491 concerned a three-year-old child whose mother claimed that she had been sexually assaulted by her father during an access visit. No evidence emerged from interviews with the child, using anatomically correct dolls, to substantiate the allegation. However, since the father did have a previous conviction for a sexual assault the mother was advised to ask the family court to vary the access by means of creating a new requirement for supervision during visits. This the court duly did and the worker attended the hearing with the mother. Here we find a cooperative mother who is able, despite the absence of evidence (except for the father's previous history), to ask for access arrangements to be varied.

We have seen that the introduction of highly proceduralised and relatively restricted practice repertoires is a conspicuous feature of child protection practice. This is child and family social work at its most efficient. There is

an interesting parallel here with the operational procedures adopted by many other organisations in the 20th
century. The drive for economy, efficiency and effectiveness, a characteristic of all modern organisations,
has been described by Ritzer (1993) as a process of
'McDonaldisation'. Ritzer defines McDonaldisation as a
process whereby 'efficiency predictability, calculability and
control through non-human technology' become the 'basic
components of a *rational* system' (p. 12). He uses the
analogy of the fast food restaurant to show how a
restricted menu, production line cooking technologies, a
relatively dehumanised eating setting and the queues in
front of the cashiers' desks produce efficiencies well
beyond what would be seen in a traditional restaurant
with waiter service, à la carte menus, personalised
cooking, a relaxed atmosphere and unique decor and fur-
nishings. Instead of being waited upon, it is the customers
who wait upon the producers. Ritzer defines technology
broadly 'to include not only machines and tools, but also
materials, skills, knowledge, rules, regulations, procedures,
and techniques. This allows us to conceive as technologies
not only obvious things such as robots, computers and the
assembly line, but also bureaucratic rules and regulations
and manuals defining accepted procedures and techniques' (p. 100). There can be few things less rational than
human relations and social practices. The variety of childrearing practices exhibited between and within classes,
cultures, generations and families, especially as they alter
and adapt under conditions of continuous social and
economic change, can give the superficial appearance of
utter and complete chaos to those with relatively static and
narrow views about the ideal nature of children and families. It is this very variety which offers infinite scope for
regulation and the deployment of technologies aimed at
the normalisation of family life. There are endless possibilities for enhancing the performance of all care-givers. The
minute observation of child/adult interactions and the
detailed inspection of domestic conditions which are predicated by child protection risk assessment procedures and
practices have a limitless potential clientele. In every

family there is always room for improvement. A recent definition of the aims of the *International Journal of Child Abuse and Neglect* declares that 'The scope [of the Journal] extends to all those aspects of life which either favour or hinder optimal family interaction.'

This definition, produced as part of a publicity leaflet in 1994[1] which announced a doubling of the frequency with which the journal was to be published, could encompass all children and families. This inevitably raises the question as to how such a potentially enormous increase in demand for service can be dealt with without an equally limitless increase in resources. The answer would appear to lie in the further refinement of measures which seem to have already increased the efficiency and effectiveness of services to children and families. In this chapter we have seen how child protection can be viewed as the McDonaldisation of child welfare services by virtue of its concentration on a very limited repertoire of interventions, a repertoire moreover which does not always bring satisfaction to the 'customer'. Its primary objective is to provide limited insurance cover. The insurance is of a ritualised 'third party, fire and theft, named driver only' nature which provides minimal cover by virtue of its specificity. In that sense, minimum insurance is given in respect of very specific matters. The liability of state child protection agents need only go as far as issuing instructions, as opposed to deploying resources or acceding to the negotiated demands of clients. McDonald's does not allow for variations in the time taken to cook hamburgers. Each burger is progressed on a conveyer belt through a grill and exposed for a very precise length of time.

In the event that child welfare agencies should seek to abandon the McDonaldised child protection version of a child welfare service, then a great deal of careful thought and re-skilling of de-skilled professionals will have to go into new types of service provision, the likes of which will never have been seen before. The analysis of advice and guidance cases in this chapter has both taken note of the limited menu of child protection and raised questions about the nature of new alternatives and the complex nature of the moral and professional resolutions which they will entail.

Conclusions

It is possible to identify three key issues arising from this analysis of advice and guidance child protection cases. They are, first, the nature of risk insurance itself and the way in which certain factors determine workers' responses to different kinds of family situation; second, the reaction of families – both care-givers and children – to these responses. Third, it can be seen that the way in which resources are used in the context of child protection procedures and practices does not always lead to efficiencies and that, if resources are to be freed up for child and family support services, some aspects of these practices will have to come under very close scrutiny.

It can be seen that the hazards to which the majority of children in this sample were exposed were for the most part unexceptional and may be common to many children in certain sectors of the population. It has to be remembered that 25 (65.8 per cent) of the children referred to suffered no identifiable harm or injury and a further eight (21 per cent) sustained only very minor injuries. The 15 per cent figure for 'serious abuse' some might claim is also an over-estimate, since the nature of emotional traumas was not defined. In the absence of harm or injury, social workers have to insure against risk and in doing so they appear to give advice in relation to the persons or actions which caused harm or injury (in those cases where these were known) or, more usually, this means selecting aspects of family life which do not appear to conform to a norm. If it is a matter of a sexual assault, then mothers are advised to inform the police and/or leave partners. If it is a matter of physical punishment, care-givers are advised to control children by other means. If neither of these matters are identified, then the focus is on preferred (white, middle-class) modes of supervision and childrearing. Additionally, many of these families were issued with warnings. This, then, is the nature of insurance against risk. The insurance covers both the worker and the agency, though their liabilities are limited. This itself raises an interesting organisational dimension which has generally been absent from child protection literature and research, but is always raised informally by workers who claim that they are doing their work as it is organisationally defined. Certainly the statistical returns required by agencies and governments represent the work, and hence their accountability, in very restricted ways. In the event that child and family support should return to child welfare, then worker and agency accountability will have to be formulated in a completely different way.

The majority of families in this sample did not appear to accept readily the limited advice and help on offer. Indeed, according to the records, for 23 of these children (60 per cent of cases), it was quite explicitly rejected and in a further three cases (8 per cent) the adults believed responsible for potentially or actually harming children were not even seen. There are those who might say, 'well, what do you expect of people like that!'. A preliminary response can only be to draw attention once more to the very small proportion of harmed or injured children in this 100 per cent sample. However this finding is interpreted, nearly 70 per cent either don't want help or don't want the kind of help that is on offer.

The third and final issue raised by these cases is concerned with the use of resources in child protection, especially as they relate to the 'sexual abuse' cases. It has already been noted in Table 7.4 that more than half of the cases in the sample were closed within three months. The exceptions were the 'sexual abuse' cases. This suggests that workers find it more difficult to negotiate and obtain risk insurance in these cases despite the extensive involvement of other agencies, most notably the police and courts. This represents the orthodoxy of child protection procedures and practices at its most intrusive yet least successful. It offers a partial explanation for some of the most spectacular child protection 'scandals', such as Cleveland and Orkney. However, and equally importantly, it is possible to see a large and arguably disproportionate quantity of resources being deployed without achieving any satisfactory outcome for those involved. If a transfer of resources is an essential prerequisite for a switch from child protection to child and family support services, then the scale and nature of attention paid to cases of this type would prove a major but highly sensitive issue.

8
Deconstructing Outcomes in Cases of Alleged Sexual Abuse

It is suggested that students of decision making may find it profitable to reconsult Cassirer's laws that describe the ways that human situations are progressively clarified. Cassirer's 'law of continuity' states that each outcome is a fulfilment of the preceding definition of the situation. His 'law of new emphasis' states that each outcome develops the past definition of the situation. These 'laws' remind us that persons, in the course of a career of actions, discover the nature of the situations in which they are acting, and that the actor's own actions are first order determinants of the sense that situations have, in which, literally speaking, actors find themselves. (Garfinkel, 1992)

This chapter focuses entirely on reports of alleged sexual abuse made to social work agencies in the UK and Australia. We have selected child sexual abuse allegations as the topic because this area of work highlights many of the issues and tensions surrounding the complexity of defining child harm and injury and deciding on warrants for intervention. In both of these areas it is probably the most troublesome field of child protection work. Sexual abuse is particularly difficult to define because an absence of signs and symptoms can be a characteristic of it. Further, as we suggested earlier, it has had an impact on child protection practices which goes beyond its mere recognition as a category for child protection intervention. Sexual abuse has reinforced the hidden nature of child abuse. Whilst previously certain injuries could be hidden, it was assumed that they were detectable with specialist scrutiny and X-rays. Their cause may have been open to dispute, but their presence could, more or less, be defined. Sexual abuse was entirely different. The emphasis for detection was in large part off the body and onto what alleged victims, persons believed responsible, witnesses, family and relevant others had to say. A proviso to this, given by the orthodox literature (Summit, 1983; Sgroi, 1982), was that not only was sexual abuse difficult to talk about, but part of the process of telling others may involve minimalising, denial and retraction. Thus, for practitioners, not only were there very few overt signs and symptoms, but it could also be expected that there would be very few overt statements about sexual abuse, and their absence could not be definitively taken to mean that sexual abuse had not occurred. An escalating number of reports, combined with this very practical problem of diagnosis, has resulted in difficulties for child protection workers. Cleveland, of course, was a very public outcome of the problem, but it was only one instance of it. Reports continue to suggest that sexual abuse should be taken as the exception in terms of rebalancing intervention (Dartington Social Research Unit, 1995). According to the Dartington Social Research Unit it is not possible to treat sexual abuse along the 'continuum of abuse' approach, where the less serious allegations and injuries can be filtered out for family support. Part of the rationale for such advice is that even apparently minor instances of sexual assault are conventionally accepted in the orthodox literature as potentially serious in outcome. But a second rationale is the difficulty associated with detection, so that all reports must be taken seriously. We would suggest that these two beliefs – that all sexual contact between an adult and a child can be serious and that sexual abuse is difficult to detect – underpin child protection practice. Thus sexual abuse has highlighted, and probably exacerbated, the problems of working in a context of risk, since most of the time it is risk and not actual harms and injuries that are being assessed. Within this context it is therefore pertinent to ask: what are the outcomes of investigations – how is the problem of working with risk of sexual abuse resolved in practice?

Efforts and resources have been moved into child protection since the mid 1970s with very little attention being paid to effectiveness and to the outcomes of the work. There has been an implicit assumption, founded on much of the research and literature reviewed in earlier chapters, that child protection is necessary and that social workers engaged in protecting children do just that. The occasional relapse into public scandal and tragedy surrounding child deaths revalidates this assumption, with the proviso that some social workers do not do their jobs properly, or that some deaths cannot be prevented. We saw in Chapter 1 that increasingly large numbers of children are being reported to child protection agencies. Outcomes for these thousands of children who have become child protection cases have not been looked at or even questioned until very recently (Dartington Social Research Unit, 1995; Thorpe, 1994). One problem has been that there is no consensus on outcome measures for child protection cases.

Since the mid 1970s the only measure of intervention in the UK has been the Child Protection Register. However, counting the number of children registered each year neither reflects the majority of child protection reports, nor tells us how many children have been harmed or injured or sheds any light on outcomes for the children involved. It simply tells us how many children reached the administrative criteria required for registration (Creighton and Noyes, 1989). There are indications that outcomes in child protection might be very difficult to measure. It is not the kind of work where inputs can be standardised, nor where the process is uniform. This chapter begins with the citation from Garfinkel who recognised that decision-making about people, whether professional or day to day, is a developing, reflexive and achieved matter. It is not, and never can be, routinised or entirely standardised except to say that it is reflexive and it is achieved. However, social workers are competent members of a particular culture and they operate in the context of certain cultural methods or 'rules'. They know, for example, how to hold a conversation, and they have certain expectations about others – parents, children, families, teachers, doctors and so forth. This is not to say that they share the same expectations, but to state that they cannot operate without some sort of anticipation of how things should be at any given time, in any given situation. These 'rules' or 'methods' turn out to be quite significant when we start to look at inputs and outcomes of the child protection process.

As we noted in Chapter 1, there has been a growing concern over the increasing numbers of children referred to child protection agencies and the parallel increase in unfounded reports. Noting how many reports are founded or unfounded represents one outcome measure of early intervention. Besharov (1988) suggests that cases are over-reported and that around 65 per cent are unfounded. Whilst the number of reports have steadily increased since the mid 1970s, the substantiation rate has fallen. Besharov maintains that this presents a threat to children, and child protection work, with scarce resources being directed wrongly. In addition, he cites the under-reporting of serious cases (despite mandatory reporting in the US) as a reflection of a growing lack of confidence in child protection professionals. Besharov's claims have come under criticism (see, for example, Finkelhor, 1990), largely because his argument has been interpreted to suggest that child abuse is less of a problem than other studies propose. However, these studies do not appear to have examined the decision-making process so that there has hitherto been no data to show what a 'substantiated'/'unsubstantiated' or 'founded'/'unfounded' child 'abuse' report might actually represent. Outcomes in child protection, however they are measured, are the product of information, decisions and actions. To understand founded or unfounded reports, cases registered or not registered, children placed in substitute care, judged to be 'at risk' and so forth, it is necessary to understand the decision-making process.

A small part of Garfinkel's work on practical reasoning was a study of jurors' decision-making practices. One of the key findings from that study was that jurors depended for the most part on the 'rules of daily life' for making decisions. A second and important proposition resulting from the study in relation to the present chapter was the possibility that jurors define decisions retrospectively. This implies that the 'outcome comes before the decision' (Garfinkel, 1992), and that the reasons or justification for the decision can then be found if called for. The task for jurors was to decide what 'actually happened'. We similarly wish to argue that child protection investigation is concerned with what 'actually happened', as a first response to information presented, but that decisions about what actually happened are rarely reached and that most cases are never resolved one way or the other. Furthermore, social workers, like jurors, are able to justify their actions retrospectively and do so daily in the records of their work.

Deciding on an Outcome Measure

During 1987 two separate studies collected data on all child protection referrals relating to child sexual abuse made in defined areas to child protection services (NSPCC, Social Services, Department of Community Services) in the UK (Wattam, 1991) and Australia (Thorpe, 1991). Both pieces of research utilised documentary evidence and coded file records from a 100 per cent sample to examine the processes and outcomes of intervention in cases of alleged sexual abuse.

The secondary analysis of this data has enabled us to clarify the process of substantiation. The Australian files appeared to be more specific in stating that there was no foundation to the allegation in 29 per cent of cases, compared to 4 per cent in the UK. There was no formally accountable place in the files to define whether a case was substantiated or not in either site at the time the data was collected. A typical example of a case, illustrating the way in which a 'not substantiated' outcome was recorded, follows.

Case A (male aged 12)

A mother was concerned about the sexual behaviour of her son and reported this to her doctor. The doctor reported her concerns to the Community Services.

> Dr C was uncertain as to what could be offered or even the 'real' nature of the problem but provided the following sketchy details.
> There appear to be a number of children involved [approx. 12–15] but S remains the central figure. Over the weekend a number of children congregated and are believed to have consumed alcohol and perhaps been involved in 'sniffing' some substances.

It is alleged that there are 3 girls aged 4–5 in the group with whom S has interfered. Exact details are not known. It is also believed that the girls have an advanced knowledge of sexuality and were sexually 'exploring' [e.g. kissing each other's nipples]. At some point during the night S is alleged to have dropped his trousers, got on all fours and allowed a dog to attempt to penetrate him. It is believed only thrusting was 'achieved'.

The Doctor contacted us after referral via Child Psych Services & Police Child Abuse Unit.

Both [the mother] and [name] of [address/phone] have enquired as to what they can offer the group of children. Dr C [phone] also has notes written by 3 boys who were present. Their notes available from his surgery.

I have agreed that we will contact both mothers in an attempt to ascertain full details and try to plan some action.

[next entry]
A referral regarding the a/n child was made by Dr C on [date]. The mother of S had approached him with concerns regarding S's sexual behaviour. It was alleged that he had been 'screwed' by a dog and, in the past, sexually interfered with his sister, M [3] and another girl, [name] [5].

K and I visited on [date]. We spoke with all children who were present at the time when the alleged 'dog' incident occurred and found that the reports provided by the boys were inconsistent and could not substantiate that the incident had actually occurred.

In relation to the allegation of sexual interference of the two young girls, it is reported that this event occurred about 3 months previous. According to A it only happened once. However, at the time A, M and S were all at home with [the mother] who is adamant that S was never alone with the girls. There are no behavioural indicators in the girls to suggest any on-going sexual abuse and I would suggest that if anything did happen, then it would have been inappropriate sexual play.

After discussion with K we are of the belief that no sexual abuse occurred. We have suggested to the mothers, however, that should they notice any changes in behaviour in the girls that causes concern they should contact either ourselves or Dr C. This information was relayed back to Dr C. Recommend NFA at present, unless further contact made.

In this and many other cases the information is third hand. The doctor who initially refers and the mother have both given versions of the event causing concern. The referred version is described as 'sketchy'. We found that a typical technique in processing the reported version was for the investigators to make the information more concise. In doing so they establish a further version containing matters of relevance to them and in this way open it up to substantiation or not.

It was alleged that he had been 'screwed' by a dog and, in the past, sexually interfered with his sister, M [3] and another girl, [name] [5].

Having reached this version they speak with the children to check it out. There were potential witnesses and these witnesses could not confirm the allegation. The sexualised behaviour was not found and alternative explanations ('inappropriate sexual play') were preferred following investigation. The investigators record that they 'could not substantiate' that the incident had occurred, and that they were 'of the belief that no sexual abuse occurred'. This is about as definite as a 'non-substantiated' or 'unfounded' finding gets in most cases. It is not stated how this conclusion was drawn, other than that reports are inconsistent, and again this is characteristic of such cases. The way in which one version is selected over another as the valid version is rarely made explicit. From observations of child protection work, it would appear that such decisions are contingent on situated moral reasoning at the time of the investigation. Decisions are achieved in and through the settings, identities of persons and situation specific factors, not all of which are accountable (Wattam, 1989).

A second group of cases were those where no conclusion about substantiation was reached but which received no further action. In general this was because informal arrangements were arrived at which made the alleged

incident of no further relevance. The matter of proof or disproof in such cases was suspended, such as where a child
told a friend that her father was 'doing things to her' but
would not give further information to investigators and an
informal out-of-home arrangement was arrived at. A third
category included children who were allegedly harmed on
access visits. This category of custody and access dispute
as a context for referral is interesting. It would appear,
from our secondary analysis at least, that cases involving
custody or access disputes often achieved informal solutions by variation of access arrangement, such as where
sexual behaviour was alleged on access visits and access
visits were stopped. Finally, a fourth category were those
where the allegation was thought to be founded but considered to be a police matter, because the family did not
require further support.

Thus, one point we make is that cases which get filtered
out after an initial visit could be substantiated or unsubstantiated. Often they are neither, since it is almost
impossible to state categorically that something has or has
not happened in any individual case. It is, therefore, not
possible to make claims about the nature and extent of
'abuse' or under- and over-reporting on the basis of cases
which receive no further action. A conclusive outcome of
'unfounded' or 'not substantiated' was rare in file records.
Furthermore, it was clear from the subject matter that such
a conclusion would be practically impossible. Indeed, in
this and other areas of life, one of the ways our culture has
developed in deciding whether or not something has
happened is through the courts, just because events are
always open to a degree of interpretation. The task for
social workers is to reach a conclusion for their own practical purposes. What became clear from the files is that they
do not do this by finding a case substantiated or otherwise.

Further and No Further Action Cases

The only predictable outcome from the files was whether
cases received further intervention or not. There was
nothing accountable about outcomes from the child
or family's point of view, or, as we stated earlier, about
whether an allegation was founded. Consequently, for the

Table 8.1   Outcome: further and no further action

	UK	Australia
Further action	41%	46%
No further action	59%	54%

purposes of secondary analysis, cases from both the UK and Australian samples were identified in relation to only two 'career' types: 'further action' and 'no further action'. Despite the finding that the Australian files seemed more frequently to note if a case was not substantiated, there were similarities in terms of 'further' or 'no further action'. The figures for both outcomes can be found in Table 8.1.

It can be seen in both countries that cases filtered out in the early stages of the investigation and which received no further action are in the majority. Given this similarity in outcome from two different countries, we were particularly interested to see how each of these different outcomes was achieved, and what factors were significant in determining the career paths for each group.

Having coded cases according to whether they received further action or not, we then examined the files to see which factors were influential in achieving either outcome. The factors identified as criteria in the decision-making process relating to whether a case received further or no further action were those which social workers recorded in the files. This is a deceptively simple statement. Coding what social workers routinely recorded as relevant to the child protection task in cases of alleged sexual assault tells us something about the inputs (the way that information is initially sorted for agency requirements), processes (the way that information is then acted on), and outcomes (what is achieved by inputs and processes).

Age, Gender and Family Structure

Details about age, gender and family structure were recorded in almost all cases in both samples. It is therefore fair to assume that these characteristics are in some way very relevant to decision-making in cases of alleged sexual harm or injury. In terms of the overall sample, half the children were aged under ten and half over. In relation to the two career types, we found that older children are more likely to receive further action and younger children no action at all. Age turned out to be an important signifier in determining whether the actions and events alleged in referrals were appropriate, and thus an important criteria affecting outcome. For example, a 13-year-old showering with her stepfather was thought worthy of reporting and resolved as not age-appropriate, whereas a three-year-old being stripped off by a neighbour was considered as acceptable age-appropriate behaviour.

We suggested in Chapter 4 that what became important, in a methodological sense, was the way in which abuse was proposed, reasoned about and talked about. Furthermore we noted that the word 'abuse' was rarely used, except by reporters to agencies. What we found were various claims about grounds for concern, and then these claims being assessed against certain criteria, including age. For example, in a case concerning a girl aged 17 the allegation was one of 'sexual interference'. The mother gave a version of events to support her claim:

-   [The father] and Laura would shower together.
-   [The brother] has seen [the father] and Laura in bed together, lying on floor together.
-   When [the mother] goes out [the brother] reported he was locked out of the house and [the father] and Laura inside together.
-   Laura is very frightened of her father and that is why she went to [town] with him.
-   [The father] is possessive of Laura won't allow her to go out, have boyfriends.
-   [The father] overly affectionate with Laura, constantly touching her.
-   [The mother] suggested medical check for Laura but she refused.
-   [The father] on sickness benefits, Laura unemployed.
-   [The mother] travelling to Perth next week.

Laura's brother and a friend were interviewed and their versions of events reinforced the allegations. However, the file contained a closing note from the social worker:

> lack of file notes but discussed with [team] – not sub-
> stantiated, most of the info. given was incorrect – basi-
> cally family conflict leading to allegation.

No 'sexual' activity is mentioned; rather the interpretation rests on the expectations of relationship behaviour between a father and a daughter who is, significantly, aged 17. The referral makes no sense unless expectable father/17-year-old daughter behaviour becomes (an unstated but ever present) part of the information. Age is therefore one criterion by which the appropriateness of behaviour is assessed.

The profile of the children in terms of gender gave a ratio of 4:1 girls to boys. This ratio remained the same in both 'further' and 'no further action' cases. An analysis of family structure showed that 35 per cent of the UK children and 26 per cent of the Australian children were living in their biological family, with 21 per cent and 36 per cent living in reconstituted families, respectively. The Australian sample had a higher rate of children in single-parent families (38 per cent) than the UK (28 per cent). Contrary to expectation, given the literature surrounding risk and the association with single parents and reconstituted families, there were more children living in their biological family in the 'further action' cases (38 per cent compared to 22 per cent in 'no further action' cases). This finding should be reviewed in the context of two further factors found to be of significance. First, where the person believed responsible (PBR) was resident in the home, cases were more likely to receive further action. Second, if the maternal response to a child living at home was observed as unsatisfactory, children were much more likely to come into care. The implications of maternal response are discussed in more detail below.

Alleged Harms, Injuries and Actions

Whilst the alleged harms and injuries were very similar in the UK and Australia, the proportions varied slightly both between countries and between career types (see Tables 8.2 and 8.3).

Children in Australia were more likely to be reported in the files as suffering from some form of emotional trauma and less likely to have no identifiable harm or injury. In addition, in Australia the alleged action was twice as likely to be couched in general terms as 'sex' than in the UK. UK referees depended more on actions to validate their report and more frequently identified alleged penetration as a reason for referral. The 'other/none' category included 4 per cent of Schedule 1 offender[1] cases for the UK sample, reinforcing the position that the presence of a previous offender was sufficient to justify concern, whatever the effect on the child.

Alleged penetration featured in 15 per cent of 'further action' cases, although even this most serious end of the sexual assault spectrum did not warrant further action in 10 per cent of cases. Of course some of these may have been unsubstantiated but, as we have already stated, it is hard to obtain proof beyond all reasonable doubt that a child has been harmed or injured at the hands of an adult.

Table 8.2   Alleged harms and injuries

Harm	UK %	Australia %	Further action %	No further action %
Emotional	24	35	21	9
Anal/vaginal trauma	8	8	3	5
STD/infection	1	6	1	3
No identifiable harm	64	46	19	35
Other	3	5	1	3

Table 8.3   Alleged actions

Action	UK %	Australia %	Further action %	No further action %
Penetration	28	22	15	10
Oral/masturbation	10	11	9	2
Touching	23	28	10	15
Non-contact	4	1	0	2
'Sex'	12	26	3	16
Other/none	23	12	8	10

Different types of harms and injuries have different symptoms but the majority of these are ambiguous and could have a number of different aetiologies. Procedurally, the task for investigators is to balance the harms, injuries, signs, symptoms, context and nature of the allegation in order to reach some conclusion about whether a child has been so harmed, and crucially whether he or she is still at risk. Assessment in sexual harm or injury is complicated by the fact that there are rarely physical symptoms (Royal College of Physicians, 1991).

In the combined sample, detailed examination of cases which received further action where the allegation concerned penetration (digital or penal), masturbation or oral sexual activity revealed that medical or physical evidence was present for only 12 per cent of the children. This suggests that the alleged harm, injury or action combined with physical evidence of it are not the criteria used to decide whether a case requires further action or not. Thus it is possible to have a case with an allegation of penetration accompanied by physical evidence which statistically would show up as a 'no further action' case, or in some samples as 'unfounded' or 'unsubstantiated'. Similarly, it is possible to have an allegation which did not concern an identifiable act and where there was no physical evidence which would show up as a 'further action' case. This is generally not because nothing or something has happened, but because other factors become significant in determining whether a case warrants further action.

'Disclosures' and Admissions

The research we report on here bears out that, in large part, any assessment as to whether a child has been sexually assaulted, or may be in the future, has to be conducted on the basis of what children, their carers and referees say or do, and the response of the alleged perpetrator. This means that the process for assessment is dependent on making sense of and making judgements about verbal accounts. This is not peculiar to sexual harm, but is predominantly a characteristic of it. Essentially the source of information for an assessment becomes versions of events and situated actions. Such an enterprise is rarely acknowledged as a task of child protection. Child protection workers, like jurors, are implicitly expected to rely on '95 per cent' common sense (Garfinkel, 1992) in order to reach their conclusions. This is not a criticism, but a recognition that this feature of child protection work opens up the question of how investigators can do otherwise and, further, that to suggest that it is possible to rationalise the process of screening through such tools as 'risk assessment' schedules may be somewhat erroneous, given that a primary skill in assessment lies in everyday practical reasoning, deciding on who is 'telling the truth'.

The majority of referrals tend to be comprised of a number of claims, some of which are more specific than others. The claims can be broken down into five types: claims of intimate behaviour between an adult and child or two children, claims of 'sex' or 'interference', specific claims about sexual acts, claims of physical symptoms, and claims of other behaviour. Some of these overlap so that two or more claims can be made about any one subject child. Examples of the first would include showering together, lying in bed/on the floor together or being 'overly affectionate'. The second type, claims of 'sex' or 'interference', tend to remain just that, with neither category being further explained. Specific claims would be detailed accounts, generally offered by the children themselves which describe sexual acts they have been involved in. The physical symptoms are usually such things as sexually transmitted diseases and infections, warts, discharges and pregnancy. The final type of claim concerns behaviour such as being withdrawn or quiet, withholding information, acting suspiciously, not sleeping, not eating and so forth. Ultimately all allegations are comprised of claims that something might be wrong, statements that intrinsically warrant the concern of the agency. Yet, as we have noted, the majority of these claims will result in no further action. Are the claims wrong, or is something else happening to filter the bulk of cases out?

In cases that resulted in no further action certain patterns emerged about the nature of claims and the supporting evidence. In 77 per cent of cases where there was a non-specific allegation there was no further action. 'Non-specific allegation' is a term used to describe referrals where no detail was given and the report amounted to vague accusations, if accusations were made at all. In some cases they constituted observations of behaviour which under certain circumstances might be thought to be indicative of abuse, but no definite accusation was made. By contrast, in the majority of 'further action' cases the allegation was specific (83 per cent). When this finding is put together with observations of how social workers go about their work, it produces important implications. On the whole, in the records social workers spend a lot of time documenting and inquiring into claims. If the claims are not specific this makes them very difficult to validate or not.

The child's account was coded as it was reported in the files as one of five types. Following Sorenson and Snow (1991) it was possible to identify the disclosure of an alleged sexual experience as 'tentative' (for example, 'it happened a long time ago', 'I dreamt it', 'it happened to a friend'), 'active' (for example, 'my father licked me there') or 'responsive' (an account given after probing).[2] In addition children sometimes denied the allegation or gave no account. Accounts of the response of the alleged perpetrator to the allegation were not always recorded on file. Where there was no report this was generally because no perpetrator had been identified, it was not possible to obtain an account (for example, the whereabouts of the alleged perpetrator were unknown) or some other factor negated an interview (for example, the child denied the allegation). Where the alleged perpetrator was interviewed their response was coded as either an 'admission' or a 'denial' of the allegation. The results of this coding are given in Table 8.4.

Table 8.4 shows clearly that 'further action' cases were much more likely to have an account from the child confirming the allegation and an admission from the alleged perpetrator that the allegation was correct. However, in 21 per cent of 'further action' cases there was no account from the child, and in almost two thirds no admission from the PBR. Furthermore, in 34 per cent of 'no further action' cases there was an account from the child recorded which confirmed the allegation to some degree, and in 4 per cent of cases there was an admission from the

Table 8.4   The accounts of subject children and alleged
perpetrators

Child's account	NFA%	FA%	PBR's account	NFA%	FA%
Tentative	9	8	Admit	4	40
Active	23	54	Deny	21	22
Responsive	2	17	Not known	49	37
Deny	4	–	N/A	26	1
None	62	21			

PBR. Thus, like medical or physical evidence, the accounts
of the people involved do not act as criteria in all cases to
warrant further or no further action, although in the majority of 'further action' cases an account from either the child
or the PBR was relevant to the decision.

Maternal Response as a Variable in Outcome

Maternal response was routinely found in the files, as frequently as age, gender, address and other more formal categories. We did not ask social workers to record it; rather the
information was recorded because of its relevance to the
task at hand. We coded the mothers' responses according
to whether they were described as supporting the child,
supporting the PBR, not satisfactory or where descriptions
were not applicable, such as where the mother was absent
or did not know of the allegation. Table 8.5 depicts the way
in which maternal response featured in outcome.

Cases with a positive and acceptable maternal response
were more likely to filter out, but 58 per cent of 'further
action' cases also recorded a maternal response which supported the child. However, the significance of a negative
maternal response comes in relation to outcome in the
'further action' cases. This revealed the nature of the
importance of maternal response as a filtering device.
Cases where the response was negative or unsatisfactory
were much more likely to warrant further action.

Beginning with 171 reports it is possible to identify the
crucial variables in outcome by envisaging each factor as a

Table 8.5   Maternal response and outcome

Maternal response	Further action	No further action
Support child	58%	71%
Support PBR	11%	2%
Not satisfactory	23%	2%
N/A or N/K	8%	25%

filter which determines whether or not cases proceed further. 21 cases had physical, medical or witness evidence and 150 did not. Concentrating in the first instance on those that did not, 89 resulted in no further action and 61 in further action. 50 of the 61 'further action' cases had a clear disclosure. Of the remaining 11 cases five had an admission by the PBR. This left six cases which had no disclosure, no admission and no supporting evidence which continued to warrant further action. Two of these cases concerned the presence of a Schedule 1 offender[3] in the home. The final variable which accounted for the four remaining open cases was that the maternal response was considered unsupportive. Conversely, taking those cases with no physical evidence which resulted in no further action (89) 59 had no disclosure and no admission from the PBR, and all but two had a positive maternal response. Of these, one was a case transferred to another area, and in the other the child left home voluntarily to live with friends. Maternal response as classified by the social worker was the most influential single factor in determining whether children came into care. This was not simply a matter of supporting the alleged perpetrator, or of having conflicting feelings of loyalty. In such cases (6 per cent of the total sample) the children were still maintained at home in 'further' and 'no further action' cases. Rather it was where the mother's response was deemed unsatisfactory that children ended up in substitute care. This finding also held for the 21 cases with medical or physical evidence. Eight of these cases received no further action and in each case a satisfactory supportive maternal response was recorded. Of the 13 cases where further action was taken, eight children remained in the home, again with a positive maternal response.

The five children who ended up in substitute care were those where the maternal response was described as unsatisfactory.

The following extracts are taken from files concerning these children. They were not placed in care as a result of the trauma experienced from the alleged and well supported sexual abuse. Rather, they were there because the assessment of the mother was such that it warranted their removal from home. This was generally couched in terms of the inability of the mother to 'protect' for different reasons in each case. In one case the mother was described as having

> limited insight into the situation and could not be relied upon to protect the children if on her own.

The children were returned to the mother's care some weeks later after the grandparents intervened. The following was recorded:

> [The mother] has considerable supports from her family, neighbours and Church. These supports are essential to her as she has an immature and dependent personality and will find the burdens of lone parenthood hard to bear. Continued Departmental involvement will also be required to ensure the protection of the children, to support [the mother] in caring for the children and to address the treatment issues for all family members.

Thus, the justification given for the mother's inability to protect her daughter was that of 'limited insight' and later her 'immature and dependent personality' are mentioned in association with her need for support. Characteristically, these assessments are not elaborated on, they stand alone and do not require justification. A further example is where a mother is described as an 'alcoholic'. Nowhere in the file is there an account of how this categorisation was arrived at, nor is there any description of behaviour that might conventionally be associated with alcoholism. This is not to suggest that these categorisations are wrong or right, but to note two points: first, the reasons given for outcomes in the most serious cases are moral categorisations of the mother; second, when mothers are articulated in the files in this way further explanation appears uncalled for. Concerns about a mother's ability to 'cope' are expressed as justification in and of themselves, without the need for the behaviour or circumstances by which this judgement is reached to be described. Where the mother may be unable to care because of her practical circumstances, these are outlined. In one case, that of an Aboriginal child aged 12, the mother agreed to place her child in care under the following circumstances:

> [The mother's] circumstances are far from ideal. She has in her care twins 8 weeks old, and three other children, 10, 8 and 5 years. She is sharing a house at [place] with one other adult and 2 children. In total there are 9 people in the one house. V is presently in [care place]. [The mother] at the conference shared our concerns about what happened to V and has stated she cannot guarantee her safety given the demands the twins place upon her. She has therefore requested her placement with an alternative caregiver until she is able to adequately provide care and supervision.

Relationship problems between the subject child and mother may also warrant removal. For example, one child from the begins care group stated:

> I ran away from home last Tuesday because I was unhappy at home. I don't get along with Mum and even when I haven't done anything wrong she hits me with the jug cord and punches me. When I ran away I went to my sister T's place.

The child remained in care, even after her sister was returned, because of

> on-going conflict between her and [the mother]. Placement was requested by [the mother] and child.

Finally, a further example of an unsatisfactory response was where a mother had not taken any action. The record notes that

During this interview [the mother] was also advised that M had disclosed sexual abuse by her father over a 3 year period. [The mother] did not show any emotion at this disclosure and said M had told her in December (last year). [The mother] went to India for 1 month in November and left M with her father. When she returned M told her dad had touched her and she spoke to her husband but it did not stop.

This mother had not reported her husband's actions and clearly viewed it as a private concern which did not warrant involvement of the state agencies. When these agencies finally did become involved at the request of the child, their assessment was that this mother had not acted in a way which adequately represented protective action.

Three main conclusions can be drawn from these findings. First, the children who receive further action in the shape of substitute care are not necessarily the most damaged, nor 'abused'. Rather they are most likely to be living in situations that are considered unsatisfactory on the basis of parental, and generally maternal, behaviour. Second, reasons for such assessments of maternal behaviour are rarely given except in broad terms such as 'drinking heavily', 'alcoholic', 'unable to cope' and so forth. These assessments are generally not made with any recourse other than the social worker's observations. Finally, to return to Cassirer's Law, there is no acknowledgement in the files as to how social workers perceive their own actions as being 'first order determinants of the sense that situations have'. Thus, and for example, there is no reflection on how a judgement of 'alcoholic mother' might give meaning to an assessment of 'a child who needs care' or even how the two may be related. This suggests that the link is taken for granted, a situation which holds for all the other moral categorisations found in the files without further information on how such categories are selected. Nor is there any recognition of the effect of this categorisation. Once judged as behaving in an unsatisfactory way, there are no accounts of attempting to address the behaviour, except much later when consideration is giving to a child returning home from substitute care. Mothers, unlike alleged perpetrators, are assessed and judged outside any legal process with very little recourse for revoking the judgement once made. Their previous behaviour and response to the current allegation act as evidence of their 'ability to protect'.

Recent research on parental perspectives shows that when subject to social work intervention parents may feel threatened and their response should be interpreted with this in mind. In addition, their perspective of the situation may be entirely different to that of a social worker used to dealing with such cases on a regular basis, and it can change over time (Cleaver and Freeman, 1995). However, attention to the parental perspective is rarely found in file records. Rather it is the social worker's perspective of the parent that is generally accountable.

Discussion

The number of cases proved 'beyond all reasonable doubt' in a court setting were in the minority,[4] and no cases were subject to a test of disproof by the same standards. The majority of cases came somewhere in between. There was no official place on the file, or in the work, where outcome categorisations such as 'substantiated', 'unsubstantiated', 'founded' or 'unfounded' were used. The words are part of professional vocabulary, and appear in case recordings, case conference minutes and, less frequently, in talk about cases. In such talk outcomes are more likely to be phrased as 'I think something's definitely happened', or 'We'll never know', or 'There's not enough evidence'. In many cases substantiation appears suspended, and remains a question of whether anything happened or not. For example, 'Nothing substantial was said – suggest case be closed'. Cases appear to remain open whilst there is any practical means available for resolving whether anything happened or not. This finding would reinforce the obser-vation that intervention is oriented by a 'forensic gaze' (Parton, 1991; Wattam, 1992), that it is not directed by the requirement to help, but to detect evidence.

Often outcomes can be observed in the files because, and only because, they are recorded as part of a conversation with another person. An example of this is in a case where the social worker telephoned the father of a child, who, amongst other things, had been suspected of 'sexually abusing' his daughter. She notes:

> Explained that investigations would go no further but that we still had concerns for the protection of the children.

Another is where a face-to-face conversation is recorded:

> I explained to [the mother] that I was only involved as a result of the incident between [the mother's sister] and her father and the repercussions of that for [the child]. As far as I was concerned the message that I wanted to get across to [the mother] was that only she and [the mother's sister] knew the truth of what had happened between themselves and their father and that the responsibility for protecting their children was theirs alone. [The mother] denied that there had been any truth in the allegations made by her sister and felt that her parents had suffered greatly as a result of the investigations. She said that she felt very sorry for people who found themselves in this predicament when it was all untrue. I reminded [the mother] that [the mother's sister] had set the process in motion by disclosing certain facts and that we always start off the investigation by believing the child. [The mother] said that in some respects she felt that this was right but that it was not right for her and [her sister]. She told me [her sister's] case was going back to court next week and that the care order would be removed. I said that a case conference was to be held and that the question of revocation of the care order would be considered at the case conference. [The mother] asked if the Social Services Department still believed [the mother's sister] in spite of the fact that she had subsequently withdrawn her statement. I said that I couldn't answer for the Social Services Department but I felt an element of doubt would always be around and it was because of that that I had to emphasise the need for vigilance.

Social workers rarely committed themselves to a definite statement at case closure, such as 'this case was substantiated'. It is as though, as in the above, they record their conclusions and reasoning for entitled file readers to see, which then stands as information which the reader can make up their own mind about. In terms of 'filtering' it would appear that drop-out points are arrived at once one of the following outcomes is established:

- something has happened and the child does not need further service – i.e. therapeutic help or substitute care (or that service is not available) – and a context has been developed in which it is unlikely to happen again;
- something might have happened and a context has been developed in which it is unlikely to happen again;
- a conclusion has been reached that there is no possibility of resolving whether something has happened or not (the 'we shall never know' case);
- in a very few cases, it can be stated with some certainty that nothing has happened at all;
- in all cases that filter out, where the presence of the mother is of relevance to the child, the mother must be categorised in a way which shows she has acted appropriately – i.e. in a way which is acceptable to the investigators.

The extract detailing the social worker's conversation with the mother above is worthy of further attention, for it can render more information about outcomes. There is always more to a case than the record provides for. This extract is recipient-designed in two ways. First, it constitutes a report of recipient-designed talk, the 'recipient' being the mother of the child. Second, it is written to be read by an entitled other, that is another social worker, a supervisor or any other person who is entitled to have access to the files. This version of the outcome is how it was put to the mother. No other outcome is recorded, but other information is offered on the file, in the same way that this is offered, not as a conclusion to the case, but as information available to any entitled party as to how the case might be judged in terms of outcome.

This method of expressing 'outcome' was also characteristic of the Australian files. Frequently, the question of doubt was left unresolved and the primary method of resolving it was to place responsibility on the 'safe parent'. For example:

> Further to our conversation of today, I am writing to confirm that following a report of inappropriate touching of children by your son [name] professional advice from child protection officer is that you are hereby informed that at no time is [your son] to be left alone with any ... children, and that he is not to be left to 'look after' these children should you need to leave your home for any reason whatsoever. You will appreciate the severity of the allegation and as such you are directed to take all care that the above request is met. This circumstance may be further considered/reassessed and you will be advised accordingly.

The identity produced by the use of descriptions of the mother's character and behaviour is of some relevance to deciphering how outcomes are arrived at. It would seem that investigation, and its outcome, further action or not, depends in the most part on the assignment of identities, particularly the identity of the mother. This emphasis on the mother, as in the two cases above, transfers the problem of substantiation onto her, and brings with it a set of expectations which may not be shared, but are expectably shared by the investigators.

A study of mothers involved in child sexual abuse investigations reveals their side of this story (Hooper, 1992). From this research Hooper reaches the view that the child protection discourse is concerned primarily with maternal responsibility.

> The responsibility accorded mothers in this discourse raises more complex issues, at least if the need for a social control role on behalf of children is accepted. Locating accountability for the abuse solely with the abuser does not resolve all issues of responsibility for child protection, which may still be contested between mothers and social workers. The problem in this context is how much responsibility women are accorded for child protection, and further whether workers attempt to

empower them to fulfil their responsibilities or simply blame them for failure. (p. 162)

As we noted earlier, mothers were, by and large, described as acting appropriately or in a supportive way. We have also shown that there were significant differences in outcomes for children whose mothers were reported as not supporting or acting satisfactorily as a protector. In 6 per cent of 'no further action' cases and 8 per cent of home-based service cases the mother was given a negative description. For those children who came into substitute care the figure was 84 per cent. The descriptions of mothers were found to be of a certain type, defining their capacity to 'protect'. There is very little attention paid to the needs or dilemmas of mothers caught up in allegations of sexual assault. For example, the mothers in the example above might be anticipated to have a number of questions as a result of the directions they have been 'officially' given. What happens when the grandparents want to babysit, or, what happens when my son wants to have children? These, however, are not acknowledged.

In Hooper's study, of ten women receiving social work support, four felt positive, emphasising the support given, four had negative feelings, emphasising what they perceived as control functions, and two had mixed feelings. Some women felt treated as children and considered the rules to be arbitrary. 'Where agencies simply take on the role of another authority setting rules for them, rather than attempting to help them gain control of their own lives, they may not only reinforce the women's "entrapment", but become the focus themselves of similar types of resistance strategy' (p. 148). Control was not just viewed in terms of instruction but was also 'implicit in the norms on which therapeutic intervention is based'. For example, 'CL had been referred for joint therapy with her husband on the basis that if they could resolve their sexual relationship it might stop him abusing again. ... She described the experience as "going through hell" and stopped it immediately the child was received into care on other grounds' (p. 149). Other elements of the monitoring function were similar to those noted by Brown (1986). These included a failure to treat mothers as equals, to recognise their strengths and to inform them fully.

Conclusions

Having stated initially that the child protection task appears to be about finding out what 'really happened' to any referred child, we are now able to qualify this. Finding out what has 'really happened' provides the orientation for the response to a report. However, this is rarely possible. Instead, there is a process underpinning the response which acknowledges that it is almost impossible to prove 'child abuse'. It is this feature of the work which places the assessment of risk at the heart of the child protection discourse. Methods for resolving the practical concern of agency accountability include the use of the 'safe parent', usually the mother, not as the arbiter of whether something has really happened or not, but whether the case warrants further intervention. These methods legitimate the filtering out of cases at various 'drop-out' points. Cases with medical, physical or witness evidence are in the minority (12 per cent), yet even these do not always warrant further action. If there is no disclosure from the child, no admission from the alleged perpetrator and a mother who is assessed as supportive then the case will almost certainly not proceed further. Cases without supporting evidence from the child (i.e. disclosures) are likely to be filtered out early on if the mother's response is supportive. If the mother's response is not considered satisfactory, however, the child is much more likely to receive further action, and to end up in substitute care.

Cases which receive no further action are not necessarily founded or unfounded. Rather they are cases where there is insufficient supporting evidence (physical and verbal) and an appropriate parental response. More importantly, in the majority of cases it is the mother who is judged, even where the PBR is not the mother's partner. Images of mothering are found repeatedly in the files, and where these images are breached children receive surveillance. We did not find the same images of fathering, but mothers were reported on ubiquitously, which implies that their behaviour is always relevant unless they are absent. In terms of identities, for women who are parents of referred children their identity formulation is almost entirely maternal. Key features of that maternal identity are that they did not know about the alleged abuse, and that when they were informed they responded in a way which was wholly maternal. That is, they made themselves always available (to the child, and others in relation to the child such as the investigators, the courts, education and health professionals), their actions could always be interpreted as supportive of the child, providing for and nurturing the child, and their insight or knowledge was articulated to show that they knew they must do this. These are, quite clearly, moral statements about maternal identity – what mothers should and should not be doing. A second feature of maternal identity is that it appears to be irrevocable in that once it is achieved, either positively or negatively, the identity holds. The same does not apply to fathers, who are rarely mentioned in the files, unless they are accused in some way.

The construction of maternal identity is integral to risk assessment. A negative maternal identity constitutes a risk factor in the child protection discourse, and as such reinforces a moral order which upholds a particular categorisation of positive maternal behaviour – one which includes the features described in the files: availability (solely by and for the child(ren)), nurturing and insight.

9
The Future(s) for Child Protection

The central purpose of this book has been to make a contribution to understanding the contemporary nature of child protection work. In part it builds on our earlier studies (Parton, 1991; Thorpe, 1994; Wattam, 1992) and draws on conceptual and empirical work we have been developing for some years. In addition, however, it has aimed to engage with a variety of debates that are currently taking place in the UK, Australia and North America about the future direction of policy and practice in child protection.

In the UK, following the publication of a number of Department of Health funded research studies in 1995 and the launch of the research overview (Dartington Social Research Unit, 1995), ministers and senior civil servants have argued that there needs to be a rebalancing of child protection work so that there is a greater concentration on children in need, that investigations should be carried out 'with a lighter touch', and that fewer children and families should be dragged into the child protection net. (See Parton 1996b for a more detailed critical analysis of the research.) The central philosophy and principles of the Children Act 1989 can be seen as being undermined because the family support aspirations and sections of the Act are being implemented partially and not prioritised (DoH, 1994). Stripped to its essentials it is argued that far too many cases are at present being dealt with under child protection procedures and that these should be dealt with under family support provisions. It is suggested that resources are being wasted by unnecessary investigations – or inquiries – under Section 47 of the Act. The primary policy change should be to prioritise Section 17 and Part 3 of the Act in terms of helping and supporting families with 'children in need' and thereby keeping notions of policing, surveillance and coercive interventions to a minimum.

A report produced by the Audit Commission (1994) argued that the amount of time and resources being used up by investigating and responding to child protection referrals could be controlled and better managed by the use of clearer guidelines and developing tighter risk indicators that trigger a full child protection investigation. Drawing on the research by Jane Gibbons (Gibbons et al., 1995) but reflected in the findings of the other Department of Health funded projects, it noted that about two thirds of referrals investigated are dropped before being considered for registration by a case conference. As we noted in Chapter 1, only about 15 per cent of original referrals ever find their way onto a child protection register, the rest being filtered out earlier usually without receiving any protection or service either. The Audit Commission report recommended that central government should provide guidance to social services on risk management and the criteria for child protection registrations. The report argued that 'the *productivity* gains which should eventually follow from better *focusing* could *free resources* for social workers to specialise in other activities – for example, in family support, work with adolescents or children with disabilities' (p. 23, our emphasis). The key questions we wish to address in this final chapter, in the light of our own research and analysis, are: How far are such strategies likely to succeed? How far are they premised on a proper understanding of child protection work and the issues and tensions it has to address in day-to-day practice? Are such strategies likely to get the genie of child protection back into the child welfare bottle or are the forces underlying these developments of much more fundamental significance? And, finally, has the nature of the problem been appropriately identified?

In Chapter 2 we characterised the contemporary nature of child protection work as the need to identify 'high risk' in a context where notions of working together are set out in increasingly complex yet specific procedural guidelines, and where the work is framed by a narrow emphasis on legalism and the need for forensic evidence. While it is clear that only a very small proportion of children subject to child protection interventions ever experience the types of harms and injuries which typify the cases which have captured the imagination of the media and have been subject to public inquiries, there is little doubt that it is these 'heavy end' cases that have driven policies and procedures and influenced day-to-day practice and decision-making. Again, while it is only a small minority of cases which are subject to statutory interventions and the removal of children, it is the court and the forensic gaze which cast a shadow over all child protection work and increasingly child welfare more generally. If this provides an adequate characterisation of child protection work, what can we learn from our detailed empirical analysis of practice to suggest how it should be reframed? Is it primarily an issue of a rebalancing, recasting the thresholds for state intervention and being more precise about what constitutes child abuse, or are there other issues at stake?

What we have argued is that, since the mid 1960s, the focus of concerns has shifted. Whereas originally the problem to be addressed was 'the battered baby', since the early 1980s the focus has been 'child abuse'. Originally it was thought there were certain *signs* on the child's body – bruises, broken bones and various lesions – which indicated that this might be a battered baby case which medical expertise, originally the X-ray, could help *diagnose*. Recent years have noted a subtle but significant shift. While the metaphor of the battered baby was key in characterising child abuse to the mid 1980s, this is no longer the case. Not only is child abuse no longer understood in essentially medico-social terms, where medical science could identify the underlying disease or syndrome, now rarely are physical or behavioural signs seen as significant. Signs of abuse have been replaced by what we call a regime of signification where notions of 'high risk' now both constitute the metaphor for child abuse and characterise the focus of the work itself.

The second half of the 1980s is the key period in which we can identify these changes taking place and there is no doubt that, in Britain, the Cleveland affair and the subsequent inquiry provided the major watershed. We would suggest that there are three contributing factors as to why this should be the case, which have pervaded the whole area of child protection since, such that they capture the essential tensions and ambiguities that are now embedded in policy and practice in terms of this regime of signification. First, the concerns were with both over- as well as under-intervention such that child protection is focused not only on protecting children from significant harm and injury, but also on protecting the family from unwarrantable state interventions. More than ever practitioners have to walk a fine balance and the costs of getting that wrong could lead to considerable public, political and media opprobrium. Second, the whole area has become contested in ways which were never evident previously. Different perspectives and arguments have developed about the nature and causes of child abuse and to what extent it exists and is harmful. More particularly, not only has traditional medical science and practice been found wanting, but arguments have developed between medical practitioners themselves as to the significance of certain signs and symptoms and whether and how far they are indicative of child abuse. As a consequence, the *signs* of child abuse have lost their traditional significance. While in Cleveland this was primarily concerned with debates about the anal dilatation test and disclosure work, it had the effect of not only undermining medical authority but of questioning both our knowledge about child abuse and, more particularly, what should be done and who should do it.

This connects with the third and perhaps most significant factor. Cleveland was about sexual abuse. The issue of sexual abuse touches a range of sensitivities which were rarely evident in earlier concerns about physical abuse and neglect: it reaches into the most intimate, hidden and private elements of family life and adult–child relations; it represents a major set of debates around patriarchy and male power and thereby opens up a range of political arguments never evident previously; and for the first time the issue threatened not just men but middle-class and professional households in ways which had never happened previously. No longer could child abuse be seen to be associated only with the marginalised and disreputable. It seemed to permeate 'normal' families.

The net result of these various factors was to problematise the issue of child abuse in quite new ways. It was not simply that the tensions and debates were most sharply exemplified in and through concerns about sexual abuse, but that they came to represent the whole area of child abuse and child protection more generally. We are not simply arguing that policy and practice have been driven in any crude or unidimensional sense by concerns about sexual abuse, but that the appearance of sexual abuse has acted to shift fundamentally the focus and priorities of child protection work. Assessing and managing risk becomes central. Thus any attempts to reformulate child protection policy and practice have to take these issues seriously and put them at the top of the agenda. The issues do not simply provide the *contexts* for child protection work, but get to the heart of the nature of the work and the tensions and ambiguities which have to be addressed in day-to-day practice. How can cases of child abuse be differentiated when in many respects the broad signs and symptoms that have come to be associated with it seem to characterise normal families and to typify adult–child relations? It is in this context that the current concerns with risk take on their particular significance.

Messages from the Department of Health Research: What Could Have Been Said

Another impact of Cleveland comes from its influence on research itself, not simply in terms of the priority afforded by central government to research on child abuse and child protection, significant though that was, but the nature of the research questions and methodologies established. Rather than being primarily concerned with researching the nature and form of child abuse, particularly clinical studies, the primary focus was the processes and outcomes of child protection interventions themselves. The launch of the Department of Health funded studies was a direct consequence of the fall-out from Cleveland and the recognised paucity of knowledge in the area of child abuse and the manifest confusion in the reactions of the investigative agencies. The programme of research aimed to explore different aspects of child abuse which would, in combination, help to provide a more comprehensive assessment. The initiative was unusual because its focus was not restricted to the deviant behaviour of children and families. It included studies of the behaviour of normal families, agency processes and decision-making. In most of the studies there was a particular concern with both short- and longer-term outcomes. What is notable is that rather than pursue more traditional positivistic research, there is a recognition that child abuse is socially constructed. The overview document, *Child Protection: Messages from Research* (Dartington Social Research Unit, 1995), quotes Jane Gibbons, who in turn references Parton (1985) by arguing that 'child maltreatment is not the same sort of phenomenon as whooping cough: it cannot be diagnosed with scientific measuring instruments. It is more like pornography, a *socially constructed phenomenon* which reflects values and opinions of particular times' (Gibbons et al., 1995, p. 12, our emphasis).

This is an approach to which, in many respects, we are sympathetic and one which has informed much of our earlier work.

However, the way social constructionism is used and developed in the Department of Health research, particularly the overview document, upon closer inspection is quite inadequate. There is an ambivalence about seriously taking on a social constructionist approach – conceptually, methodologically and practically. For example, the conclusion to the research overview states that 'the message from the 20 studies is that decisions about children in need are, *to some extent*, socially constructed and that the same need *may* require different inputs in different historical eras' (Dartington Social Research Unit, 1995, p. 55, our emphasis). The first thing to note here is that there is an interesting move from the social construction of child abuse or child maltreatment to the social construction of children in need. By the end the research overview is not sure whether its prime concern is child abuse or children in need. In part this is because of its recognition that, when considering harms and injuries and longer-term outcomes for the cases studied, the predominant finding was that child protection cases were better understood, by the researchers, as children in need cases. What is also evident is that the research never takes on a social constructionist perspective wholeheartedly. The central concern is that certain cases, particularly those of 'emotional neglect' are quickly and inappropriately filtered out of the system at an early stage. The research overview wants to reconstruct the system so that these receive services and support. However, it seems that this only becomes feasible if it is recognised at the outset that certain cases are inherently severe and thus self-evidently abusive: for example, *'with the exception of a few severe assaults and some sexual maltreatment ... where the decision is clear cut,* as a society we have to decide which of the several million potentially harmful situations that occur each year require intervention' (Dartington Social Research Unit, 1995, p. 53, our emphasis). It seems to assume that the problems associated with defining what constitutes 'severe assaults and some sexual maltreatment' can be easily resolved or that the phenomena are/will be self-evident. In fact the term 'assault' almost implies this. The net result is that while for the vast majority of the child protection cases studied in the research, child abuse can be conceptualised in social constructionist terms and can therefore be *reconstructed* as children in need, for the severe cases this is not so. The latter are seen as self-evident and not necessarily socially constructed in the same way.

The research studies would have provided a remarkable and methodologically 'rich' opportunity to treat the definition of child abuse as problematic (Wise, 1991) and to examine how its construction, by different professionals, by parents, by children, by policy and guidance, impacted on and related to constructions of responses, effects, consequences and outcomes. Rather than do this, the overview seeks to arrive at a consensus about definition by suggesting that this

> complex situation is clarified by introducing the idea of a continuum of abuse. Several research teams concluded that abuse was better understood if the focus of concern was on behaviour which children ordinarily encountered but which in certain circumstances could be defined as maltreatment. *Once this step has been taken, questions for researchers and practitioners tend to be about chronicity and severity of behaviours, such as how much shouting at children can be said to be harmful.* (p. 14, our emphasis)

The point of the emphasis is that it demonstrates that the overview document rejoins the orthodox community. Having suggested that abuse is constructed, it then goes on to reconstruct it for practical purposes, to arrive at a definition which enables practice and research to get on with their job of deciding how best to intervene in this social problem, or report on good outcomes. At key points this juxtaposition of researchers and practitioners is quite unreflexive. For example, Cleaver and Freeman's (1995) study is reported in the following ways:

> From the first part of the study it emerged that many *allegations* were not *substantiated*…. (p. 59, our emphasis)

> Mothers and fathers were equally likely to come under suspicion as *perpetrators of physical abuse*, but in *cases of neglect* and *emotional abuse*, it was more commonly mothers …. (p. 59, our emphasis)

> … there was much else to suggest that the *child protection system* did succeed in protecting the majority of *children at risk*. (p. 60, our emphasis)

Or consider the following:

> In particular, the withdrawal of *support* from *non-abusing parents* adversely affected their ability to assist in their children's recovery and could delay the return of those children who had been *removed*. (p. 62, our emphasis)

> By the end of the study most of the *sexually abused children* were living with a *non-abusing parent*. (p. 63, our emphasis)

> *Case outcome* was evaluated on three fronts: whether the children had been *protected*, their general *welfare* had been enhanced and the *needs* of parents or carers met. (p. 63, our emphasis)

Such citations are entirely consistent with the whole report. The emphasised words are treated unproblematically; they appear as orthodox descriptive terms. They are, along with the word 'abuse', constantly recurring words in the child protection discourse. But having stated that child abuse (and, we would add, all these other terms too) are socially constructed, they are then utilised as they are utilised within the child protection discourse to make judgements about that discourse's practices, without any reference to their construction. This is wholly unsatisfactory, both from an academic standpoint and from a practical one, since many of the problems facing practitioners, both in the legal and therapeutic arenas, relate to the way these terms have been constructed and are used.

There is also a strong indication that these terms are problematic for individuals who have experienced, or are alleged to have experienced, specific harmful actions. For example, take the term 'substantiated'. This is professional parlance for whether a specific action can be said to have occurred. A substantiated case is not one that is tested to a standard of proof in a legal setting, either civil or criminal (although it may be in a minority of cases). A substantiated case is one where practitioners, usually police and social workers, believe that something has occurred – and it may not be the action reported; it could be something else that is definable as 'abuse' which has occurred. In a practical sense problems derive from the point of view of legal practitioners who must work on specified evidential criteria to 'substantiate' a case, parents who may take the view that a particular harm has not occurred in contrast to the practitioner's judgement, and the child who may not view the action as 'abuse'. What is interesting from a research point of view is how one particular version is preferred above other versions of events, and the ensuing practical consequences of that preference. The fact of something actually occurring is almost always contestable, even when proved by the highest standards in a criminal court. Treating the language as problematic and looking at how certain versions become authorised tells us something not only about the construction of child abuse, but about the wider social and political framework in which it is responded to. Those who have the power to define the terms have the power to shape the discourse. From the document we get no sense of the problematics of substantiation – it is just there to be reported on. The same can be said of 'abuse' (having established that it is on a continuum), 'allegation', 'perpetrator', 'physical abuse', 'sexual abuse', 'emotional abuse', 'neglect', 'support', 'non-abusing parents', 'removed', 'case', 'protected', 'welfare' and 'needs', and a host of other descriptive terms utilised throughout the overview document as they are utilised by those who carry out the work.

Our approach has been somewhat different, for the central question which has been the focus of this book, and which we discussed at some length in Chapter 4, is: how is child protection work *accomplished*? Child abuse for official organisational accounting purposes is not only in the eye of the beholder (a subjective definition), it is an inter-subjective phenomenon whose meaning and import can only be understood in the cultural and organisational contexts in which it is, not simply constructed, but negotiated and constituted.

This is much more than being just concerned with issues of labelling, mis-labelling and operational practices. We have to understand the nature and significance of child abuse in the way it is made sense of by lay people and professionals and acted upon. Our concern is with the way child abuse and child protection have been constituted and how they have developed and changed, in both the macro and micro spheres. A key difference between our approach and that of the Department of Health research is that we move beyond recognising that child abuse is a social construction to analyse the significance of the term and consider what work it does in both contemporary culture and organisational practices. Only then will we be in a position to gauge how far and in what ways policy and practice might change. This is not simply a question of trying to change individual professional attitudes and day-to-day operations. Much wider issues are at stake.

One of our central concerns in this book has been to make social work decisions and judgements about individual cases transparent. What quickly became apparent from our research was that in the vast majority of cases the level and form of intervention is not based on whether the allegation or concern is substantiated or not. Invariably it is impossible to make such a judgement as there are no identifiable harms or injuries. Similarly it is almost impossible to establish what really happened. As a consequence methods for resolving the practical concerns for agency accountability are substituted, and the primary focus is that of making judgements about risk. We demonstrated in Chapter 4 that discussions of *child abuse* were rarely mentioned in the file texts – only by referrers. Essentially we were analysing the way *child protection* work is socially organised. Similarly, children were virtually absent or silent from the files – their voices were only present as they became relevant to the concerns or allegations under investigation. It is here that the recent concerns about sexual abuse are central. The increased willingness to let children speak is not primarily in order to listen to their wishes and views as subjects, but to help resolve the disputes about allegations and to make a judgement about the level and type of risk. In other areas of child protection work the voices of children themselves were rarely drawn upon. It seems that children as subjects with their own views and interests are very marginal to child protection policy and practice.

This position is reflected and reinforced in the Department of Health research. Lorraine Fox Harding (1991) has provided a conceptual framework for analysing child-care policies in terms of four perspectives or ideal types: laissez faire and patriarchy; state paternalism and child protection; the birth family and parental rights; and children's rights and child liberation. If we draw upon these perspectives for analysing the Department of Health research studies we find a significant missing voice.

The operational child protection perspective appears to be a mixture of paternalism/protection (which authorises intervention and directs it where harms and injuries have occurred), laissez faire (where it is established that protective action is not required), and an emerging trend towards a defence of the birth family with an invocation to support and work in partnership with parents. The perspective which is completely absent, in all the studies and in the overview document itself, is that of children's rights. The body, on whom all this attention is directed, including practices directed specifically at protecting it, and research directed at finding out how well it is being protected, is not only mute, it is depicted in very specific ways – as one which is having various 'normal' and 'abusive' things done to it, and one whose normality and abnormality is judged in relation to its parents. Take, for example, the studies on what happens in normal families by Smith and Grocke (1995) in which children were actually interviewed. However, the findings as they are reported in the overview document focus almost exclusively on what had been done to these children, or what they reportedly had done themselves in relation to violent or sexual behaviour. For example, the categories offered in the overview document by which normality should be judged reflect the focus of the research:

A touched mother's breasts
B touched father's genitalia
C drawn genitalia
D been seen masturbating
E seen 'simulated' sexual intercourse on films or TV
F seen pornographic material
G seen horror movies
H bathed with parents

(Dartington Social Research Unit, 1995)

Whilst it is reported that children's hobbies, activities, family and social relationships were explored in interview with the children themselves, nothing of this content is mentioned as relevant. Indeed the distinction between what the children said and what their parents said is not clear from the document. Whilst their voice was sought, even in this limited way, it was clearly not relevant to record in relation to the 'messages from research'. The child's voice is missing in the overview document in the same way that it was missing from our files.

In Chapter 6 we were concerned with pinpointing the risk-identifying criteria evident in the files. It started from the analysis of Case 167 which was referred following allegations but where, following investigation, the case was closed and the social worker was reassured in all areas. This allowed us to identify 12 categories which approximated to a set of norms about family life and child-rearing practices.

These 12 criteria were then analysed in relation to four other quite different cases. We argued that these risk criteria provided insights into the moral reasoning whereby practitioners came to a judgement. Each of the 12 categories had the potential for identifying abnormality in *any* childrearing setting. Child protection practices are not particularly concerned with the condition and experiences of children. The primary concern is with the physical and social circumstances of families, particularly the moral character of parents – essentially the mother. The primary focus of the work is the construction of parental identity – particularly maternal identity. As we discovered on numerous occasions, the attitude and response of the mother is key in judging risk. In effect if the mother's response is not considered satisfactory, the case is much more likely to be subject to further action, ultimately resulting in the removal of the child. Images of mothering were found repeatedly in the files, and where these images were breached, children and families received surveillance. Women are articulated, by and large, only in terms of their maternal identity which was found to include certain expectations – namely their constant availability and their ability to 'protect'.

This finding was also reflected in the Department of Health research carried out by Farmer and Owen (1995) who found that whenever mothers were regarded as responsible for abuse, the children were more likely to be registered. In addition they suggest that 'the difficulties of children and their mothers deepened when assistance was withdrawn' and that 'although physical injuries were inflicted in equal numbers by father figures and lone mothers, social work focused almost exclusively on mothers' (p. 63). However, this focus on mothers is not drawn out in *Messages from Research*. It is not commented on in terms of what it has to say about the perspective of social work intervention, nor is the term 'mother' treated problematically in terms of questioning how it is constructed within the discourse. In observing that the professional discourse reinforces a particular identity for women, the notion of family support becomes questionable. 'Family' is, not unsurprisingly, another term which is treated unproblematically in the overview report. The absence of any mention of maternal focus and identity in the overview indicates that family support may mean even more responsibility to women for what many regard as a male problem. This is not to deny that women could do with some more support in childrearing, but to expose something of the assumptions on which a support framework may be based. There is nothing in *Messages from Research* to suggest that mothers would be anything other than reaffirmed in their position as primary carers, thus perpetuating a particular, some would say patriarchal, perspective. This is reinforced by Farmer and Owen's finding that after 20 months 70 per cent of the children were considered to be protected largely as a result of the 'abuser' being separated from the 'abused child'. Given that in the majority of sexual abuse cases the person believed responsible is male, that those who were prioritised for service were those cases where the PBR was a family member, and that an equal number of male and females are PBRs in physical abuse cases, the carer left with the child is most likely to be the mother. These are important issues if we are seriously attempting to shift the emphasis in child protection work and closely relates to the type of service offered.

Where cases are not closed after investigation the major form of 'intervention' is advice and guidance while the children remain at home. Only a very small proportion of children are ever removed from their families on a short- or longer-term basis. In Chapter 7 we analysed 30 advice and guidance cases in detail. What became apparent was that the services received were not on the child's or the parents', usually mother's, terms. Not only are those on the receiving end unwilling volunteers, but a very restricted menu of help and services was on offer. In many respects the services are not made available ostensibly to meet needs but as a mechanism for risk insurance. The household is thereby opened up to surveillance and monitoring while the agency can be seen to be doing something in a context of partial substantiation or risk, and where case closure or child removal is neither warranted nor provable. This is not to say that individual family members do not get something out of the contact; clearly some do. However, what the cases demonstrated was that a considerable amount of negotiation is built into the process and those on the receiving end, primarily mothers, spend much of their efforts trying to present an appropriate 'face' and manoeuvre out of the clutches of the social workers and the gaze of child protection. Essentially they do not want the advice, guidance and services on offer, or the way it is offered, and do what they can to get out of it. They develop imaginative ways of dealing with their problems and avoiding contact.

We also found that cases entered and left the system not just because something had or had not happened, but also because of the various remedies that children themselves came up with. For example, they left home, refused to cooperate with interviews and so forth. This option was only open to the child when what had happened to them was in dispute, or where they were old enough or articulate enough to take such action. However, it is worth bearing in mind in relation to family support, since nowhere in *Messages from Research* is there any indication that this was inquired into. Instead the recommendation is a focus retained on family support for those cases that are reported and assessed as needing it. Nowhere are the views of those who claim to have experienced 'abuse' solicited in terms of the service they might require, a service which would be taken up and might therefore go some way to helping the individuals not 'netted' by the system.

This provides a fairly salutary picture and certainly suggests that simply shifting towards a child welfare response in terms of Section 17 of the Children Act will not overcome the problems. The choice of services is restricted and a whole range of possibilities are simply not on the menu. More fundamentally, however, the uncertainties and tensions which current policy debates are attempting to address cannot be changed by remedial action aimed at redefining child protection as child welfare, child abuse as children in need or investigations as inquiries. The regime of signification based on the assessment and management of risk invokes a number of categories of the moral order where notions of maternal identity and children's identity are central, together with the responsibilities and accountability of a whole range of health and welfare professionals, particularly social workers. In effect the focus of attention is no longer the physical harms and injuries to children themselves implied by the 'battered baby syndrome', but the policing and surveillance of childrearing practices through the construction of specific maternal and child identities.

This brings us to a major point. There is an assumption in *Messages from Research* that large numbers are 'netted' but then fall out of the net with no service once claims of child abuse have been dealt with or dismissed. This assumption underpins the advocacy of family support – as if those who have been referred have a need for support notwithstanding their child protection status. This is the only real criticism of the child protection system itself: that it is not meeting the needs of those referred to it. Nowhere is there any criticism of a child protection system which is quite clearly inefficient in addressing the needs of those it seeks to service. If a business sets out to corner the market on a particular product, it would be entirely unsatisfactory if the majority of clients approached said that they did not want this product in its current form. The company would do everything it could to reach the right group of people with the right product, and it would dismiss the marketing company who got the wrong group and the wrong product. An analogy with commerce is not always appropriate. Tangible products and commercial markets are not culturally constructed and defined in the same ways as 'abused children', but it makes a point. *Messages from Research* describes briefly three cases where the rights to justice and prosecution were denied and the frustrations that resulted. It is now familiar knowledge within the child protection world that only a minority of cases reach prosecution, and only some of them succeed (Wattam, 1992; Davies et al., 1995). This is just one service that some might want, which clearly does not work. What the DoH research shows is that we have a very ineffective system for those who are legitimately entitled to use it. Rather than question this legitimacy of use and suggest that other issues might be lurking in the background which could more usefully address the problems created by poverty, long-term unemployment, relationship difficulties and even domestic violence, the social worker is remonstrated for being too focused on finding those children who have harms and injuries and not focused enough on responding to a wealth of social problems largely beyond their, or any other individual agent's, control.

The research overview argues that it is important that child protection should be defined broadly and that contexts and outcomes are key. On reflection it is evident that what is being suggested is that *practitioners* should develop a broader approach and should give greater priority to contexts and outcomes without suggesting how that might be done. It is sad indeed that wider political and economic contexts are hardly mentioned, particularly in the *Messages from Research* overview. For example, while we are told to take a broad definition of child abuse and there is considerable evidence in the studies that the vast majority of children and households subject to child protection interventions are living in poverty and come from the most marginalised and deprived sections of society, nowhere is it suggested that policies which reinforce and deepen these social ills are themselves abusive. Issues of patriarchy, social class, racism and the implications of increasing social divisions in British society (Barclay, 1995; Hills, 1995) are never discussed. It is as if improvements can be brought about by small ameliorative changes in social workers' attitudes, re-labelling and modifications to operational practices. There is a real danger that social workers and social service departments will be expected to resolve problems which are well beyond their remit, thereby increasing their sense of confusion and bewilderment.

The research overview has not really addressed *why* children's services are constructed in the way they are, *why* the tensions have become so sharply focused and *why* professionals respond in the way they do. We have suggested this partly arises from the failure to address the nature of child protection *work*. But it also arises because the detailed empirical work has itself not been located in the context of wider social and economic changes, particularly in terms of public policy over recent years and the impact this has had in influencing and informing the way practice is carried out. The changes suggested are not something which social workers can resolve alone.

The Nature and Significance of Risk in Child Protection

It is in this context that the contemporary nature of risk in child protection is central and which most recommendations for change, including those from the Audit Commission (1994) and the Dartington Social Research Unit research overview (1995), fundamentally underestimate.

As we argued in Chapter 2, the development of social work in the area of child care, in the post-war period, was based on optimistic notions of improvement and rehabilitation and played a small but key element in the growth of welfarism. However, the collapse of welfarism and the growth of neo-liberal critiques has ushered in a quite new situation in which notions of risk are not simply re-cast but given a much greater significance. No longer is the emphasis on governing through 'society' but through the calculating choices of individuals (Rose, 1993). For neo-liberalism the political subject is less a social citizen with powers and obligations derived from membership of the collective body, society, than an individual whose citizenship is active. It is an individualised conception of citizenship where the emphasis is upon personal fulfilment and individual responsibility. At the same time, the impact of global market forces has hastened dislocation in most areas of economic and social life, reinforcing a whole variety of insecurities, uncertainties and fears. Not only can changes in social work be seen to reflect these wider and rapid social and economic transformations, but the nature of social work is such that it is intimately implicated and involved. The growing concerns about risk in social work with children and families can thus be understood as both reflecting these increased anxieties, uncertainties and insecurities and as providing a rationale for coping, understanding and responding to the new situation (Parton, 1996a).

For much of the post-war period there was a general mood of optimism that science and technology, together with the activities of the welfare state, had generally ushered in a period of prosperity and permanent improvement. There was an enthusiasm and support for experts and professionals and a perception that science had made things different and better for everyone. As a result it was believed that we were able to recognise real danger, whose causes could be objectively identified, backed by the authority of research and theory. Chance and mystery had been reduced to the margins not yet claimed by science.

But generally it was believed that, because of our objective, accurate knowledge of the world and our powerful technologies, our blaming behaviour was capable of going directly to real causes. Real blaming was possible because of its objective basis in scientific knowledge. It was assumed that human order by the development and application of science could be subject to human control so that things could be regular, repeatable and predictable. Notions of reason and rationality informed the development of a blaming system that was primarily positivistic and believed that not only could causes be objectively identified but that they could be subject to improvement and change. This was essentially the situation in child abuse following the 'discovery' of the 'battered baby syndrome' up until the early/mid 1980s.

Increasingly, however, contemporary society has become characterised by widespread scepticism about providential reason – the idea that increased secular understanding of the world leads to a safer and more rewarding existence. There is now a growing recognition that science and modern technologies are double-edged, creating new harms and negative consequences as well as offering beneficial possibilities – the era we are now living through and ushered in by Cleveland. One of the messages to emerge is that the system which had been set up to identify, predict and prevent abuse is itself culpable. The scientific basis by which we had attempted to tackle child abuse seems to have as many negative consequences for children, families and professionals as it does positives.

However, having argued that concerns about risk are central to the regime of signification in relation to child protection, it is important that we be clearer about what is meant by risk and how this has come about. The concept originally emerged in the 17th century in the context of gambling. For this purpose a specialised mathematical analysis of chance was developed. Risk then meant the probability of an event occurring, combined with the magnitude of the losses or gains entailed (Hacking, 1975). Subsequently the analysis of probabilities became the basis of scientific knowledge, transforming the nature of evidence, of knowledge, of authority and logic. Any process or activity had its probabilities of success or failure. In the

18th century the analysis of risk had important uses in marine insurance. The chances of a ship coming safely home took account of the probability of gains and losses. The calculation of risk became deeply entrenched in science and manufacturing as a theoretical base for decision-making. In the process, notions of probability became embedded in modern ways of thinking.

However, as Mary Douglas has argued (1986; 1992), while notions of risk have become more central to politics and public policy, their connection with technical calculations of probability has weakened. While it continues to combine a probabilistic measure of the occurrence of the primary event(s) with a measure of the *consequences* of those events, the concept of risk is now only associated with negative outcomes – hazard, danger, exposure, harm and loss. For example, the Royal Society Study Group recently defined risk 'as the probability that a particular *adverse* event occurs during a stated period of time, or results from a particular challenge' (Royal Society Study Group, 1992, p. 2, our emphasis). Risk that is the central concept for policy debates no longer has much to do with *neutral* probability calculations. 'The original connection is only indicated by arm-waving in the direction of possible science: the word *risk* now means danger; *high risk* means a lot of danger' (Douglas, 1992, p. 24, original emphasis).

Whereas originally a high risk meant a game in which a throw of the die had a strong probability of bringing great gain or great loss, risk now only refers to negative outcomes. Whereas previously 'danger' would have been the right word, 'danger does not have the aura of science or afford the pretension of a possible precise calculation' (Douglas, 1992, p. 25). The language of danger having turned into the language of risk thus gives the impression of being calculable and scientific. But this is not simply about linguistic style. The possibility of a scientifically objective decision about exposure to danger is part of the new complex of ideas. Not only is risk superficially scientific, it is also future oriented and predictive. It looks forward to assess the dangers ahead.

However, Douglas argues that while this is an important shift, it is not the major significance of the contemporary emphasis on risk. 'The big difference is not in the predictive uses of risk, but in its forensic functions' (1992, p. 27). The concept of risk emerges as a key idea for contemporary times because of its uses as a forensic resource. The more culturally individualised a society becomes, the more significant becomes the forensic potential of the idea of risk. Its forensic uses are particularly important in the development of different types of blaming systems and 'the one we are in now is almost ready to treat every death as chargeable to someone's account, every accident as caused by someone's criminal negligence, every sickness a threatened prosecution' (pp. 15–16).

Ulrich Beck (1992a; 1992b) characterises contemporary society as a 'risk society'. This does not simply refer to the fact that contemporary social life introduces new forms of danger for humanity, but that living in the 'risk society' means living with a calculative attitude to the open possibilities of action with which we are continually confronted. In circumstances of increasing uncertainty and apparent doubt the notion of risk has a particular purchase.

In the shift from the modern society to the risk society, the quality and nature of communal concerns and values shift. According to Beck, in the former the focal concerns are with substantive and positive goals of social change, attaining something good and trying to ensure that everyone has a stake and a fair share. However, in the risk society the normative basis is safety and the utopia is peculiarly negative and defensive – preventing the worst and protection from harm. As a result, statements on risk become the 'moral statements' of society (Beck, 1992a, p. 176). The axial principle is the distribution not of goods but of bads – the distribution of hazards, dangers and risks.

The concept of risk becomes fundamental to the way both lay actors and experts experience and organise the social world. Risk assessment and risk management are crucial to the colonisation, understanding and control of the future, but at the same time they necessarily open up the unknown. Risk assessment suggests precision, and even quantification, but by its nature is imperfect. Given the mobile character of the social world and the mutable and controversial nature of abstract systems of knowledge, most forms of assessment contain numerous imponderables. This issue – the central yet uncertain nature of risk management and risk assessment – is key to understanding the changing nature and role of science and knowledge and hence the role of experts in contemporary society (Luhman, 1993).

The risk society is thus also a self-critical, reflexive society. Risks come into being where traditions and assumed values have deteriorated. Determinations of risk straddle the distinction between objective and value dimensions. Moral standards are not asserted openly but in quantitative, theoretical and causal forms. But notions of risk are never settled and are continually moving. 'The concept of risk is like a probe which permits us over and over again to investigate the entire construction plan, as well as every individual speck of cement in the structure of civilisation for potentials of self-endangerment' (Beck, 1992a, p. 176).

Risk becomes central in a society which is taking leave of the past but also opening itself up to a problematic future. Risk becomes closely interrelated with reflexivity. For to assess risk in contemporary society requires the process of 'reflexive scientization' (Beck, 1992a) or 'reflexivity' (Giddens, 1990; 1991) in what we do and the way we do it both individually and institutionally. The 'reflexive monitoring of risk is intrinsic to institutionalised risk systems' (Giddens, 1991, p. 119).

Beck differentiates between 'reflexive scientization' and what went before, 'primary scientization'. The model of primary scientization is based on the 'naïveté' that the methodical scepticism of science can be institutionalised but reserved for the *objects* of science and not applied to itself. However, scientific methods and pronouncements carry within themselves the standards for their own critique and possible abolition. Scientific developments undermine their own foundations through the continuity of their own success. 'In the course of the *triumph* and generalisation of the norms of scientific argument, a completely different situation arises' (Beck, 1992a, pp. 164–5, original emphasis). This unbinding of scepticism lies at the heart of the conditions of reflexive scientization. While scientific and professional dogma are undermined their original authority and foundations themselves become increasingly uncertain and shaky. So while science becomes indispensable in the risk society, it also becomes devoid of its original validity claims. Science thus experiences a loss of security and confidence in both its internal and external relations and hence a decline in its power. This results in increased conflict between experts and lay people. Beck suggests that one good indicator of this is the increase in 'medical malpractice' lawsuits, but others would include the increased proceduralisation of child protection work and the focus on forensic evidence, together with the growth of parent groups and their willingness to take their grievances to courts of law.

However, while science is increasingly being seen as 'human' and therefore packed with errors and divergent interpretations, the risk society cannot do without it. The recourse to scientific analysis and results for the socially binding definition of truth and decision-making becomes more and more necessary but less and less sufficient. As a result of this growing disparity between the necessary and sufficient conditions of truth, the number and range of grey areas open to dispute grow. 'The target groups and users of scientific results become more dependent on scientific arguments in *general*, but at the same time more independent of *individual* findings and the judgement of science regarding the truth and reality of its statements' (Beck, 1992a, p. 167, original emphasis).

Risk and science are very dependent on each other in the contemporary situation. Whereas previously hazards and dangers were directly perceptible to the senses – the *smell* of neglect or the *sight* of the battered baby – the ways risks are increasingly thought about almost escape perception. Because something does not assault our senses does not mean it is not a risk. Risk in effect 'exists' in the formulas, theorems or assessments which construct them. They remain essentially invisible and are based on causal *interpretations* and predictions , and thus 'exist' in terms of the knowledge about them. We are dealing with a theoretical and hence a scientized consciousness, even in the everyday consciousness of risk. They must always be imagined, implied and ultimately *believed* – what we referred to in Chapter 5 as the difference between category-organised *knowledge* and category-organised *belief*. The suggested causality always remains more or less uncertain and tentative. Risks can thus be changed, magnified or minimised within the knowledge of them, and to that extent they are particularly open to social redefinition and social reconstruction. The mass media and the scientific and legal professions thus play key political roles in the defining, redefining and reconstituting of risks.

It is in this respect that it becomes evident that contemporary concerns with risk in child protection reflect ways of *organising* and *thinking* about the world, rather than some external or hidden reality. Thus while a significant part of expert thinking and public discourse is about risk profiling – analysing what, in the current state of knowledge and in current conditions, is the distribution of risks in the given milieu of action – such profiles are subject to continual critique and revision. No longer does expert knowledge create stable inductive arenas, for it is liable to produce unintended or unforeseen consequences or its findings may be open to diverse interpretations. The self and the wider institutional arrangements have to be continually assessed, monitored and reviewed and thereby reflexively made. Nothing can be taken for granted. So while science has become indispensable to this process, it is incapable of truth. 'Where science used to be convincing qua science, today, in view of the contradictory babble of scientific tongues, the *faith* in science or the *faith* in alternative science (or this method, this approach, this orientation) becomes decisive' (Beck, 1992a, p. 169, original emphasis). Under conditions of reflexive scientization, the production or mobilisation of *belief* becomes a central source for the social enforcement of validity claims – whether a child is safe or 'at risk'.

Thus the emergence of the risk society arises because of the undermining of science, knowledge and the various truths and power of experts – doctors and social workers – in the area of child abuse. However, rather than replace these emerging doubts and uncertainties with new certainties, they have been replaced by the *faith* and *belief* of practitioners who operate in a context of contradictory publicity played out via the media and public inquiries. It is not by chance then that the increased focus on risk in child protection work coincided with the decline in *trust* in social workers and their knowledge and practices. As trust has been undermined, audit has increased, and this process is intimately related to our pervasive concerns about risk (Rose, 1993) which plays a key role in the 'blaming system' and new forms of accountability. As Michael Power (1994a; 1994b) has argued, audit in a range of forms has come to replace the trust once accorded to professionals both by their clients and by the authorities which employ, legitimate and constitute them. The constant demands for audit both give expression to and contribute to the erosion of trust, and the expertise and positive knowledge of human conduct on which it was based.

In short, the pervasiveness of risk in a context where the trust in science and experts is replaced by audit can lead to new forms of organisational defensiveness and authoritarianism. It is as if once concerns about risk become all-pervasive, the requirement to develop and follow organisational procedures becomes dominant and the room for professional manoeuvre and creativity is severely limited. Ironically, once risk becomes institutionalised, the ability and willingness of professionals to take risks – in the original sense of possible positive as well as negative outcomes – is curtailed.

The vocabulary of risk attempts to provide a bridge between the known 'facts' and experiences of existence and the construction of a new moral community. It aspires to provide a generalised mechanism whereby the needs of welfare and the needs of justice can be met. As Douglas has argued, 'the idea of risk could have been custom-made. Its universalising terminology, its abstractness, its power of condensation, its scientificity, its connection with objective analysis, make it perfect. Above all, its forensic uses fit the tool to the task of building a culture that supports a modern industrial society' (1992, p. 15). Notions of risk have thus become central in a culture which needs a common forensic vocabulary with which to hold individuals accountable – particularly mothers and social workers in the context of child protection.

Towards the New Child Welfare?

Our argument is clearly very sceptical about how far changes can be introduced into current practice via a shift

from child protection to family support or from investigations to children in need in the ways suggested. For in
many, almost surprising and contradictory, ways the
current initiatives and debates instigated by the Department of Health appear to want to recreate the era of the
1950s and 1960s before the 'discovery' of child abuse. It is
as if we are trying to turn the clock back and deny what
has been happening since the early 1970s. Yet it is probably
more appropriate to read the recommendations as a
serious attempt to reinforce and make real the central aims
and principles of the Children Act 1989. However, as we
argued in Chapter 2, the nature and timing of the Act
always indicated that the focus of policy and practice
would be narrowly defined child protection and that child
welfare more generally would be legalised and proceduralised. More particularly it helped to institute the concentration on the identification, assessment and management
of risk as the main priority. Not only did we find evidence
for this in the files we analysed, but we have subsequently
demonstrated how this concentration on risk relates to a
range of social and cultural changes. Concerns about risk
lie at the heart of child protection work and are centrally
concerned with professionals both accounting for their
decisions and ultimately being held to account themselves.
While the concept of need draws attention to the deficits in
a situation, the concept of risk is concerned with the *consequences* of those deficits – and it is this which has become
central (J. Packman, personal communication). We would
argue that the current recommendations for change do not
fully grasp the nature of practice in child protection nor
these wider social changes which have both contributed to
and reflected this. Further, the advocated policy shifts are
in danger of making an already complex and difficult situation – for parents, children and social workers – worse. To
expect frontline social workers, and social service departments, to resolve these dilemmas may have the unintended consequence of putting them in a further double
bind – taking responsibility for the rebalancing of family
support and child protection – for all the best of intentions.
The recommendations for change fail to locate the current
situation in any wider social and political analysis. As a
consequence they fail to ask *why* children's services are

experiencing difficulties, *why* the tensions have become so sharply focused and *why* professionals respond in the way they do. This is not something that can be resolved by social workers alone. Not only are the police, the courts, the crown prosecution service, health and education professionals and agencies involved, but so are the full plethora of the media and central and local government, including the Social Services Inspectorate and the Department of Health. All have to take responsibility for the current situation and developing ways of responding. We have also demonstrated that this is not something particular to Britain but is reflected in Australia and North America. While lessons and experiences can be learnt from abroad, this is something facing most countries in the Western world. It is almost a global phenomenon. As we have argued, many of the issues are endemic to child protection as it has developed since the early 1970s. This is not meant to be a message of doom and foreboding but one of caution where we should be as clear as possible about why the situation has come about and about the nature of child protection practice. Recommendations that social workers need to be clearer about risk before embarking on an investigation do not resolve the problems – they simply shift their location.

Apart from the research by Jane Gibbons and her colleagues (1995), none of the Department of Health research looked at child protection cases at the point of referral. Most were concerned with cases further along the process often from the initial case conference stage. What we have argued is that once a case has been categorised at the point of referral as child abuse – which we have seen has been subject to 'diagnostic inflation' – it is very difficult not to treat it as a child protection case at least until it has been investigated or 'not substantiated'. To treat it as any other in the current climate seems very difficult. This is not to say it may not be treated with 'a lighter touch', but it is still a child protection case where notions of risk are embedded from the outset. Central government needs to recognise that until clear indications and criteria are given as to how, from all the allegations and referrals that come to official attention, frontline workers are to sift out the high risk and who, ultimately, takes responsibility for those decisions, it is naive to assume that they cannot be treated as 'high risk' until proven otherwise.

Simply re-labelling these allegations and referrals as Section 17 'children in need' does not overcome the issue. A closer look at the way the personal social services prioritise their work, particularly for the purposes of allocating scarce resources and holding professionals to account, demonstrates further the increasing role played by notions of risk. For example, in a study of the approaches developed by four local authorities in relation to responding to 'children in need' under the Children Act 1989, the issue of risk is demonstrated as key in determining case priority (Giller, 1993). Social workers and managers explicitly referred to the increased 'bombardment' and the increasingly severe limitations in available resources, so that prioritisation not only took place at the point of initial assessment but continued into service planning and delivery. One of the areas studied clearly illustrated the central role played by risk in prioritising. The tool employed for case prioritisation in the authority at the time was that contained in the workload management system and was developed prior to the implementation of the Children Act and thus applies to client groups other than children. The priority weightings were as follows – where 9 is the top priority and 1 the lowest:

9   Any situation where a *serious* and *immediate risk* of physical injury has been identified for adults or children, or where there is an immediate risk of reception into care. This would include all children on the Child Protection Register who are living at home.
8   Any situation where there is a *risk* of physical injury or reception into care for adults or children occurring in the short term, but where this is not considered immediate.
7   Children who are the subject of statutory intervention who are not living at home.
6   Children who are the subject of statutory orders for purposes other than child protection, who are living at home.
5   Situations where a longer-term risk of reception into care for adults or children has been identified but this is not considered immediate or short-term.

4   Situations involving the rehabilitation of vulnerable adults to the community, e.g. mental health after-care.

3   Requests for assessments for services for vulnerable older people or people with disabilities, e.g. day care, CSDP Act Telephone, TO services.

2   Situations involving 'distress' where there is no apparent risk to life or admission to care of any kind.

1   Requests for social inquiry reports for criminal and Non-School Attendance proceedings should be allocated within 4 weeks of the final hearing.

(adapted from Giller, 1993)

What is of particular note, and it is not untypical of criteria for the allocation of cases and the rationing of resources in other social service departments, is that attempts to prioritise need essentially to become framed in terms of risk. Notions of risk take on a particular significance even when the focus of attention is apparently needed.

This is even more evident in a study recently completed into the provision of services for children in need and their families under Part 3 of the 1989 Act (Colton et al., 1995a; 1995b). The research, funded by the Welsh Office, studied the way policies for children in need were defined and prioritised in all eight Welsh local authorities and eight comparable English authorities, together with more in-depth analysis in two of the Welsh authorities. The second part of the study included interviews with 103 social workers, 21 team leaders and six principal social services officers. The problems identified in the failure to develop the family support services were seen to have been exacerbated by consistent underfunding over many years, so that services were inadequate even before the potential client population was increased by the introduction of the Children Act.

Child-care managers were asked to rank nine categories of children in two ways. First, in order of the actual service priority each category receives and, second, in the order which each category, in the manager's opinion, should ideally have. 'Actual' ranks given by the managers indicated 'that social services departments in Wales are clearly concentrating their efforts on children *at risk of abuse and neglect*' (Colton et al., 1995a, p. 204, our emphasis).

However, when asked how they would prioritise under ideal circumstances, managers were far more likely to give equal ratings to a number of categories, an indication of their desire to give more emphasis to family support work so that fewer children would be in need of statutory intervention. The actual and ideal rankings provided by the social workers and team leaders were similar to those of the managers and reflected the same emphasis on child protection. Just over one third of the social workers interviewed indicated that their assessments of need were influenced at least as much by their knowledge of resources as by the child's needs.

It seems remarkable that research of this sort has neither influenced the thinking at the Department of Health nor is reflected in the Dartington Social Research Unit research overview (1995). As a consequence there is a failure to grapple with the full complexities of the current situation and to recognise that calls to prioritise family support without much more fundamental change are naive and potentially dangerous. Crucially it fails to grasp fully the significance of the notion of risk in the current context.

Notions of risk have thus taken on a strategic contemporary significance for rationing services and holding professionals and others to account in a changing political and economic context, where potential need and demand is increasing but where there are insufficient resources. What we are also arguing is that statements about risk have become the key *moral* statements of society and lie at the heart of child protection work. They represent a more general societal gauge on the way we value and treat children and the people who take prime responsibility for looking after them and bringing them up – usually mothers. To assume that the responsibility for assessing and managing risks to children is exclusively or even primarily the responsibility of social workers is both naive and potentially dangerous. Until this issue is grasped it is unrealistic to expect any major changes in the nature and priorities of those given responsibility for child protection. The words may change but they may only act to obfuscate an already shrouded and complex sphere of professional, personal and social life. While the current system has many problems, it does essentially do the work demanded of it. There is little evidence that children are being missed and in many ways practitioners are very good at detecting the few who might suffer injury. But this is at a cost. The myth is to suggest that, with current resources and in the current political and economic climate, practitioners can do this in a fundamentally different way. As we have argued throughout, current practice very much carries out the child protection *work* that is asked of it. The problem with much recent research and policy debates is that they fail to understand what the nature of that work is and *why* it takes the form that it does.

Notes

Chapter 2

1   Under Section 3 of the 1980 Children Act (Section 2 of the 1948 Children Act) a local authority could assume full parental rights of children who came into care with the 'voluntary' agreement of their parents (Section 2 of the 1980 Children Act or Section 1 of the 1948 Children Act). It was an administrative decision taken within the local authority and only if the parents objected did the case go before a court.

2   Place of Safety Orders (POSOs) date back to the 1870 Infant Life Protection Acts and were legal mechanisms for removing a child or young person from a situation of risk to 'a safe place'. A place of safety was defined in Section 107(1) of the Children and Young Persons Act 1933 as a community home, police station, hospital, surgery or other suitable place, the occupier of which was willing temporarily to receive the child or young person.

    While there were a number of statutory provisions which empowered such a removal, the most important was that embodied in Section 28(1) of the Children and Young Persons Act 1969. Under that Section, any person could apply to a magistrate for authority to detain a child or young person and take him/her to a place of safety; in practice this was normally done by local authority social workers, officers of the NSPCC and, sometimes, the police. The magistrate had to be satisfied that *the applicant* had reasonable cause to believe that grounds existed for a care order under the Act as set out in Section 1(2)(e): that is, neglect, ill-treatment, moral danger, beyond control of parent, not receiving full-time education. Under the order, the child or young person could be detained for up to 28 days or less as specified. The application was *ex parte* and the order was not appealable and could not be renewed. It was primarily intended to ensure that children at risk of abuse or neglect or beyond control could be removed from immediate danger until a decision was made as to their long-term future.

    Available statistics suggest that the use of POSOs had increased dramatically during the 1970s. For example, official statistics show an increase from 204 in force on 31 March 1972 to 759 in force on 31 March 1976. Since 1977 figures were published for orders made within each year. These figures indicate a further increase until

247

the end of the decade followed by a slight decrease (see the table below).

Year (1 April to 31 March)	Aged under 5	5–16	16+	Total
1977/8	2,101	3,117	253	5,471
1978/9 (excludes Wandsworth, no figures available)	2,335	3,109	261	5,705
1979/80	2,556	3,788	269	6,613
1980/1	2,390	3,513	309	6,212
1981/2	2,550	3,400	301	6,251
1982/3	2,390	3,027	309	5,726
1983/4	2,162	2,731	314	5,207

3 Jasmine Beckford died on 5 July 1984 at the age of four and a half at the home of Morris Beckford, her stepfather, and Beverley Lorrington, her mother, in North-West London, of cerebral contusions and subdural haemorrhage, as a direct result of severe manual blows inflicted on the child's head. She was also emaciated as a result of chronic undernourishment. She and her sister, Louise, were made the subject of Care Orders to the London Borough of Brent in August 1981 after both children had been admitted to hospital with severe injuries, including a broken arm and broken femur. From September 1981 to April 1982 they had been living with foster parents but were returned 'home on trial' in April 1982, still being subject to the Care Order. When Jasmine was discharged from hospital after being taken into care, she weighed 18 lbs 14 oz. Serveral months later when she was returned home after being fostered she weighed 25 lbs 5 oz. When she died she weighed 23 lbs. Morris Beckford was convicted of manslaughter and was sentenced to ten years' imprisonment, while Beverley Lorrington pleaded guilty to child neglect and was sentenced to 18 months' imprisonment. At the trial, Judge Pigot said that the social worker, Gun Wahlstrom, had shown a 'naivete almost beyond belief' and called the Assistant Director of Social Services to be examined on oath about the work of his department in relation to the case. The panel of inquiry was set up by Brent Borough Council and Brent Health Authority.

4 Under Part 3 of the Children Act 1989, local authority responsibilities for support for children and families were outlined. Section 17(1) of Part 3 of the Act says that:

It shall be the general duty of every local authority (in addition to the other duties imposed on them by this Part) –

a) to safeguard and promote the welfare of children within their area who are in need; and

b) so far as is consistent with that duty, to promote the upbringing of such children by their families,

by providing a range and level of services appropriate to those children's needs.

The specific duties and powers were set out in Part 1 of Schedule 2 of the Act.

Chapter 4

1 To some degree the enterprise of the orthodoxy in child abuse research is paralleled by the enterprise of positivism – the establishment of a method which would overcome scepticism. Ironically, for positivism this was a reaction to theology (or belief), whereas for the child abuse orthodoxy, this was a reaction to scepticism itself. The method therefore came to substantiate a belief – that there was such a thing as child abuse, that this was a major social problem and that something 'should' be done about it. The dominant entrepreneurs have been ISPCAN who, particularly through their journals, have sought to offer a 'credentialled version' (Pollner, 1975) of a social problem as they see it.

2 Fuchs and Ward (1994) suggest that DECONSTRUCTION is a 'destabilising' enterprise: 'The point of DECONSTRUCTIVE reading, then, is not to find the meaning of a text of system of signs, but to destabilise the very notion that there is such a thing as literal or "true" meaning' (p. 482).

We would want to distance ourselves from this essentially destabilising position, just as we would distance ourselves from a 'realist' position. The status of the statement that there is no 'truth' is no different, in our opinion, from the status of the statement that there is truth. This is to make the transition from sociology to epistemology, to say 'what passes for knowledge' is 'knowledge', without investigating how things come to be known. For social actors there are 'truths' which have to be arrived at for practical purposes. Looking at how truths are arrived at could be said to destabilise in that it enables actors to critically reflect on how they come to arrive at 'truths' in the first place. But it is only destabilising in that it encourages this critically reflexive practice, which may ultimately become a stable position.

3 Lightup quotes T. Wilson (1974), 'Normative and Interpretive Paradigms in Sociology', in J. Douglas (ed.), *Understanding Everyday Life*, London: Routlede and Kegan Paul, p. 69.

Chapter 5

1 Taking a single case in this way may open up suggestions that another example could have been treated differently. However, it is not the case, *per se*, that is being scrutinised here. Rather it is the way in which the work is made accountable for organisational purposes. The fact that it is one case is less important than the fact that the record is organisationally acceptable. It was not remarked that the reasoning or methods used were in any way unusual to the social worker, or the organisation. On the contrary, the text stands as a description of the work treated routinely. It is this notion of routine which renders validity rather than any claims about the particular characteristics of the case, or any others used in this chapter.

2 Qvortrup (1990) notes the absence of measurement of children; they are only measured in relation to adults in statistical accounting – for example, social class is always defined by adult occupation. James and Prout (1990) suggest that there are available ways of reconstructing stratification of children through age, but acknowledge that this too is an adult method of stratifying children, particularly through age groupings in school, and that age may have different meanings for children themselves.

3 Sacks took, for example, the statement 'The baby cried, the Mommy picks it up', and analysed the work it did. We don't hear it as any baby or any Mommy – the category bound activity (picking up a crying baby) links the identities. It is the expectation that a mother will pick up *her* baby when it cries that allows the sentence to be heard as referring to the Mommy of the baby. The organisation of knowledge which the use of pairs provides for is complex. Sacks gives a description of their use as follows:

(1) If any Member X knows his own pair position with respect to some Member Y [e.g. if someone knows that he can properly be categorized as a 'boyfriend' of a particular person], then X knows the pair position of Y with respect to himself [e.g. he knows that that person may correctly be categorized as his 'girlfriend']. X also knows that if Y knows what pair position Y has to X, then Y knows what pair position X has to Y.

(2) If any Member Z (neither X nor Y) knows what X takes to be X's pair position to Y, then Z knows what pair position X takes it that Y has to X. Z also knows that X takes it that if Y knows that X stands to Y in the pair position X supposes, then Y takes it that Y stands to X in the pair position X supposes. Z knows too that the converse holds for Y. Z knows further, as X and Y know,

what the rights and obligations are that obtain between X and Y given a convergence in their determination of their respective pair positions. (Sacks, 1992)

4   For a critique of the standard model of child development and its consequences in constructing a particular version of childhood see James and Prout (1990) and Woodhead (in James and Prout, 1990).

5   The UK sample drawn on here comprised 106 cases. This was a 100 per cent sample of all the cases referred to social work agencies in a local authority area in the North of England between 1987 and 1988 that were classified as both (a) child sexual abuse reports and (b) appropriate for investigation. For further details see Wattam (1992).

6   RIC is social work shorthand meaning 'Received into care'.

7   'Schedule 1 offender' refers to a person convicted under Schedule 1 of the Children and Young Persons Act 1933. These offences include murder or manslaughter, assault or battery, abandonment, cruelty, causing a person under 16 to be used for begging, allowing a person under 16 to be in a brothel, exposing a child under 12 to risk of burning, and taking away or detaining a child with intent to deprive a person having the lawful care or charge of such child. Schedule 1 was extended by amendments and includes offences under the Sexual Offences Act 1956, Indecency with Children Act 1960, Suicide Act 1961 and Protection of Children Act 1978.

8   Solberg (1990), for example, shows how children are perceived differently in Norway in terms of responsibilities for themselves and others in the family. There it is not unusual for children of ten to be in the home alone and preparing the family tea before the adults return.

Chapter 7

1   In March 1994, Pergamon Press, the publisher of *Child Abuse and Neglect*, distributed an eight-page publicity pamphlet to potential readers of the journal. The pamphlet described the journal as the 'Official Publication of the International Society for Prevention of Child Abuse and Neglect'. It contained a letter from the editor, announced a doubling of the frequency of publication from six to twelve annual issues, invited contributions from potential authors and invited requests for a free sample copy from potential subscribers. This quotation is extracted from a section of the pamphlet entitled 'Aims and Scope'.

Chapter 8

1   See Chapter 5, note 7.
2   Many of the studies of children 'disclosing' sexual abuse have been criticised for their clinical nature, and also for potential bias in relation to prejudging whether children have in fact been abused. The study by Sorenson and Snow (1991) which we report on here does not have these limitations. Cases were selected from a large sample where there were definite indications of sexual harm or injury (for example, prosecution, admission by perpetrator, medical evidence) and these cases were examined for information on the way in which children bring their abuse to the attention of others. Whilst the term 'disclosure' was discredited in Cleveland (Secretary of State, 1988) this was only in so far as it was attached to the word 'interview', such that interviews should not prejudge that there is something to hide. In relation to children telling about sexual assault, where these children have been assaulted, it remains a useful clinical concept. The Sorenson and Snow study reinforced the clinical view that disclosure – that is, the giving of information about a sexual assault – is a process rather than a one-off event. Furthermore, the process was found to have stages (depicted below).

The Disclosure Process

Denial	Tentative	Active	Recant	Reaffirm
72%	78%	96%	22%	93%

These results show that in the majority of substantiated cases children will deny all or some part of allegations of sexual assault, give tentative information (hints, 'it happened to my friend', 'it happened a long time ago'), but will actively tell their story at some future point. A minority retract this information, and the majority of those that do retract reaffirm it later.
3   See Chapter 5, note 7.
4   A prosecution was considered in 36 cases (21 per cent). Of the overall sample, a successful prosecution was obtained in 13 per cent of cases, and in 8 per cent the prosecution either was dropped or failed or the outcome was not recorded.

Bibliography

Aldridge, M. (1994) *Making Social Work News* (London: Routledge).

Allan, L. J. (1978) 'Child abuse: a critical review of the research and theory', in J. P. Martin (ed.), *Violence in the Family* (London: John Wiley).

Ammerman, R. T. (1991) 'The role of the child in physical abuse: a reappraisal', *Violence and Victims*, 6(2), pp. 87–100.

Ariès, P. (1973) *Centuries of Childhood* (Harmondsworth: Penguin).

Armstrong, D. (1983) *Political Anatomy of the Body: Medical Knowledge in Britain in the Twentieth Century* (Cambridge: Cambridge University Press).

Asogwa, S. E. (1986) 'Sociomedical aspects of child labor in Nigeria', *Journal of Occupational Medicine*, 28, pp. 46–8.

Audit Commission (1994) *Seen But Not Heard: Coordinating Child Health and Social Services for Children in Need* (London: HMSO).

Baccus, M. (1986) 'The visibility criterion of real world social theorizing', in H. Garfinkel (ed.), *Ethnomethodological Studies of Work* (London: Routledge and Kegan Paul).

Baher, E., C. Hyman, C. Jones, R. Jones, A. Kerr and R. Mitchell (1976) *At Risk: An Account of the Work of the Battered Child Research Department* (London: Routledge and Kegan Paul).

Baker, A. W. and S. P. Duncan (1985) 'Child sexual abuse: a study of prevalence in Great Britain', *Child Abuse and Neglect*, 9, pp. 457–67.

Barclay, P. (1995) *Joseph Rowntree Foundation Inquiry into Income and Wealth, Volume One* (York: Joseph Rowntree Foundation).

BBC (1986) 'Childwatch – overview of results from 2,530 self-completion questionnaires' (BBC Broadcasting Research, unpublished).

BBC (1987) 'Childwatch – national survey on child abuse' (BBC press briefing, 9 July, unpublished).

Beck, U. (1992a) *Risk Society: Towards a New Modernity* (London: Sage).

Beck, U. (1992b) 'From industrial society to risk society: questions of survival, social structure and ecological enlightenment', *Theory, Culture and Society*, 9(1), pp. 97–123.

Belsky, J. (1980) 'Child maltreatment: an ecological integration', *American Psychologist*, 35, pp. 320–35.

Berger, P. and T. Luckman (1984) *The Social Construction of Reality: A Treatise in the Sociology of Knowledge* (Harmondsworth: Penguin).

Besharov, D. J. (1988) 'The need to narrow the grounds for state intervention', in D. J. Besharov (ed.), *Protecting Children from Abuse and Neglect: Policy and Practice* (Springfield, Ill: C. C. Thomas).

Besharov, D. J. (1990) *Recognising Child Abuse: A Guide for the Concerned* (New York: The Free Press).

Birchall, E. and C. Hallett (1995) *Working Together in Child Protection* (London: HMSO).

Blagg, H. (1989) 'Fighting the stereotypes – "ideal" victims in the inquiry process', in H. Blagg, J. Hughes and C. Wattam (eds), *Child Sexual Abuse: Listening, Hearing and Validating the Experiences of Children* (Harlow: Longman).

Bottoms, A. E. (1977) 'Reflections on the renaissance of dangerousness', *Howard Journal of Penology and Crime Prevention*, 16(2), pp. 70–96.

Brindle, D. (1995) 'Row over child abuse claim', *The Guardian*, 15 June, p. 8.

British Paediatric Association (1996) 'The battered baby: a memorandum by the Special Standing Committee on Accidents', *British Medical Journal*, 601, 5 March, pp. 601–3.

Brown, C. (1986) *Child Abuse Parents Speaking: Parents' Impressions of Social Workers and the Social Work Process*, Working Paper 63 (University of Bristol, School for Advanced Urban Studies).

Brown, M. and N. Madge (1982) *Despite the Welfare State: A Report on the SSRC/DHSS Programme of Research into Transmitted Deprivation* (London: Heinemann).

Browne, K. (1993) 'Home visitation and child abuse: the British experience', *American Professional Society on the Abuse of Children*, 6(4), pp. 11–31.

Browne, K. and S. Saqi (1987) 'Parent–child interaction in abusing families: its possible causes and consequences', in P. Maher (ed.), *Child Abuse: The Educational Perspective* (Oxford: Blackwell).

Browne, K. and S. Saqi (1988) 'Approaches to screening families at high risk for child abuse', in K. Browne, C. Davies and P. Stratton (eds), *Early Prediction and Prevention of Child Abuse* (Chichester: John Wiley).

Butler, I. and H. Williamson (1994) *Children Speak: Children, Trauma and Social Work* (London: NSPCC/Longman).

Campbell, B. (1988) *Unofficial Secrets* (London: Virago).

Cant, R. and R. Downie (1994) *A Study of West Australian Child Protection Data: A Report for the Department for Community Development, Western Australia* (Perth: Social Systems and Evaluation).

CIBA Foundation (1984) Ruth Porter (ed.), *Child Sexual Abuse Within the Family* (London: Tavistock).

Ciccheti, D. and V. Carlson (eds) (1989) *Child Maltreatment: Theory and Research on the Causes and Consequences of Child Abuse and Neglect* (New York: Cambridge University Press).

Cleaver, H. (1983) and P. Freeman (1995) *Parental Perspectives in Cases of Suspected Child Abuse* (London: HMSO).

Cohn, A. H. 'The prevention of child abuse: what do we know about what works?', in J. E. Leavitt (ed.), *Child Abuse and Neglect: Research and Innovation* (London: Martinus Nijhoff).

Colton, M., C. Drury and M. Williams (1995a) *Children in Need: Family Support Under the Children Act 1989* (Aldershot: Avebury).

Colton, M., C. Drury and M. Williams (1995b) 'Children in Need: Definition, Identification and Support', *British Journal of Social Work*, 25(6), pp. 711–28.

Corby, B. (1993) *Child Abuse: Towards a Knowledge Base* (Milton Keynes: Open University Press).

Court, J. (1969) 'The battered child: (1) Historical and diagnostic reflection; (2) Reflection on treatment', *Medical Social Work*, 22, pp. 11–20.

Creighton, S. J. (1993) 'Children's Homicide: An Exchange', *British Journal of Social Work*, 23(6), pp. 643–4.

Creighton S. J. and P. Noyes (1989) *Child Abuse Trends in England and Wales 1983–1987* (London: NSPCC).

Crittenden, P. M. (1985) 'Social networks, quality of child rearing and child development', *Child Development*, 56, pp. 1299–313.

Dartington Social Research Unit (1995) *Child Protection: Messages from Research* (London: HMSO).

Davies, G., C. Wilson, R. Mitchell and J. Milsom (1995) *Videotaping Children's Evidence: An Evaluation* (London: Home Office).

De Mause, L. (1974) *The History of Childhood* (New York: Psychohistory Press).

Department of Family and Children's Services (1995) *Focus on Protecting Children* (Perth: DFCS).

DoH (1988) *Protecting Children: A Guide for Social Workers Undertaking a Comprehensive Assessment in Cases of Child Protection* (London: HMSO).

DoH (1991) *Child Abuse: A Study of Inquiry Reports 1980–1989* (London: HMSO).

DoH (1993) *Children Act Report 1992* (London: HMSO).

DoH (1994) *Children Act Report 1993* (London: HMSO).

DHSS (1970) *The Battered Baby*, CMOZ/70.

DHSS (1972) *Battered Babies*, LASSL 26/72.

DHSS (1974) *Non-Accidental Injury to Children*, LASSL 74/13.

DHSS (1980) Child Abuse Central Register Systems, LASSL 80/4.

DHSS (1982) *Child Abuse: A Study of Inquiry Reports 1973–1981* (London: HMSO).

DHSS (1985a) *Review of Child Care Law: Report to Ministers of an Interdepartmental Working Party* (London: HMSO).

DHSS (1985b) *Social Work Decisions in Child Care: Recent Research Findings and their Implications* (London: HMSO).

DHSS (1986) *Child Abuse – Working Together: A Draft Guide to Arrangements for Inter-Agency Cooperation for the Protection of Children* (London: DHSS).

DHSS (1988) *Working Together: A Guide to Inter-Agency Cooperation for the Protection of Children from Abuse* (London: HMSO).

Dingwall, R. (1989) 'Some problems about predicting child abuse and neglect', in O. Stevenson (ed.), *Child Abuse: Public Policy and Professional Practice* (Hemel Hempstead: Harvester Wheatsheaf).

Dingwall, R., J. Eekelaar and T. Murray (1983) *The Protection of Children: State Intervention and Family Life* (Oxford: Basil Blackwell).

Donzelot, J. (1980) *The Policing of Families* (London: Hutchinson).

Donzelot, J. (1988) 'The promotion of the social', *Economy and Society*, 17(3), pp. 395–427.

Douglas, M. (1986) *Risk Acceptability According to the Social Sciences* (London: Routledge and Kegan Paul).

Douglas, M. (1992) *Risk and Blame: Essays in Cultural Theory* (London: Routledge).

Driver, E. and A. Droisen (1989) *Child Sexual Abuse: Feminist Perspectives* (London: Macmillan).

Drotar, D. (1992) 'Prevention of neglect and nonorganic failure to thrive', in D. J. Willis, E. W. Holden and M. Rosenberg (eds), *Prevention of Child Maltreatment: Developmental and Ecological Perspectives* (New York: John Wiley).

Dukes, R. L. and R. B. Kean (1989) 'An experimental study of gender and situation in the perception and reporting of child abuse', *Child Abuse and Neglect*, 13, pp. 351–60.

Famularo, R., K. Stonem, R. Barnum and R. Whaton (1986) 'Alcoholism and severe child maltreatment', *American Journal of Orthopsychiatry*, 56, pp. 481–5.

Farmer, E. and M. Owen (1995) *Child Protection Practice: Private Risks and Public Remedies* (London: HMSO)

Ferguson, H. (1990) 'Rethinking child protection practices: a case for history', in The Violence Against Children Study Group, *Taking Child Abuse Seriously: Contemporary Issues in Child Protection Theory and Practice* (London: Unwin Hyman).

Finkelhor, D. A. (1986) *Sourcebook on Child Sexual Abuse* (London: Sage).

Finkelhor, D. A. (1990) 'Is child abuse overreported?', *Public Welfare*, 46(1), pp. 22–9.

Finkelhor, D. A. and L. Barron (1986) 'Risk factors for child sexual abuse', *Journal of Interpersonal Violence*, 1(1), pp. 43–71.

Flavell, J. H. (1963) *The Developmental Psychology of Jean Piaget* (New Jersey: Van Nostrand Reinhold).

Foucault, M. (1972) *The Archaeology of Knowledge* (London: Tavistock).

Fox Harding, L. (1991) *Perspectives in Child Care Policy* (London: Longman).

Franklin, B. (ed.) (1986) *The Rights of Children* (London: Basil Blackwell).

Franklin, B. (ed.) (1995) *The Handbook of Children's Rights: Comparative Policy and Practice* (London: Routledge).

Franklin B. and N. Parton (eds) (1991) *Social Work, the Media and Public Relations* (London: Routledge).

Franklin, W. and R. E. Kahn (1987) 'Severe asthma due to household pets: a form of child abuse and neglect', *New England and Regional Allergy Proceedings*, 8(4), pp. 259–61.

Freeman, M. D. A. (1983) *The Rights and Wrongs of Children* (London: Frances Pinter).

Freeman, M. D. A. (1987–88) 'Taking children's rights seriously', *Children and Society*, 1(4), Winter, pp. 299–319.

Friedrich, W. N., P. Grambsch, D. Broughton, J. Kuiper and R. L. Beilke (1991) 'Normative sexual behaviour in children', *Pediatrics*, 88, pp. 456–64.

Frost, N. and M. Stein (1989) *The Politics of Child Welfare: Inequality, Power and Change* (Hemel Hempstead: Harvester Wheatsheaf).

Fuchs, S. and S. Ward (1994) 'What is deconstruction, and when and where does it take place? Making facts in science, building cases in law', *American Sociological Review*, 59(4), pp. 481–500.

Garbarino, J. and G. Gilliam (1980) *Understanding Abusive Families* (Lexington: Lexington Books).

Garfinkel, H. (1992) *Studies in Ethnomethodology* (Cambridge: Polity Press).

Geach, H. and E. Szwed (eds) (1983) *Providing Civil Justice for Children* (London: Arnold).

Gelles, R. J. (1982) 'Problems in defining and labelling child abuse', in Starr, 1982.

Gelles, R. J. and M. Straus (1987) 'Is violence towards children increasing? A comparison of 1975 and 1985 national survey rates', *Journal of Interpersonal Violence*, 2(2), pp. 212–22.

Ghate, D. and L. Spencer (1995) *The Prevalence of Child Sexual Abuse in Britain: A Feasibility Study for a Large-Scale National Survey of the General Population* (London: HMSO).

Gibbons, J., S. Conroy and C. Bell (1995) *Operating the Child Protection System* (London: HMSO).

Gibbons, J., B. Gallagher, C. Bell and D. Gordon (1995) *Development after Physical Abuse in Early Childhood: A Follow-Up Study of Children on Protection Registers* (London: HMSO).

Giddens, A. (1990) *The Consequences of Modernity* (Cambridge: Polity Press).

Giddens, A. (1991) *Modernity and Self-Identity: Self and Society in the Late Modern Age* (Cambridge: Polity Press).

Gil, D. (1979) 'Societal Violence and Violence in Families', in J. M. Eekelaar and S. N. Katz (eds), *Family Violence: An International and Interdisciplinary Study* (Toronto: Butterworth).

Giller, H. (1993) *Children in Need: Definition, Management and Monitoring* (London: DoH).

Giller, H., C. Gormley and O. Williams (1992) *The Effectiveness of Child Protection Procedures: An Evaluation of Child Protection Procedures in Four ACPC Areas* (Manchester: Social Information Systems).

Giovannoni, J. M. (1982) 'Prevention of child abuse and neglect: research and policy issues', *Social Work Research and Abstracts*, 18(3), pp. 23–31.

Giovannoni, J. M. and R. M. Beccera (1979) *Defining Child Abuse* (New York: Free Press).

Goffman, E. (1961) *Asylums* (Harmondsworth: Penguin).

Gordon, L. (1988) 'The politics of child sexual abuse: notes from American history', in 'Family secrets: child sexual abuse', *Feminist Review*, 28, Spring, Special Issue, pp. 56–64.

Graham, H. (1994) 'The changing financial circumstances of households with children', *Children and Society*, 8(2), pp. 98–113.

Greenland, C. (1987) *Preventing CAN Deaths: An International Study of Deaths Due to Child Abuse and Neglect* (London: Tavistock).

Hacking, I. (1975) *The Emergence of Probability: A Philosophical Study of Early Ideas about Probability, Induction and Statistical Inferences* (Cambridge: Cambridge University Press).

Hallett, C. (1995) *Interagency Coordination in Child Protection* (London: HMSO).

Hallett, C. and E. Birchall (1992) *Coordination and Child Protection: A Review of the Literature* (London: HMSO).

Hamilton, C. J. and J. J. Collins (1982) 'The role of alcohol in wife beating and child abuse: a review of the literature', in J. J. Collins (ed.) *Drinking and Crime: Perspectives on the Relationship between Alcohol Consumption and Criminal Behaviour* (London: Guildford Press).

Hammond, J., A. Perez-Stable and C. G. Ward (1991) 'Predictive value of historical and physical characteristics for the diagnosis of child abuse', *Southern Medical Journal*, 84, pp. 166–8.

Hartmann, C. R. and A. W. Burgess (1989) 'Sexual abuse of children: causes and consequences', in Cichetti and Carlson, 1989.

Health Committee Second Report (1991) *Public Expenditure on Personal Social Services: Child Protection Services, Vol. 1: Report together with the Proceedings of the Committee* (London: HMSO).

Helfer, R. E. and C. H. Kempe (1976) *Child Abuse and Neglect: The Family and the Community* (Cambridge, Mass: Balinger).

Higginson, S. (1990) 'Under the influence', *Social Work Today*, 22(14), pp. 20–1.

Hight, D. W., H. R. Bakalar and J. R. Lloyd (1979) 'Inflicted burns in children', *Journal of the American Medical Association*, 242, pp. 517–20.

Hills, J. (1995) *Joseph Rowntree Foundation Inquiry into Income and Wealth, Volume Two* (York: Joseph Rowntree Foundation).

Home Office in conjunction with DoH (1992) *Memorandum of Good Practice on Video Recording Interviews with Child Witnesses for Criminal Proceedings* (London: HMSO).

Home Office, DoH, DES and Welsh Office (1991) *Working Together Under the Children Act 1989: A Guide to Arrangements for Inter-Agency Cooperation for the Protection of Children from Abuse* (London: HMSO).

Hooper, C. A. (1992) *Mothers Surviving Child Sexual Abuse* (London: Routledge).

Households Below Average Income 1979–1990/91 (1993) (London: HMSO).

Howe, D. (1992) 'Child abuse and the bureaucratization of social work', *The Sociological Review*, 40(3), pp. 491–508.

Howitt, D. (1992) *Child Abuse Errors: When Good Intentions Go Wrong* (Hemel Hempstead: Harvester Wheatsheaf).

Hughes, J. A. (1990) *Philosophy of Social Research* (Harlow: Longman, 2nd edition).

James, A. and A. Prout (1990) *Constructing and Reconstructing Childhood* (London: Falmer Press).

Jayyusi, L. (1984) *Categorization and the Moral Order* (London: Routledge and Kegan Paul).

Johnson, H. and P. Chisholm (1989) 'Family homicide statistics, Canada', *Canadian Social Trends*, Autumn, pp. 17–18.

Kempe, C. H. (1979) 'Recent developments in the field of child abuse', *Child Abuse and Neglect*, 3, pp. 9–15.

Kempe, C. H., F. N. Silverman, B. F. Steel, W. Droegemueller and H. K. Silver (1962) 'The battered child syndrome', *Journal of the American Medical Association*, 181, pp. 17–24.

King, M. and C. Piper (1995) *How the Law Thinks About Children* (Aldershot: Gower, 2nd edition).

King, M. and J. Trowell (1992) *Children's Welfare and the Law: The Limits of Legal Intervention* (London: Sage).

Kinsey, A. C., W. B. Pomeroy and C. E. Martin (1948) *Sexual Behaviour in the Human Male* (Philadelphia: W. B. Saunders).

Kinsey, A. C., W. B. Pomeroy, C. E. Martin and P. H. Gebhard (1953) *Sexual Behaviour in the Human Female* (Philadelphia: W. B. Saunders).

Kirschner, R. H. and R. J. Stein (1985) 'The mistaken diagnosis of child abuse: a form of medical abuse', *American Journal of Diseases of Children*, 139(9), pp. 873–5.

Kitzinger, J. (1990) 'Who are you kidding? Children, power and the struggle against sexual abuse', in James and Prout, 1990.

Korbin, J. (ed.) (1981) *Child Abuse and Neglect: Cross Cultural Perspectives* (Berkeley, Ca: University of California Press).

La Fontaine, J. (1990) *Child Sexual Abuse* (Cambridge: Polity Press).

La Fontaine, J. (1994) *The Extent and Nature of Organised and Ritual Sexual Abuse of Children* (London: HMSO).

Lamb, S. and M. Coakley (1993) '"Normal" childhood sexual play and games: differentiating play from abuse', *Child Abuse and Neglect*, 17, pp. 515–26.

Ledbetter, D. J., E. I. Hatch, K. W. Feldman, C. L. Ligner and D. Tapper (1988) 'Diagnostic and surgical implications of child abuse', *Archives of Surgery*, 123, pp. 1101–5.

Lightup, R. W. (1982) *A Micro-Study of Some Interactional Features of Social Worker–Client Relationships*, Ph.D. (University of Manchester, Department of Sociology).

Lindsey, D. (1994) *The Welfare of Children* (New York: Oxford University Press).

London Borough of Brent (1985) *A Child in Trust: Report of the Panel of Inquiry Investigating the Circumstances Surrounding the Death of Jasmine Beckford* (London: London Borough of Brent).

London Borough of Greenwich (1987) *A Child in Mind: Protection of Children in a Responsible Society: Report of the Commission of Inquiry into the Death of Kimberley Carlile* (London: London Borough of Greenwich).

London Borough of Lambeth (1987) *Whose Child? The Report of the Panel Appointed to Inquire into the Death of Tyra Henry* (London: London Borough of Lambeth).

Luhman, N. (1993) *Risk: A Sociological Theory* (Berlin: Walter de Gruyter).

Lynch, M. A. and J. Roberts (1977) 'Predicting child abuse: signs of bonding failure in the maternity hospital', *British Medical Journal*, 1, pp. 624–6.

McCurdy, M. A. and D. Daro (1993) *Current Trends in Child Abuse Reporting and Fatalities: The Results of the 1992 Annual Fifty State Survey* (Chicago: National Committee for the Prevention of Child Abuse).

Madge, N. (1983) 'Identifying families at risk', in N. Madge (ed.), *Families at Risk* (London: Heinemann).

Markowe, H. L. J. (1988) 'The frequency of childhood sexual abuse in the UK', *Health Trends*, 20 (1), pp. 2–6.

Melnick, B. and J. R. Hurley (1969) 'Distinctive personality of child-abusing mothers', *Journal of Consulting and Clinical Psychology*, 33, pp. 746–9.

Milner, J. S. and C. Chilamkurti (1991) 'Physical child abuse perpetrator characteristics: a review of the literature', *Journal of Interpersonal Violence*, 6(3), pp. 345–66.

Morgan, S. (1987) *My Place* (Fremantle: Fremantle Arts Press).

Morris, A., H. Giller, E. Szwed and H. Geach (1980) *Justice for Children* (London: Macmillan).

National Research Council (US) Panel on Research on Child Abuse and Neglect (1993) *Understanding Child Abuse and Neglect* (Washington, D.C.: National Academy Press).

Nelson, S. (1987) *Incest: Fact and Myth* (Edinburgh: Stramullion).

Oates, R. K., A. A. Davis, M. G. Ryan and L. F. Stewart (1979) 'Risk factors associated with child abuse', *Child Abuse and Neglect*, 3, pp. 547–53.

Okell, C. and C. H. H. Butcher (1969) 'The battered child syndrome', *Law Society Gazette*, 66, p. 9.

Orme, T. C. and J. Rimmer (1981) 'Alcoholism and child abuse', *Journal of Studies on Alcohol*, 42, pp. 273–87.

Parke, R. D. and C. W. Collmer (1975) 'Child abuse: an interdisciplinary analysis', in E. M. Hetherington (ed.), *Review of Child Development Research 5* (Chicago: University of Chicago Press).

Parker, R. (ed.) (1980) *Caring for Separated Children: Plans, Procedures and Priorities. A Report by a Working Party Established by the National Children's Bureau* (London: Macmillan).

Parton, C. (1990) 'Women, gender oppression and child abuse', in The Violence Against Children Study Group, *Taking Child Abuse Seriously: Contemporary Issues in Child Protection Theory and Practice* (London: Unwin Hyman).

Parton, C. and N. Parton (1989a) 'Child protection: the law and dangerousness', in O. Stevenson (ed.), *Child Abuse; Public Policy and Professional Practice* (Hemel Hempstead: Harvester Wheatsheaf).

Parton, C. and N. Parton (1989b) 'Women, the family and child protection', *Critical Social Policy*, 24, pp. 38–49.

Parton, N. (1985) *The Politics of Child Abuse* (London: Macmillan).

Parton, N. (1990) 'Taking child abuse seriously', in The Violence Against Children Study Group, *Taking Child Abuse Seriously: Contemporary Issues in Child Protection Theory and Practice* (London: Unwin Hyman).

Parton, N. (1991) *Governing the Family: Child Care, Child Protection and the State* (London: Macmillan).

Parton, N. (1994a) 'Problematics of government, (post) modernity and social work', *British Journal of Social Work*, 24(1), pp. 9–32.

Parton, N. (1994b) 'The nature of social work under conditions of (post) modernity', *Social Work and Social Science Review*, 5(2), pp. 93–112.

Parton, N. (1996a) 'Social work, risk and "the blaming system"', in N. Parton (ed.), *Social Theory, Social Change and Social Work* (London: Routledge).

Parton, N. (1996b) 'Child protection, family support and social work: a critical appraisal of the department of health studies in child protection', *Child and Family Social Work*, 1, pp. 3–11.

Payne, M. (1992) 'Psychodynamic theory within the politics of social work theory', *Journal of Social Work Practice*, 6(2), pp. 141–9.

Pearson, G., J. Treseder and M. Yelloly (eds) (1988) *Social Work and the Legacy of Freud* (London: Macmillan).

Pecora, P. J. and M. B. Martin (1989) 'Risk factors associated with child sexual abuse: a selected summary of empirical research', in P. Schene and K. Bond (eds), *Research Issues in Risk Assessment for Child Protection* (American Association for Protecting Children, Denver: The American Humane Association).

Pfohl, S. J. (1977) 'The discovery of child abuse', *Social Problems*, 24(3), pp. 310–23.

Philp, M. (1979) 'Notes on the form of knowledge in social work', *Sociological Review*, 27(1), pp. 83–111.

Pithers, D. (1989) 'A guide through the maze of child protection', *Social Work Today*, 20(18), pp. 18–19.

Polansky, N. A., J. M. Gaudin and A. C. Kilpatrick (1992) 'Family radicals', *Children and Youth Services Review*, 14, pp. 19–26.

Pollner, M. (1975) 'The very coinage of your brain: the anatomy of reality disjunctures', *Philosophy of the Social Sciences*, 5, pp. 411–30.

Pollock, V. E., J. Briere, L. Schneider, J. Knop, S. A. Mednick and D. W. Goodwin (1990) 'Childhood antecedents of antisocial behaviour: parental alcoholism and physical abusiveness', *American Journal of Psychiatry*, 147, pp. 1290–3.

Power, M. (1994a) *The Audit Explosion* (London: Demos).

Power, M. (1994b) 'The audit society', in A. G. Hopwood and P. Miller (eds), *Accounting as Social and Institutional Practice* (Cambridge: Cambridge University Press).

Pritchard, C. (1992) 'Children's homicide as an indicator of effective child protection: a comparative study of Western European statistics', *British Journal of Social Work*, 22(6), pp. 663–84.

Pritchard, C. (1993) 'Re-analysing children's homicide and undetermined death rates as an indication of improved child protection: a reply to Creighton', *British Journal of Social Work*, 23(6), pp. 645–52.

Qvortrup, J. (1990) 'A voice for children in statistical and social accounting: a plea for children's rights to be heard', in James and Prout, 1990.

Ritzer, G. (1993) *The McDonaldisation of Society* (California: Pine Forge Press).

Roberts, J. (1988) 'Why are some families more vulnerable to child abuse?', in K. Browne, C. Davies and P. Stratton (eds), *Early Prediction and Prevention of Child Abuse* (Chichester: Wiley).

Rose, N. (1985) *The Psychological Complex: Psychology, Politics and Society in England, 1969–1939* (London: Routledge and Kegan Paul).

Rose, N. (1989) *Governing the Soul* (London: Routledge).

Rose, N. (1993) 'Government, authority and expertise in advanced liberalism', *Economy and Society*, 22(3), pp. 283–99.

Rose, N. and P. Miller (1992) 'Political power beyond the state: problematics of government', *British Journal of Sociology*, 43(24), pp. 173–205.

Royal College of Physicians (1991) *Physical Signs of Physical Abuse in Children: A Report of the Royal College of Physicians* (London: RCP).

Royal Society Study Group (1992) *Risk: Analysis, Perception and Management* (London: The Royal Society).

Roycroft, B. (1987) *Statement of the President of the Association of Directors of Social Services (to the Cleveland Inquiry)* (Newcastle upon Tyne: ADSS).

Sacks, H. (1972) 'An initial investigation of the usability of conversational data for doing sociology', in D. Sudnow (ed.), *Studies in Social Interaction* (New York: Free Press).

Sacks, H. (1992) *Lectures on Conversation*, ed. G. Jefferson (Oxford: Blackwell).

Schene, P. (1987) 'Is child abuse decreasing?', *Journal of Interpersonal Violence*, 2(2), pp. 225–7.

Schorr, A. L. (1992) *The Personal Social Services: An Outside View* (York: Joseph Rowntree Foundation).

Schutz, A. (1964–67) *Collected Papers. Volume 1: The Problem of Social Reality* (The Hague: Martinus Nijhoff).

Schwartz, R. H., P. Pearcy and D. Mistretta (1986) 'Intoxication of young children with marijuana: a form of amusement for "pot-smoking" teenage girls', *American Journal of the Disease of Children*, 40, p. 326.

Secretary of State for Social Services (1974) *Report of the Inquiry into the Care and Supervision Provided in Relation to Maria Colwell* (London: HMSO).

Secretary of State for Social Services (1988) *Report of the Inquiry into Child Abuse in Cleveland*, Cmnd 412 (London: HMSO).

Seebohm Report (1968) *Report of the Committee on Local Authority and Allied Personal Social Services*, Cmnd 3703 (London: HMSO).

Sgroi, S. M. (1982) *Handbook of Clinical Intervention in Child Sexual Abuse* (Toronto: Lexington Books).

Sharland, E., D. Jones, J. Aldgate, H. Seal M. and Croucher (1995) *Professional Intervention in Child Sexual Abuse* (London: HMSO).

Sharrock, W. and W. Coleman (in press) 'Unconstructive', in I. Velody (ed.), *The Politics of Constructionism* (London: Sage).

Skinner, A. K. and R. L. Castle (1969) *78 Battered Children: A Retrospective Study* (London: NSPCC).

Smith, M. and M. Grocke (1995) *Normal Family Sexuality and Sexual Knowledge in Children* (London: Royal College of Psychiatry/Gorkill Press).

Social Services Committee (HC360) (1984) *Children in Care* (London: HMSO).

Solberg, A. (1990) 'Changing constructions of age for Norwegian children', in James and Prout, 1990.

Sorenson, T. and B. Snow (1991) 'How children tell: the process of disclosure in child sexual abuse', *Child Welfare*, 70(1), pp. 3–15.

Spinetta, J. J. and D. Rigler (1972) 'The child abusing parent: a psychological review', *Psychological Bulletin*, 77(4), pp. 296–304.

Stainton Rogers, R. and W. Stainton Rogers (1992) *Stories of Childhood: Shifting Agendas of Child Concern* (London: Harvester Wheatsheaf).

Starr, R. (ed.) (1982) *Child Abuse Prediction: Policy Implications* (Cambridge, Mass: Balinger).

Steele, B. F. and C. B. Pollock (1968) 'A psychiatric study of parents who abuse infants and small children', in R. F. Helfer and C. H. Kempe (eds), *The Battered Child* (Chicago: University of Chicago Press).

Stenson, K. (1993) 'Social work discipline and the social work interview', *Economy and Society*, 22(1), pp. 42–76.

Straus, M. A., R. J. Gelles and S. K. Steinmetz (1980) *Behind Closed Doors: Violence in the American Family* (New York: Anchor/Doubleday).

Suchman, L. (1987) *Plans and Situated Actions: The Problem of Human–Machine Communication* (Cambridge: Cambridge University Press).

Summit, R. (1983) 'The child sexual abuse accommodation syndrome', *Child Abuse and Neglect*, 7, pp. 177–93.

Taylor, L., R. Lacey and D. Bracken (1980) *In Whose Best Interests?* (London: Cobden Trust/Mind).

Taylor, S. (1989) 'How prevalent is it?', in W. Stainton Rogers, D. Hevers and E. Ash (eds), *Child Abuse and Neglect: Facing the Challenge* (London: Batsford).

Thoburn, J., A. Lewis and D. Shemmings (1995) *Paternalism or Partnership? Family Involvement in the Child Protection Process* (London: HMSO).

Thorpe, D. (1989) *Patterns of Child Protection Intervention and Service Delivery*, Report for the Standing Committee of Social Welfare Ministers and Administrators of Australia (Perth: Department for Community Services, Western Australia).

Thorpe, D. (1991) *Patterns of Child Protection: Intervention and Service Delivery – Report of a Pilot Project*, Research Report No. 4 (University of Western Australia: Crime Research Unit).

Thorpe, D. (1994) *Evaluating Child Protection* (Milton Keynes: Open University Press).

Thorpe, D. and S. Thorpe (1992) *Monitoring and Evaluation in the Social Services* (Harlow: Longman).

Tite, R. (1993) 'How teachers define and respond to child abuse: the distinction between theoretical and reportable cases', *Child Abuse and Neglect*, 17, pp. 591–603.

Unsworth, C. (1987) *The Politics of Mental Health Legislation* (Oxford: Oxford University Press).

Utting, D. (1995) *Family and Parenthood: Supporting Families, Preventing Breakdown* (York: Joseph Rowntree Foundation).

Valentine, D. P., D. S. Acuss, M. I. Freeman and T. Andreas (1984) 'Defining child maltreatment: a multidisciplinary overview', *Social Work Information Bulletin*, 62(6), pp. 497–509.

Warner, J. E. and D. J. Hansen (1994) 'The identification and reporting of physical abuse by physicians: a review and implications for research', *Child Abuse and Neglect*, 18, pp. 11–25.

Wattam, C. (1989) 'Investigating child sexual abuse: a question of relevance', in H. Blagg et al. (eds), *Child Sexual Abuse: Listening, Hearing and Validating the Experiences of Children* (Harlow: Longman).

Wattam, C. (1990) 'Adultcentrism and child protection', presented at the 8th International Congress on Child Abuse and Neglect, Hamburg, September.

Wattam, C. (1991) *Truth and Belief in the Disclosure Process*, NSPCC Research Policy and Practice Series (London: NSPCC).

Wattam, C. (1992) *Making a Case in Child Protection* (London: NSPCC/Longman).

Westcott, H. (1993) 'Perceptions of casework in NSPCC teams: interviews with parents, children and child protection officers', unpublished, available from NSPCC Hedley Library.

Westcott, H. (1995) 'Perceptions of child protection casework: views from children, parents and practitioners', in C. Cloke and M. Davies (eds), *Participation and Empowerment in Child Protection* (London: Pitman Publishing).

Winch, P. (1991) *The Idea of a Social Science and its Relation to Philosophy* (London: Routledge, 2nd edition).

Wise, S. (1991) 'Child abuse: the NSPCC version', *Feminist Praxis*, 32.

Wolfe, D. A. (1985) 'Child abusive parents: an empirical review and analysis', *Psychological Bulletin*, 93(3), pp. 462–82.

Wolfe, D. A. (1991) *Preventing Physical and Emotional Abuse of Children* (New York: Guilford Press).

Wolfner, G. D. and R. J. Gelles (1993) 'A profile of violence toward children: national study', *Child Abuse and Neglect*, 17, pp. 197–212.

Wyatt, G. E. and S. D. Peters (1986) 'Issues in the definition of child sexual abuse in prevalence research', *Child Abuse and Neglect*, 10, pp. 231–40.

Index